KT-218-776

Anna Birch is a vet, farmer's wife and mother of two small children. They live together on a farm in beautiful North Dorset with a herd of Red Devon cows, twenty Wiltshire Horn sheep, the occasional Gloucester Old Spot pig, four rescue chickens, two farm cats, two Jack Russells and one Labrador. This is Anna's first memoir about vetting and rural life.

Call the Vet

Call the Vet

Farmers, dramas and disasters –
my first year as a country vet

Anna Birch and Deborah Crewe

2 4 6 8 10 9 7 5 3 1

Published in 2014 by Virgin Books, an imprint of Ebury Publishing
A Random House Group Company

Copyright © Anna Birch and Deborah Crewe 2014

The authors have asserted their right under the Copyright, Designs
and Patents Act 1988 to be identified as the authors of this work

All rights reserved. No part of this publication may be
reproduced, stored in a retrieval system, or transmitted in any form
or by any means, electronic, mechanical, photocopying, recording
or otherwise, without the prior permission of the copyright owner

This book is a work of non-fiction based on the life, experiences
and recollections of Anna Birch. In some cases names of people,
places, dates, sequences or the detail of events have been changed
to protect the privacy of others. The authors have stated to the
publishers that, except in such respects not affecting the substantial
accuracy of the work, the contents of this book are true

The Random House Group Limited Reg. No. 954009

Addresses for companies within the Random House Group
can be found at www.randomhouse.co.uk

A CIP catalogue record for this book is available from the
British Library

The Random House Group Limited supports the Forest
Stewardship Council® (FSC®), the leading international forest-
certification organisation. Our books carrying the FSC label are
printed on FSC®-certified paper. FSC is the only forest-certification
scheme supported by the leading environmental organisations,
including Greenpeace. Our paper procurement policy can be found
at www.randomhouse.co.uk/environment

Printed and bound in Great Britain by Clays Ltd, St Ives plc

ISBN 9780753555071

To buy books by your favourite authors and register for offers visit
www.randomhouse.co.uk

To my children,
a real-life bedtime story for you,
how Mummy and Daddy met.

Contents

Contents

PART ONE

Autumn

CHAPTER ONE

Cows, coffee and cling film

It is December, three o'clock in the morning, and I am standing naked and shivering in the garden of my tiny cottage, up half a mile of muddy track in rural West Dorset. I am covered from hair to feet in every kind of liquid that comes out of a labouring cow, and trying to scrub it off with half a flask of tepid sugary coffee. I smell bad. My mother Helga's clipped, Germanic, don't-even-try-arguing-with-me words always come into my head at moments like this: 'Oh, Anna, such a glamorous job, vetting.' I am not feeling glamorous. But – tired, cold and sticky – I am feeling overwhelmingly lucky and fantastically happy.

Exactly three months earlier, on a quiet Wednesday afternoon in early September, I had arrived in the beautiful sleepy town of Ebbourne. That first day, I parked my tiny car next to a stray seagull, and unfolded myself from its battered interior. As I stretched from the journey, my stomach jerked tight and I took another hit of adrenalin. Finally – finally – I was going to get the chance to do the job I had been training for through all these years: the job I had wanted since I was six years old. Today was the day.

Taking a few calming breaths of the warm sweet air, I took in the sights and sounds of my new home. Around the market square that doubled up as a car park were arranged the usual landmarks of a comfortable country town: post office, bank, a gift shop, two butchers and a mini-market (with an impressive-looking deli counter in the window, I noted). Gulls swooped and cawed around the ornate butter-cross memorial, clearing up the only litter visible, a rather tempting abandoned strawberry ice cream. Narrow streets splayed out from the square like spider's legs, some climbing steeply before opening out onto fields scattered with houses built in the local soft yellow stone. I spotted a colourful playground with two swings, a slide and a hopeful-looking elephant on a spring. It was all smart, picturesque, and completely deserted. Apart from the gulls, and some distant washing waving in the wind, there was nothing moving. Were there any people here? Could I really live here for the next three years? My nervous excitement gave way to pure nerves.

Before I had time to get back in my car and turn around, an explosion of noise and activity broke the peaceful scene. A tall, shambling, ranting man hove into view and I was startled for a moment before I recognised him as Stanley, the jovial junior partner of Ebbourne's veterinary surgery. He was striding towards me in his vet's scrubs, waving and smiling. 'Anna, Anna, you're here, you're here, terrific. Come on, I'll give you a quick tour – or do you want to get settled in first? Cup of tea, sit down? Yes, quick tour, I think.'

Seeing Stanley was enough to remind me of all the reasons I'd accepted this job: he and the senior partner Mike both seemed kind and competent; the practice was in a beautiful spot; and because it was so remote, it had to cover everything, so I'd be working both with large animals on the local farms, and with cats, dogs and other pets. Maybe some wildlife too. I took a deep breath, returned Stanley's enthusiastic handshake, and smiled broadly. Before I could answer his question, he was bundling me and my rucksack of belongings into his dirt-caked Land Rover, and muttering about sorting me out with a decent veterinary vehicle.

I'd seen the sights already as part of the job interview. I'd also sampled Stanley's exhilarating driving style.

'A cup of tea would be lovely, actually.'

'Right, great. Let's take you over and fix you up at Mike's house then. They can get the kettle on there.'

I lived with Mike and his wife Natasha for my first three months in the job. They were generous to open their home to me, but I became impatient to move out. I felt that they must be sick of having me hanging around. And, at the grand old age of 29, having lived with my parents or fellow students my entire life, I was excited about moving into my own place for the first time.

In fact, I was so excited that I moved in prematurely. The cottage I was to call my own had previously been occupied by an elderly couple who were now getting infirm and wanted to live closer to their children. This couple appeared to have done no work at all on the place for the thirty years they had lived there, and there were white rings on the yellowing wallpaper where plates had once hung. The practice had taken the cottage on as accommodation for me and those who would come after me, and Mike and Stanley had decided it needed a new kitchen, new carpets, paint job, everything. When, in the dead of winter, I insisted on moving in, it still wasn't anywhere near finished. For the first couple of days that hadn't bothered me in the slightest, but now, tonight, it had suddenly become an issue.

This particular December night, the local builder, plumber, plasterer, carpet-layer, calf-rearer and philosopher known to us all as Cauli (he had magnificent ears from years of playing in the local rugby club's scrum) had been working hard all day, pouring new concrete throughout most of the ground floor of the cottage, to level it out for the new flea-free carpets. Upstairs was all in working order but downstairs there was simply a plank from the bottom of the stairs to the front door.

I was on duty overnight and I'd already been in bed and dozing for an hour when the phone rang. I shook myself out of sleep to answer, hoping it might be something I could make go away so I could snuggle back under my warm duvet.

It was Tom Stevens, a farmer I'd not yet met, with a cow that had prolapsed. He sounded calm enough, but I knew a prolapse was nasty. When the uterus turns itself inside out and appears on the outside of the animal, it needs returning smartish. It can happen after a cow has given birth, especially when the calf is on the big side. The uterus kind of clamps itself around the calf as it's making its way out, and then this vast organ follows the calf out of the cow. You see it in sheep too. It's definitely an emergency and I was suddenly completely awake.

In the three months I'd been working as a vet I'd never replaced a prolapse on my own and I was both excited and petrified, but mainly petrified. This was a real test. Could I go out on a farm all on my own and convince the farmer I was a vet, not a frightened child, and remember the theory, and put it into practice, and do what vets do? Come on, Anna.

It was blinking cold, so I kept my pyjamas on and just slipped my vets-issue heavy green cotton boiler suit on top. I checked I had all the kit with me, jumped into my ludicrously white Land Rover Defender and set off at pace down the dark country roads. This was well before satnav and I'd not been to the Stevens' farm before. After a couple of nifty U-turns in the pitch black, praying nothing else would be hurtling along these roads in the middle of the night, I found it and jumped out.

Tom Stevens, poker-faced, big-bellied and straight-backed, was waiting out by the road for me. He introduced himself and gave me a long stare before seeming to decide I would do. 'Lock your car,' he advised as we set off towards the cow. Lock my car? On a farm set back from a country lane in the middle of the night? 'Workshop got broken into. Everything taken. Insurance came through last week. All new tools. Got broken into again last night.' This gruff farmer with his military bearing spat his story out, jaw firmly locked, he was betrayed only by the tiniest quiver at his cheek. I let him lead on while he composed himself.

'Here we are,' said Tom, as he closed the gate and we walked into the field. He was recovered now and back to his full scary, staring style. And there she was, with this huge inside-out organ hanging out of her. I could see immediately that she was freshly calved because the mucus membrane was still nice and moist, and a reddish-pink colour. And I could see the cotyledons, mushroom-like structures that act like great big mushy buttons, connecting the placenta to the cow, all hanging out too. She was down, which was on balance a good thing. But she was down under a tree, so there were leaves and twigs all over what ought to have been the inside of this uterus, and there was blood and placental fluids around from the birth, and she'd crapped on it too, of course.

I had put my waterproof trousers on over my boiler suit, and then the big calving gown over them – like a massive plastic cloak. I knelt down, slid the gown underneath the uterus and sloshed several buckets of water over it, trying to wash off as much of the crap and other muck as I could.

It was at this point that I realised it was wrong to have worn my pyjamas. You do a lot of kneeling in this job, and the waterproofing on my 'waterproof' trousers had worn away. So I now had freezing cold, sopping wet, poo-covered knees. But there was nothing for it. The uterus needed to be put back in.

The uterus can be a friable, fragile organ, so I knew I couldn't just grab it with my fingers. I had to take it in the palms of my hands and slowly twist it and push it at the bit nearest the cow. Imagine trying to coax a floppy piece of raw pastry dough through a small hole. Only the pastry weighs ten kilos and is engorged with blood and if you tear it, you're going to have a dead cow on your hands. I pushed slowly at first, just gently teasing it in. For a long time – probably only thirty minutes but it felt like hours and days – I was getting nowhere. I badly wanted to do this on my own: I needed to show Tom Stevens, Stanley, Mike, and most of all myself that I could do it. If I called either of the partners they would gladly come, I knew that, but I would feel humiliated and useless, and I suspected Tom would never trust me near his cows again. So I wasn't going to do that. But was my need to prove myself getting in the way of my judgement? Was I going to let some poor cow suffer and possibly die because I wanted to feel like a competent vet? In the silence and darkness of Tom Stevens' field, with a cow's heavy uterus in my hands, these thoughts went round and round my head. I was starting to shake with the physical effort when suddenly the organ started to go back in.

At that point, knees now numb, fingers aching, I remembered something. I asked Tom, standing impassively watching, could he go to my Land Rover, and bring me the wine bottle that was in the back. Tom looked at me like he'd seen a lot of things before but he'd never seen a vet on the bottle with her arm elbow-deep inside a cow. He blinked once, took my keys, and set off to the car.

'Bottle-opener's up at the house,' said Tom darkly on his return, as he handed me a bottle of the local Spar's cheapest, nastiest white wine.

A cow's uterus has two horns, making it the shape of a short-armed Y. Both horns can turn themselves inside out when prolapsed and once I had finished pushing the uterus back in, I had to fix this. The technique is a bit like when the fingers of your gloves turn inside out as you take them off. The easiest way to turn your gloves the right way round is to stick your fingers into the inside out bits, and push. Only my arms weren't long enough to reach all the way inside the uterus to the uterine horns. That's what the wine bottle was for. With minimal finesse, a moderate amount of grunting and maximum heaving, I duly returned the uterus to its correct anatomical position, right way round, inside in. Cow number 327 reluctantly lurched forward onto her feet and turned her head around to stare at me – nonplussed, but calm. I stared back, shaking with the exertion and sweating profusely despite the cold night air.

With everything back in the right place, cow 327's great big cow bladder could work again. Without breaking eye contact, she had a five-litre pee on me. Terrific. Now I had the full house.

But I didn't care in the slightest. I was elated. I had done it, it had worked. And Tom's wife had found the calf in a ditch, still alive. Now the cow was up we brought her her calf, who started sucking straight away. What a beautiful sight. The night covered up my face-splitting grin of relief and joy.

I had a quick hose-down in the yard, shook hands with Tom and his wife, trying not to look too surprised at myself (they didn't know I'd never done it before) and got back into my white Land Rover, exhausted, wet, shivering, but on a huge high.

Halfway back to my little cottage, my pager went off. This was early days for mobile phones. Mine was a huge brick that mostly had no reception. I stopped at a phone box. And I am genuinely sorry to the person who next tried to use it. I have no idea what you will have thought on being assaulted by the sight and smell of pee, poo, blood and other assorted cow matter. All I can say is, it was an emergency.

I phoned the number on my pager. At the other end was Simon Porritt, a very experienced, gentle old dairy farmer. He had a freshly calved cow with a vaginal tear – another genuine crisis. The birth canal of a full-term cow is engorged with large blood vessels the width of a finger, geared up for getting blood to a huge uterus. On its way out of its mother, this calf had stuck its foot into her soft tissues, tearing one of these vessels, and the mother was now spurting out blood like something from a horror movie. I needed to get there and clamp off the vessel but it was a 20-minute drive to his farm, deep down in the valley, and the cow was going to bleed to death in that time. I told Simon to do like the little Dutch boy with the dam. He needed to try to find where all the blood was coming from and either pinch the vessel closed with his finger and thumb, or literally stick his finger in it.

Adrenalin pumping, I got back in the Land Rover. I thought I'd sounded quite competent on the phone but actually this was another procedure I had never done before. The fog was rolling in off the sea by now – even with a full beam I couldn't see more than a few yards ahead of me on the unlit country roads – but I'd been to the Porritt farm before and I found my way there with no problems.

I screeched into the farmyard and there was Simon just like I'd asked, holding back the tide. Bless him, this man had two new hips and terrible arthritis and here he was in the middle of a chilly December night with his hand in his cow. His son Michael was standing by, and from the amount of blood on him, had presumably been taking turns with his dad. The last time I had seen Michael Porritt, he had been in black tie and I had been in my posh frock. My stomach gave a little squeeze as I caught his eye. I wondered whether he was remembering that too, and how his feelings about me would be affected by seeing me covered in muck.

But Simon and Michael didn't bat an eyelid at my sullied state. This was their lifestyle, and they were covered in all sorts themselves; I fitted right in. With a slight shake of my head I pulled my shoulders back and put myself firmly in professional mode. I donned a clean boiler suit and calving gown, picked up my calving box, walked round to the back of the cow … and my mind went blank. 'Sorry, Simon, Michael, I'll be right back, I left something in the car.' Back at the Defender, I rifled through my textbook and found the pages I needed. Breathe, Anna, focus. I ran back, empty-handed. If Simon and Michael noticed, they decided not to comment.

'Okay girlie, let's sort you out,' I murmured to the injured cow. I got out my artery forceps – they're like scissors but with a clamp end instead of shearing blades – and attached a piece of white cloth to them. It's an old vet's trick that the senior partner, Mike, had taught me. If you have to leave artery forceps inside a cow because you can't get at the artery to tie it off – as I could see I was going to have to do here – the white cloth makes them easier to either retrieve later, or to spot in the farmyard if they've fallen out. Using my hand as my eyes inside this cow, I quietly chatted to her as I felt for the tear where the whooshing arterial blood was escaping and clamped it off to seal it.

From the bloodbath I was standing in, she'd clearly lost a lot of blood, and she wasn't looking too strong, so before I started tidying up and cleaning around the back end I thought it would be prudent to put her on some fluids. To the accompaniment of the weak bleating of the newborn calf beside us in the calving box, I went about setting up a drip: big catheter in the big jugular vein; large bag of fluid. That was another first: I'd never put a catheter in a cow before. 'There you go, girlie, that should sort you out.' Off I went round the back and

I was halfway through finishing up when Michael asked anxiously, 'Should there be a football on the side of her neck?' I ran back round to the front and either from her moving her neck around, or more likely from me not putting the catheter in properly, it had slipped out of the vein, and all this fluid was being pumped in just under the skin.

It wasn't a fatal mistake, thank goodness, just a stupid and dramatic one. And it meant more prodding and poking for this new mum who was now dripping milk and looking round plaintively for her calf. Gentle bleating had turned to blaring: mother and child were both impatient to get bonding.

I performed my second-ever catheterisation, into the vein this time. 'Sorry girlie, let's try again.' This time the fluid ran rapidly into her vein. Five minutes later, job done, I needed to check the uterus to make sure there was no twin or further tear. I picked up my lubricating gel and squeezed a big dollop into the palm of my hand. Vets and prostitutes, I thought – we must surely be the main customers for these huge litre bottles of all-purpose lubricant. I wondered how big the intersection was in that particular Venn diagram … vets and prostitutes … I suppose there were probably a few. Come on, Anna, focus, focus, concentrate.

My examination completed to my satisfaction – there was no twin, no further damage – I escorted my patient into the calving box. Mum immediately set to licking her calf. I fussed around them both, making sure my patient had straw to keep her comfortable. Michael then gently raised the calf onto its wobbly legs. We all watched wordless as, supported and guided by Michael, the calf started to softly nudge his mother's underside with his nose, helping the milk to flow. At the same time, guided only by instinct, the cow twisted herself around to put her nose to the back end of the calf, pushing him gently towards her udder. Contented slurping noises took the place of the bleating and blaring. I caught Michael's eye for a second time and we smiled at the precious family scene.

Poor beast, she went through a lot that night. But I'd saved her. She was going to live.

I took another bone-chilling hose-down with freezing cold water, the bare minimum I felt I could get away with before sitting back in the Land Rover. The adrenalin was wearing off and in its place was a dazed happy weariness.

I'd pulled it off. I'd saved two cows, and two calves had their mothers still. No one had laughed me off their farm, no one had queried whether I really knew what I was doing, no one had asked me to go away and send a proper vet. It was only the running commentary inside my head whispering that I was a fraud, an impostor – and even that had been silenced for this one delicious moment. I was doing it, I was living the rural vetting dream.

I drove back to the house in this trance-like state.

It was only as I opened the front door that my spirits fell. I had no heating, no running water. My second hose-down had left me sopping wet but still covered in filth. My happy heart sank. Then I remembered I had a flask of still-quite-warm coffee in the Land Rover. I'm tall – five foot eleven and a half, lanky really – and I've got a really fast metabolism. I get very hungry, very suddenly. So I always keep sugary snacks on hand. Immensely cheered, I went back to the Land Rover and fished out the sweet coffee.

I crossed my fingers that the neighbours were asleep as I stripped off my layers and washed myself down in the little garden, wishing I hadn't put quite so much sugar in it (it was very sticky).

It didn't really work, to be honest. I got some of the big bits off, but the sugary coffee had also acted as an adhesive with some of the other bits. I surveyed my handiwork and sighed a deep, deep sigh, putting off the moment when I admitted it to myself. I was now covered in a kind of heady mix of cowshit, wee, bloody mucus, sugar and coffee. I couldn't lie in or even on my bed like this. My Territorial Army training at the front of my mind, I considered my options. The best I could come up with was this: if I could somehow make it into the kitchen, I could get the cling film from on top of one of the boxes I was using as a makeshift cupboard, and wrap myself up in it, to prevent contamination of the rest of the house. One foot in the setting concrete and I would not be popular with Cauli in the morning, but it was a small cottage. It might just be possible.

Back to the Land Rover again. I grabbed a second pair of artery forceps – like the ones I'd left inside the Porritt cow an hour earlier. I stood right on the edge of the plank running from the front door to the stairs, leant forward as far as I dared, and used the long forceps to grab hold of the cling film. Success!

But as usual, it took forever to find the free end of the wrap. Free end identified, my first attempt to tear a piece off with my cold clumsy fingers left me with a tiny, ragged, useless little specimen. My second attempt yielded a lovely big bit that immediately crumpled itself into a ball. Finally, feeling like a contestant in a particularly humiliating game show, I managed to wrap my torso. Next, legs. But should I do them together (pro: quicker, uses less cling film; con: seriously compromises my ability to move) or separately? I decided to do them together. Finally, my left arm. Doing the right one was too difficult and I didn't want not to be able to bend either arm. My handiwork finally complete, there was, sadly, no applause. I waddled over to the bannister-free stairs and jumped up them like a slug. I tried to put out of my mind all images of toppling over and being discovered in the morning, wrapped like a mummy and stuck in the cement. I slept with my penknife by my side, ready to cut myself out in case of (further) emergency.

A couple of hours later, the alarm went off. I'd set it early so I could get into work before anyone else.

Wearing a new boiler suit – I couldn't bear to put the old one back on – I crept into the practice, checked three times to make sure no one was around, and stepped into the dog shower. It was just a tray in the floor, with a hand-held shower attachment, but once I'd swilled the dog-hair down the drain, it did me just fine.

*

By the time everyone else started arriving for the day's surgery, I felt fresh and ready to go – or as fresh as is possible on two hours of cling-film-wrapped sleep.

As always, Judith, our long-standing receptionist, and the rock on whom the whole surgery rested, arrived first. As she bustled around, putting the kettle on, wrestling the photocopier into life, and fixing a shonky door handle, she asked me about my night. She was sympathetic, congratulatory, warmly aghast.

Over the course of the next thirty minutes, the rest of our little family arrived. Each got the bulletin from Judith – the story getting slightly more dramatic, the details more lurid as she hit her stride. Lois, the accounts clerk, tutted, pursed her lips, and clicked noisily on her high heels over to her little office. Penny, the young nurse, oohed and aaahed at all the right points, asking a series of wide-eyed questions and slipping in what she really wanted to know right at the end: 'So, how was Michael?' Stanley, so tall and square and capable that somewhere in the back of my mind I realised I thought of him as Superman – he even had the geeky glasses and the cleft chin – guffawed and promised me a stiff drink that night.

Finally, fifteen minutes after the first appointments had started turning up, Mike arrived, resplendent in a new striped tank top, having already ticked off the first farm visit of the morning, a routine fertility call. I braced myself but 'Anna's had a bit of a tough night,' was all that Judith said. Mike nodded knowingly and Judith left it at that. Mike had been doing this job – which had never been 'just a job' to him – day in day out, for over twenty years. It would take more than a couple of messy cow emergencies and a lost night's sleep to impress him.

I spent most of my morning quietly neutering cats. The only remarkable cases that came in were Sophie, a Labrador puppy belonging to one of my favourite Ebbourne residents, and Charlie, a splendid old spaniel on his last legs.

I had become very fond of both Sophie and her owner Tamara, who misguidedly believed me to be some kind of genius veterinary talent.

Tamara had long streaked blonde hair and wore a paint-spattered white boiler suit (in which she managed to look stunning) and sunglasses all year round. I could always smell cigarette smoke on Sophie's coat and, though she made a big play of having given up, I liked to imagine Tamara reclining on a chaise longue with a long cigarette holder, Audrey Hepburn style. I wasn't sure what Tamara's husband did, but he was able to keep her, their nine-year-old animal-mad daughter Amelia, Sophie and their menagerie of other birds and animals in fine style. Tamara was a very frequent shopper with us. She couldn't bear to carry out even the most mundane of procedures, so I clipped Sophie's nails, cleaned her ears out, and pulled her out of whatever her latest scrape was. 'This has to be the most gold-plated dog in Dorset,' Tamara would sigh as she wrote out yet another Coutts' cheque. When Tamara brought Sophie in this time, she was obviously in big disgrace. Even her tail, usually wagging like a metronome, seemed to have turned itself off.

'She ate all the slug bait the gardener had left in the shed,' wailed Tamara, raising a hand to her brow like a Southern belle prone to fainting fits. Tamara knew how to poke fun at herself. 'The gardener caught her but not before she'd snuffled up the lot. Can you believe this dog, she's a disaster.' Labradors are such happy dogs, but they can be greedy – and Sophie in particular would eat pretty much anything.

'Okay, Tamara.' (She insisted we were on first name terms.) 'We're going to have to make Sophie sick or the metaldehyde toxin in slug bait could make her convulse and overheat.' Tamara looked like she might be sick herself at this. I gave Sophie an injection and up came piles of the blue slug bait, plus a matted piece of beige material.

'Oh, disgusting. Naughty, naughty Sophie,' chided Tamara fondly. 'That's Amelia's riding glove.'

But dogs know tone, and Sophie knew she was out of trouble now. Her tail started up again, and she jumped up in a puppyish show of affection. With her paws on my tummy and her black eyes smiling up at me, I was helpless. I ignored the inner vet voice telling me not to encourage such behaviour and happily returned her love, giving her a good long pat and a cuddle.

I sent Tamara home and kept Sophie in for the afternoon for observation. It wasn't strictly necessary but I knew if I sent Sophie home with Tamara, it would mean a series of panicky phone calls as Tamara watched her like a hawk for any signs of a setback.

Charlie came in a little later. He was a liver-and-white spaniel, who must have been glorious in his day, but I had only ever seen him in discomfort. And yet he was still always so pleased to see everyone, giving each of us in turn his trademark 'paw' like a perfect gentleman. His owner, Lucy, was a sad, dignified lady in her mid-40s, whose husband, a local solicitor, had died just before I had arrived in Ebbourne. They had no children, just the immaculately groomed old Charlie. Lucy was bringing him in for an X-ray so that I could see whether his recent coughing fits that I couldn't get under control were due to his heart condition, or whether something else was going on. She handed me a leather-bound notebook. 'His breathing gets worse at night,' she said, pointing to the appropriate places in her meticulous notes. I guessed from these comprehensive records of Charlie's every symptom that Charlie probably slept in her bedroom; and that Lucy was getting up to comfort him several times a night. She couldn't be getting much sleep.

The X-ray brought bad news: the heart was massive and the lungs congested – he was slowly drowning from heart failure. I suggested to Lucy that we tinker with Charlie's meds a little. I also had to broach the topic of when enough would be enough for Charlie. 'Charlie and I will talk it through,' said Lucy. 'It's so hard to know how much pain someone can take before their life isn't worth living, isn't it?'

I made it through the rest of the day without further incident.

Brushing my teeth in the bedroom of my cold, no-water, no-heating, half-finished cottage that evening, I spotted something in my hair. Something sticky, and smelly. My hair is quite curly and messy at the best of times so perhaps, I thought, no one had spotted it. Perhaps no one had noticed that I had been walking around all day with a piece of placenta in my hair. Oh yes, Mum, it's a glamorous job.

CHAPTER TWO

Welcome to Ebbourne

All things considered, it was pretty miraculous that I was a vet at all.

Aged fourteen, I had what turned out to be a momentous interview with the careers adviser at yet another new school. (My father was in the army so we moved about a lot.) This well-meaning schoolteacher, with his weary eyes and his ancient shirts, indelibly sweat-stained at the armpits, must have entered his profession in the 1950s. The sexual and social upheavals of the 1960s had passed him by; the ambitions of a school-full of girls in the 1980s completely bewildered him. And I, in particular, seemed to bewilder him. 'Ah, young Anna. So ... ' He flicked slowly through the pages in front of him. I assumed they were my reports from my old school. 'You've been at a mixed comprehensive school ... ' Each word was given distinct emphasis. He appeared to fall into a reverie, contemplating the amazingness of this fact about me. I briefly wondered whether he was going to fall asleep. Then he roused himself.

'You'll find things a bit different here, eh?' Here he smiled weakly and distractedly. 'Most of the gals here have already chosen their timetabled lessons so we'll have to fit you in where we can. No promises. What are your interests?'

Eagerly, I outlined my love of PE, woodwork and metalwork. The careers teacher quietly laid his elbows on the desk in front of him, and with his ink-and-nicotine-stained fingers, made a careful tent in front of his mouth. 'Yes, well, I'm afraid, Anna, it will have to be needlework and home economics here.'

Crestfallen, I battled on. I liked science, I offered, especially biology; I thought I might like to be a vet. The master frowned and peered at me over his tented fingers. He appeared to sink back into his reverie before blinking himself back to our conversation. 'We're not very good at science here. Because we're all girls. You wouldn't do well, I'm afraid. I wouldn't bother trying for vet school if I were you.'

'Christ, they're in the dark ages!' exclaimed my father, Colonel Julian Barrington – first a teacher, then commissioned into HM forces, and an educator through and through – when I unveiled my timetable that evening.

But that was that. I buried my childish ambitions, threw myself into hockey and running and generally being a teenager, and three years later, at yet another school, embarked on a completely eccentric set of A-levels – German, Economics and Biology. It was impossible to get into vet school on those, but somehow I did manage to snag a place at Oxford to study the equally eccentric Philosophy and Psychology.

Well, that would have been that, but for 52 rats and my then boyfriend, Allen. Yearning to do something practical, I opted to conduct a psychology experiment in my final year at university. After diligent preparation, including sheaves of paperwork to obtain a license from the Home Office, I was granted permission to run an experiment testing a model of schizophrenia. Into my care were given 52 white Wistar rats, whom I immediately set about naming and training. On my last day in the lab I liberated my two favourites – Harry and B52 – and cycled them home in a shoebox on the front basket of my bike (I got some strange looks at the traffic lights, as Harry and B52 made the box twitch and shake all the way home). They lived in my room in a house on Cowley Road, ranging freely, chewing my duvet, stashing the apple cores from my bin under the bed, leaving little poops around the place and generally wreaking ratty havoc.

Those 52 lovely creatures made me realise how much I liked working with animals. Allen saw it too, and decided to do something about it. He told me about a friend of his who had gone to vet school after her first degree; he researched what to do about my missing chemistry and maths A-levels – I had to take a year out and go back to school to take chemistry, and I had to persuade a veterinary college of the laughable idea that I had done enough maths as part of my psychology degree. We told my parents it was a possibility, and they were fully behind me too. Back then, students were still fortunate enough to have one degree funded by the government, but two was pushing it, so this time I would have to pay the tuition fees as well as living costs. But there was no loans system available for tuition fees back then either – and unlike Allen's friend I didn't have wealthy parents to bankroll me. So Allen even helped me to write hundreds of letters to charitable trusts, begging for some grant money, and also to identify the more affordable vet schools in the country. He and I may not have stood the test of time, but I will be forever grateful to him for helping me pursue a career that I could love my whole life long.

To my great joy, Bristol, the most affordable of them all, offered me a place.

I had not been a particularly brilliant student at Oxford. I spent too much time on the river, and I am sure my tutor found me completely exasperating as I postponed tutorial after tutorial. I vowed that when I got to veterinary college, I was going to be an exemplary student. After all, I had done it before, I knew the whole drill. I knew how to set my notes out, how to write an essay, how to study.

That resolve remained firm all the way through the first week of my five-year course. The first three 'pre-clinical' years were mostly tedious, dry bookwork. We were taught vast amounts of detailed information with little sense (at least to me) of why we might ever need to know it. Biochemistry, physiology, anatomy, pathology, histology; rote learning, sometimes in Latin, with no clues about its relevance to the clinical years. *The bladder of a bitch sits under its rectum, and the reproductive tract lies between the two.* This anatomical information is a very boring thing to learn or know, until you are rootling away inside someone's pet (with a nurse drumming her fingers on the operating table) unable to find the wretched uterus. Then it becomes terrifically fascinating and useful, and you will wish you had paid more attention. Similarly, learning every facet on a bone is mind-numbing and would have been less so if I'd understood its relevance to the important question of where to apply a plate in case of a fracture.

I was supporting myself through vet school partly by waitressing and partly by working for the Officers Training Corps (the OTC), a sort of student army. This gave me the perfect excuse to spend my weekends in a field somewhere getting muddy, rather than in the library bashing the books. I don't think I'm a particularly warlike person, but I did love being in green, going on my belly through the mud, firing weapons and being allowed to trash HM's clothing.

I enjoyed the vacation practical placements and the last two clinical years of the course much more than those first three years of book learning. We all moved out of the centre of Bristol to the Mendips, where the college farm was, and the clinical school with horses and cows and so on. We were all assigned foster practices that we went back to repeatedly, and little by little we were given more responsibility, until by the end we were carrying out minor procedures. At last, we were getting our hands on some animals.

Towards the end of my fourth year I realised I didn't have much experience with ruminants – animals with more than one stomach. So I got myself a goat, a British Saanen cross called Fanny. I thought I could watch her ruminating cycle – how often she would burp and bring up the cud to re-chew, that sort of thing. But poor old Fanny had a kid called Ada and developed raging mastitis just as my fourth year exams were coming up, so I had to go out to the field and milk her three or four times a day to strip out the infection. I would sit in the field with my notes, trying to revise, waiting for the next milking time, and Fanny would wander along and try to eat my notes, eat my hair, eat my clothes, whilst Ada jumped all over me.

Eventually I decided I would have to foster my goats out for a few weeks whilst I took my exams. I put them in the back of my car and Fanny nibbled my ear contentedly as we circumnavigated Bristol. To the man in the Mercedes stopped at the lights in Congresbury, with the manically barking Alsatian: yes, you and your dog did see a goat in the back of a Mini Metro.

Throughout my five years at veterinary college, I watched in bemused and slightly anxious amazement the focused preparations of many of my fellow students for their glittering futures.

My always cheerful flatmate, Sally, was utterly conscientious about both her bookwork and her clinical work, and fantastic with animals. She genuinely loved all creatures and empathised with them deeply; she was a good nurse, as well as a good vet, understanding that it is no good treating a problem and then ignoring all the other things a sick animal needs – has it got a litter tray, is the water bowl okay, is it getting enough food? We were close, but Sally was probably one of those vets who found animals better company than people, and she spent many happy hours clipping and combing and cuddling my rescue spaniel, Nellie. Sally knew what she wanted: a suburban small animal practice.

My other two great friends could not have been more different from each other. Athena, all thick dark eyebrows and long black hair, was terribly academic, and one of the top students in our year. She hadn't always been; by all accounts, she had spent most of her first year partying. But she had dropped down to our year after a car accident had laid her up in hospital for months. The accident must have given her a St Ignatius of Loyola moment, because when she came back to college Athena threw herself into her studies with the same intense, all-or-nothing energy she had previously dedicated to drinking and dancing. It was dispiriting revising with her because she had a photographic memory. If I asked her a question she would squint one eye shut and say, 'It's in my yellow file, midway through, top right hand corner, halfway through the first paragraph.' And there it was. I couldn't compete with that and nor could anyone else. Athena had her heart set on an internship in London at the Royal Veterinary College – a sort of houseman's job in a thriving academic environment – and I had no doubt she would achieve her goal.

Lena was a bit of a hippy with hennaed hair, home-knitted jumpers and a gently reassuring manner. She wasn't interested in material success at all, nor in settling down

– concerned that premature domestication would stifle all the adventure out of her life, she had recently transferred her affections from a lovely boyfriend to a mountain bike that she took on annual tours of the Highlands and islands of Western Scotland. Lena was going to use her qualification to travel the world, having amazing experiences and doing good. In a genuine doing-good way.

Huddled together in each others' flats or in the College library, I envied my friends their clear-eyed vision. I felt, by comparison, a bit lost. I'd made it to vet school but what kind of vet was I cut out to be?

Then there was the small matter of my job interview.

On one of my many, many breaks from studying that summer, I was standing and staring slightly aimlessly at the big noticeboard that flanked the entry to the library. Most of the notices had been on the board for so long that they had become wallpaper rather than conveyors of information, and I was thinking more about the training schedule for my next marathon than anything else. (Training for my first marathon the previous year, in the middle of my clerking rotations, had been a pretty poor idea. It was a huge time commitment, and my long-suffering clerking partner, Mary, had taken more than her fair share of the ICU work one particularly trying week when I was at peak 20-mile training. But it had been such an amazing experience that I had immediately decided to enter again. I wanted to improve on my time, I knew I would go nuts without some kind of physical outlet, and my rescue spaniel, Nellie, loved training too. But it had been another poor idea: now my knees were regretting it, and some of my cattle medicine notes were rather sparse.)

As Felix Urquhart, the large-animal supervising vet, passed by, he pointed at a notice that had just gone up for an Assistant Veterinary Surgeon at Dryden and Dalyrimple Veterinary Practice in Ebbourne and said, 'That's a nice mixed practice; good people, and it's near the sea. You should apply.' And on he walked. 'What?' I thought. And then, 'why not?' That evening, back in our digs above a traditional country pub, I lay in the bath listening to pints of cider being poured and breathing in the smell of cigar smoke. When Sally had finished her regular call with her parents I jumped out and dialled the West Dorset number.

The following Tuesday, I set off for Ebbourne in my younger sister Henry's cast-off mini-Metro. The bodywork was mostly rust – I don't know how it had passed its MOT – and the interior smelt strongly of lactating goat but it was in fact by far the best car I had as a student. Perhaps because I always went for the cheapest car I could find but also hankered after something with a bit of character, I had had several disastrous cars before this one: a Trabant Estate, with panelling made from something like Bakelite and a two-stroke engine, that drew funny looks in petrol stations because I had to fill up the tank with a mixture of oil and petrol; and a Hillman Imp that, though it was fabulous for Bristol because it was so short I could park it sideways, had never been the same after I had managed to melt the fan belt onto the engine one night.

I had a crisis of confidence about what to wear for this, my first real job interview. I had been brought up to think one ought to look smart on such occasions, but I knew I was heading to a mixed practice where the dress code would be trousers, a shirt and sturdy footwear for all. I didn't want to look like an ignorant townie who had never encountered mud before. Backwards and forwards I went in my mind: I hadn't fretted this much about what I was going to wear since Allen had taken me to the Caledonian Ball five years ago. In the end, on the third attempt, I had come up with something I was more or less happy with: a plain blouse, a pretty-but-sensible skirt with an unobtrusive flowery pattern, and flat shoes – with a pair of trousers to change into if we did a farm visit. I was annoyed that my nails looked so ragged, and regretted the nervous attack I had led on them the previous evening.

I set off about an hour earlier than I needed to, 'just in case'. Bristol to Ebbourne was a straightforward drive down the A37, though I made it slightly more difficult for myself by deciding to drive it with a two litre bottle of water between my legs. (Drinking huge quantities of water was part of my marathon training regime.) I spent a pleasant hour hurtling down a nearly-empty road, singing loudly, drinking water, and rehearsing interview answers. At about the halfway point, when I was fully focused on thinking of something sensible to say about how to treat a fitting dog, a roundabout loomed up out of nowhere. I slammed on the brakes and skidded my way around it, Grand Prix-style. The movement fountained the remaining litre of water out of the bottle and onto my lap, my seat and the floor – where it mixed with the dust and crud underfoot to create a kind of muddy paste. Bugger.

I hauled myself over to a lay-by to assess the damage. It was the late 1990s, and an item of clothing known as a 'body' was in vogue. A body was like a dancer's leotard and its point was that it created a smooth line under a blouse. It could also be worn by the reasonably flat-chested like me instead of a bra. My knickers, body and pretty-but-sensible skirt were all sopping wet. My shoes had a thin coating of muddy paste on them.

I sloshed the two inches of water I had left over my shoes. The skirt and body I removed and hung out of the back window of the Metro, winding the window up as tightly as I could with the stiff handle. I drew the line at the knickers though and put the spare trousers on over those. So now my trousers were wet as well. As I resumed my journey, my clothes might have been flying out proudly behind me, but I was feeling deflated, chastened – and really rather soggy.

Arriving in Ebbourne I had no time to take in the town beyond a general impression of comfortable sunlit sleepiness. I was too focused on looking for a secluded spot where I could, first off, hide my filthy car, and second, change my clothes unobserved.

I had to settle for an empty but actually fairly exposed car park, where I hurriedly removed my skirt-and-body flags from the car windows and put them back on – crumpled

41

but at least dry – over my still-soaking knickers. Should I 'go Scottish'? No, best not.

A rangy and rather disheveled man appeared at reception the moment I announced myself, grinning widely. He looked me up and down, established that I was indeed Anna, pumped my outstretched hand energetically, and introduced himself as Stanley Dalyrimple, the junior partner at Dryden and Dalyrimple.

Stanley whisked me upstairs to the 'vets' room' – a small, low-ceilinged affair with filing cabinets and bookshelves around three of its bare white walls – hardly giving me time to take in the layout of the reception and consulting area on the ground floor, or the peering faces of the three women populating it. 'Sorry; the building's designed around the needs of the horse and five-foot-tall people and it's listed,' he said, as we both ducked our heads under the doorway.

The room was furnished with two matching standard-issue brown desks, pushed together so that if you were sitting on the standard-issue swivel chair at one of them, you would be looking straight into the eyes of whoever was sitting at the other. In the corner was a third, smaller desk with a straight-backed chair that looked like it had been rescued from someone's dining room. Mike and Stanley clearly did not have interior decorating high on their list of priorities. Each of the three desks was piled high with files, loose paper and reference books, and from deep behind the tallest tottering pile emerged Mike, the senior partner. Mike was as short and deliberate as Stanley was tall and excitable. He shook my hand warmly and firmly and offered me the dining chair. Mike and Stanley did an awkward shuffle with their swivel chairs until we were sitting roughly opposite each other in the middle of the room and the interview could begin.

It wasn't what I had been expecting at all. There were no clinical questions, nothing to test the vast tracts of knowledge I had crammed into my poor brain over the past five years. Instead they conducted what I can only describe as a friendly chat. Perhaps, I thought, they had had some more difficult questions planned but retreated from them when I made such a fidgety meal of their opening salvos.

'So Anna, where are you from?' Mike lobbed me a straightforward question but it didn't have a straight forward answer.

'I'm not really from anywhere. I was born in Tidworth, near Middle Wallop in Hampshire, but I only lived there for a year or so. My father is in the army and we moved about all the time as children; the longest we lived anywhere was three years, in one place in Germany. I'd been to ten schools by the time I was fourteen.' I shifted my weight, and tried casually to readjust the wet knicker elastic cutting into my hips.

'And do you have brothers and sisters?' Another easy question from Mike.

'I've got a sister, Henrietta but we all call her Henry, who's 11 months younger than me, and a kind-of-adopted brother, Angus. Not really adopted, not formally, but I think of him as a brother and he thinks of my parents

43

as parents.' Another squirm as I realised I had pulled my knickers up above the waistband of my skirt.

After a slightly stunned beat, Stanley weighed in. 'What do you do in your spare time, Anna?' he beamed. We were on safer ground here as I waxed lyrical about marathon running and the OTC, and Stanley and Mike described in return the many outdoor leisure options available around Ebbourne. 'Stupendous recreational facilities around here if you like out-and-about things,' urged Mike. 'Salt water, fresh water, hills, you name it. Shooting and fishing and working dogs are my things,' he added. 'Stanley likes the water – scuba diving and kayaking.'

I fidgeted my way through a couple more interchanges and then they were bustling me back out of the practice and over to Stanley's Land Rover. 'It's a beautiful day, let's show you a bit of the country and get you something to eat,' Stanley suggested in a way that brooked no argument. 'Mike and his wife will meet us there.' And then: 'Sorry – yes – just throw all that rubbish into the back.' This last was a reference to the debris piled up on the passenger seat – old banana skins and apple cores, a pair of muddy socks, and several other items I didn't want to inspect too closely.

Stanley set off at the racing pace favoured by country folk who know every bend and pothole of every lane. I spotted, with mild alarm, a lone policeman standing on the narrow verge between the road and the buildings, and pointing his speed trap equipment at us as we careered past. 'Don't take any notice,' grinned Stanley as I turned to him quizzically. Stanley was definitely driving too fast. 'Gordon's just trying to impress you. A couple of months ago we all found out it's just a hoover nozzle. He says it works better for everyone – cuts down on speeding *and* paperwork.'

Stanley talked non-stop and every time he wanted to emphasise a point he would take his eyes off the road and turn to me to make sure I was appreciating the import of what he was saying. Stanley had a lot of points he wanted to emphasise.

'The oldest buildings in Ebbourne are typical golden stone picture-postcard affairs – look at those on the left. Great stuff. Bridport and the sea are seven or eight miles to the south. Crewkerne is the closest town to the north, same kind of distance. These hedgerows are typical for the area by the way, look at the way they are laid on top of the banks, wide and low. Do you know Hooper's rule of hedgerows? I can't quite remember it myself. Where was I? Yes: Ebbourne's population is around 3,500. Large towns aren't close and cities are even further – Exeter, Bournemouth, Taunton, Bristol are all an hour or more away. And the access roads are slow, you probably noticed. But we like it that way! It's why we are like we are!' Stanley took a particularly long break from watching the road to twinkle at me at this point. 'I've been here since 1989. I don't really have one area I'm particularly keen on – I'm enthusiastic about it all. I like dermatology though. And birds of prey. And I'm keen to get the lab busier.' Another long twinkle, followed by a wrenching of the steering wheel as we approached a bend at full pelt. 'Look at these beasts, beautiful creatures.'

'Sheep,' I said.

'They're cows, Anna.' Even Stanley's positivity was challenged by this enormous clanger.

'No. Sheep. Not in the field, on the road. Up ahead.'

Stanley braked hard. There was a flock of around two hundred sheep ambling along the road and completely blocking our way. 'Nip out, Anna,' said Stanley, as he jumped out himself. 'This is all part of the plan. We need to test your large animal handling skills.'

I knew that two hundred escaped sheep couldn't possibly be part of any plan, but that didn't mean it didn't matter how I performed now. I felt two pairs of eyes – Stanley's, and the farmer's – watching my every move as I tried to quietly shoo my recalcitrant new friends along the high hedgerows and through the five-bar gate that led into their field. Two damp patches appeared under my arms.

Ten minutes later, the farmer gave us a cheery wave as Stanley sped off down the newly cleared lane.

The Poachers' Inn, our chosen destination, was a pub that sat on a high point about five miles from the practice, with views from its sunny beer garden of gently rolling hills stitched by hedgerows and scattered with ancient oak trees.

Mike and his smartly dressed wife, Natasha, must have gone a different way because they were there already, and had chosen a table on the edge of the garden, overlooking the valley. Despite the warm sun on my back, the patchwork of green fields beneath us, the still silence, and the deliciousness of my shandy and Ploughman's lunch, I couldn't relax; the formal interview might be over, and my clothes were at least now dry, but I was still being assessed.

So I picked my way painfully and ignorantly through the conversation about important local issues – the cost of housing, the rise in rural crime, the possible closure of the post office – hoping that listening and nodding would count in my favour.

'And another thing,' Mike was saying, as I contemplated the pickled onion nestling between a hunk of cheddar and a slab of stilton on my plate. (My meal choice had been based on a 'no social faux pas' policy. I'd ruled out the sirloin steak for fear of seeming decadent; and I'd got yolk on my shirt the last time I had attempted gammon and egg. The Ploughman's had seemed like the safest option.) 'Christ, this new government doesn't have the first idea about the country. Have any of them actually ever been here? Ban hunting? Over my cold dead twitching body.'

I didn't know what I felt about hunting, nor what I should do about my pickled onion. My cheese was just calling out for it: the vinegary hit, the delightful crunch. But should one eat such a thing at an interview? Would it make my breath smell?

In my confusion I cut into the fragrant morsel just as Mike was coming to the peak of his frenzy. My knife went in, Mike banged the table, and to my horror the pickled onion shot off my plate, across the table and down Natasha's silk blouse, coming to rest gently in her lap.

The world seemed to stop moving. But two seconds later, Natasha gathered herself and seemed to decide to direct her irritation at Mike. Everyone kindly joined in with the charade, but the bread in my mouth suddenly seemed very dry. I drained my shandy.

Perhaps my careers teacher had been right after all, I pondered, as I made my way back to Bristol and cringingly turned over the events of the last few hours: the wet fidgeting, the crumpled clothing, the coarse table manners that would have made my mother weep. Perhaps I shouldn't have bothered. Perhaps it wasn't to be.

Three days later, though, a lovely letter came in the post:

'Our little world is changing and our practice should have the energy and enthusiasm to change and prosper with it! With you in the team we are excited by the future.'

I did a little dance of joy in my tiny kitchen. It had finally happened. I was going to be a vet.

CHAPTER THREE

What do you know about hamsters?

There was, I remembered quickly after my kitchen jig, the small matter of passing my exams. People did fail the things, with worrying regularity. But with the prospect of an actual job dangled so tantalisingly in front of me, I knuckled down, and that July, standing proudly alongside Sally, Lena, Athena, Mary and the rest of the class of '97, I finally graduated.

Eight weeks of glorious summer with no studying and no responsibilities stretched in front of me. I spent half of it getting some much-needed experience, spaying and castrating at the RSPCA in Bristol, and the other half backpacking through Chile with Sally. (I had been lucky enough to see a lot of the world already, but had never been to South America, and Sally loved llamas.)

And so, on the 3rd of September 1997, at the relatively ripe age of 28, I finally embarked on my chosen career path. I had not followed a traditional route to get there and wondered what twists and turns lay ahead. 'You are the master of your destiny' was the mantra I repeated in the car on the way down, to try to calm myself: but a mix of excitement and nerves was driving regular jolts of adrenalin through me. 'You're ready,' I told myself. And I was. Nevertheless, as I approached my destination on that dazzlingly bright Wednesday afternoon I realised that my armpits were sweaty, my lips bitten raw and I felt a little bit sick.

The reassuring appearance of the junior partner, Stanley Dalyrimple, calmed my breathing a little. Yes, this was going to be alright. Stanley ushered me off as if he thought a flurry of activity and a non-stop monologue could settle my nerves, and deposited me safely with the senior partner Mike and his wife Natasha at their grand pile of a manor house. Built of the local stone and covered in wisteria, it was set back up its own gravel path from one of the little lanes leading off the main square. There was ample room in the driveway for the three Land Rovers parked like privates on parade, all in a row.

'Mine,' said Natasha, pointing at the Discovery fitted out with car seats. 'Mike's,' pointing at the more utilitarian Defender in standard mud-spattered khaki, 'and yours.' I wasn't sure whether she was joking. 'My' Defender was pristine white.

'It belonged to Mr Hudson,' Natasha added, as though this were explanation enough. When I continued to look confused she explained further. Apparently, the former senior partner had seen this as a natural mode and colour of transport after years vetting in Africa.

Behind the handsome house I glimpsed a large backyard, home to an impressive wooden swing set, a regimented vegetable patch, a smart hen house, balls of every shape and size and a diesel tank. Natasha took me inside, showed me to the room that would be mine until the practice cottage had been renovated, and introduced me to a succession of well-trained working dogs and equally well-trained but exuberant children. The former consisted of two Labradors and two spaniels who followed Natasha devotedly around the place and made me long for my own lovely spaniel, Nellie, whom I had had to leave in London with my friend Sally, as I knew she couldn't have lived alongside Mike's pack of dogs. The latter consisted of three blond boys, who shook hands beautifully before returning quickly to their business. In fact, each child seemed to have one sole preoccupation which was to physically dominate his siblings. There was a lot of wrestling, and their constant entwinement did not help me in remembering which name went with which small face. Mike had obviously developed the ability to zone out the sound of grunting, squealing offspring and go about his life oblivious to it all. They seemed like nice boys but, understandably, wholly uninterested in their new guest, so I thought it might be wise to try to copy Mike's example.

Natasha did her best to make me feel at home but there was a certain awkwardness to making small talk with my boss's wife and I eagerly took up Mike's offer to show me round the town as soon as I had unpacked. With everything centred around the quaint main square, dominated by a grandiose war memorial, the tour would have been over within ten minutes if Mike hadn't been stopped by almost every passer-by. Most were simply passing the time of day; a few wanted some quick veterinary advice; and they all wanted to know who his companion was. I did a lot of smiling and tried to commit some of the names to memory. I also took particular note of the French patisserie hidden away down one of the side streets – 'that's an exotic development for Ebbourne' muttered Mike; and the well-maintained homes – old workers' cottages interspersed with thatched cottages and a surprising number of large manor houses, all with smartly painted front doors. Good, I thought, that means the clients won't shy away from work-ups (diagnostic tests) and treatments for their pets when they need them. I was keen to use my new knowledge to reach diagnoses and treat appropriately. I had seen practices in less affluent areas where vets had to take an educated guess at what was wrong, and sometimes even euthanise, if the work-up or treatment was prohibitively expensive. Frustrating for all.

Dinner was a delicious, if loud, affair. It was every man for himself as Natasha placed a great dish of glistening pork chops on the table, accompanied by huge buttery platters of potatoes and carrots from the garden, and a bowl of chunky home-made apple sauce. What conversation there was revolved around how many chops each of us had had, and preparations for going back to school for the start of the new academic year the following day.

My dreams when I finally dropped off that night were filled with puzzling symptoms that made no sense, and meds whose names I couldn't remember. It was a relief to wake up and find that my first day at work was still all to play for.

Breakfast was another rowdy and satisfying meal. There was absolutely no expectation of conversation so I helped myself to a bit of everything – toast, cereal *and* a fresh egg – and let the 'getting ready for school' chaos happen around me. Mike too appeared to be a calm island in a frothing sea of packed lunches, PE bags and missing shoes. When he quietly put his coat on I took it as my cue to do the same and followed him out of the house.

Even at Mike's measured pace it was probably only a two-minute walk to the practice, but we needed our Land Rovers there in case of farm calls. So after a brief induction into the mysteries of the Land Rover's transmission system, and a tour of the contents of the large animal kit in the back – calving ropes, those familiar unchanged tools of my trade for decades and perhaps centuries; a voluminous blue PVC calving gown; the surgery kit all wrapped up in its crinkly sterile bag; and an assortment of needles, syringes and medications that I couldn't imagine I would ever be able to remember, to which I added a pair of spotless wellingtons, two cereal bars, a banana and a litre bottle of water – we drove the 80-yard journey in our separate vehicles. I was quite pleased that by the time I had manoeuvred myself into my parking space, Mike had disappeared inside. It gave me time to take a deep breath of the crisp first-of-autumn morning air, test myself on whether I could remember the large animal kit checklist Mike had given me five minutes earlier (I couldn't), and gather my thoughts.

The practice building and its courtyard and outbuildings, built in the 18th century I guessed, in more of the local stone, filled the apex of a triangular piece of land that was enclosed by two narrow lanes that met each other at the top and then each led down to the main square. Next door to the practice was a NatWest bank that formed the base of the triangle, with a frontage on the main drag. I was just trying to decide what would look stranger – entering the practice via the back door from the courtyard where I'd parked, or going in the front door, which would require me to leave the courtyard and walk around the side of the building – when Stanley came bounding out to greet me like a big old dog.

'Fantastic to see you, Anna. Fantastic. Well done for getting here early, it means I can give you the grand tour of the surgery before I head out on my morning calls. Everyone's dying to meet you.'

Stanley bustled me inside and across a narrow corridor into the clean, bare reception area with its obligatory notices about hamster cages for sale and stacks of leaflets about vaccination, worming and other hot topics. 'Waiting room, obviously. Judith's domain. Judith – Anna, our brilliant new vet: Anna – Judith, our wonderful receptionist.' A competent-looking woman with kind eyes and a reassuring presence came out from behind the low desk and shook my hand with a strong, cool grip. She was solidly stocky with thick brown hair cut in an ageless style. I guessed she was probably in her late 30s. 'Anna, so lovely to finally meet you,' she said, in a way that made me believe she really meant it. 'I don't know what you were thinking of, coming to work with this pair of old reprobates in the back of beyond. But good luck to you. At least you've got a decent nurse.' It felt like being the new girl at school, and discovering that the girl I was to share a desk with was the nicest girl in the class.

Stanley propelled me around the rest of the set-up: downstairs, arranged in a horseshoe shape around the reception area, were two sparsely-furnished consulting rooms; the large animal drug store full of medieval-looking kit; and the accounts room. 'We're too small for a practice manager but Lois does our accounts,' said Stanley as he opened this last door and gave me five seconds to peer inside. 'Mmmm – not quite nine, so Lois won't be in yet,' he murmured, glancing at his watch. I made a mental note that this little cubbyhole was where the kettle and biscuit tin lived.

Upstairs was the vets' room I'd already seen; the lab room with a binocular microscope and stains, biochemistry and haematology analysing machines; an autoclave; and the darkroom for developing X-rays. It all smelt reassuringly like every other practice I'd ever entered – a top note of cleaning fluids and surgical spirit, with a slight but persistent whiff of veterinary malevolence (surgical waste plus wet dog). Like the town itself, the practice seemed small, cheerfully unmodern, and at ease with itself.

Back downstairs, we crossed the open courtyard to a converted outbuilding that contained a small operating theatre, a set of kennels, a dog shower, and the freezer room that doubled as a laundry. 'It's not ideal,' admitted Stanley. 'Not what you'd call ergonomic. You do end up struggling across the courtyard with collapsed dogs a bit more than I'd like. And I'd love to be able to kennel dogs and cats separately so they wouldn't upset each other. Ah' – a delighted exclamation – 'good morning, Penny. Penny, meet Anna. Anna, Penny.'

The practice nurse Penny, a diminutive blonde in a neat ponytail and crisp uniform, and surely only just out of school, was crouched amongst the kennels preparing them for the day. We exchanged broad, shy smiles.

'Okay?' broke in Stanley. 'All good? Good. Sorry to have to rush off on your first morning but we've kept the diary pretty clear for you, and Mike will either be consulting or in the vets' room catching up on paperwork if you get stuck.' Stanley bounced off to his mucky Land Rover, banging his head as he jumped in.

I wandered into 'my' consulting room and closed the door. It was 40 minutes into the first day of my first proper job: the culmination of five years of studying. I was Anna Barrington, Member of the Royal College of Veterinary Surgeons, and it was time to get my teeth into what I'd been trained to do. Mike was next door consulting and Stanley was out on a call; I was in charge of my destiny, elated in my brand new green high-collared consulting smock. (Judith had had the foresight to order one for me, since Stanley's would have been too long, and Mike's too short, and I had proudly put it on, enjoying the sensation as each popper clicked shut.) My loins were girded. I was ready for action.

But there was no action.

I opened and closed each drawer of each of the white-fronted cabinets in my room. Syringes, nail clippers, scissors and thermometers were all laid out neatly in their labelled places. I opened the door and wandered out into the empty waiting room, where Judith was swearing gently and intently at the computer screen, trying to make something print. I headed off to the drug store and looked through all the medications, familiarising myself with the trade names and testing myself on what they each did – the antibiotics, the analgesics, the hormones in brown glass bottles for the manipulation of cattle breeding cycles, the calcium and glucose and magnesium for collapsed cows. I went over in my head what I'd do if a fitting dog came through the door and checked for rectal diazepam. I went back to my room. I wondered whether it was too early for a cup of tea and a bun: would it be considered poor form if I nipped over to the patisserie? I thought of Athena, and wondered how her first day at the Royal Veterinary College was going.

Just as I was cleaning the consult table for the third time I heard the front door being buzzed over and over again, then the door opening and slamming shut. A small plaintive voice wailed, 'Get the vet, get the vet, please get the vet.'

Judith came charging through to my room. 'Quick. Anna. What do you know about hamsters?' What did I know about hamsters? The gestation period, which seemed unlikely to be very useful at this point. Not much more. My mouth went dry and I felt an old familiar tightening in my gut.

In the waiting room was a small hysterical girl with long plaited hair, dressed in her school uniform and holding a motionless hamster. In between sobs she managed to gasp that her name was Amelia, his name was Mr Jennings, and she'd dropped him. Mummy was trying to find somewhere to park the car. She was going to be late for school.

Mr Jennings the hamster was looking pretty blue and I could see he wasn't breathing well. I gently scooped him up, took him across the courtyard and into the operating suite, and laid him on the stainless steel operating table, where he looked very still and very small. I turned on the oxygen, and put the nozzle at the end of its corrugated tube to his nose. Come on, Mr Jennings.

Startlingly, Mr Jennings woke up instantly. Great! And shot straight up the corrugated tube towards the anaesthetic machine. Not great! My thoughts raced, flashing back to the time my pet rat B52 had disappeared into my sofa for a week. I could not let the little chap make it into the anaesthetic machine, he'd never make it out alive. An image came unbidden to my mind and I considered, for about half a second, swinging the tube round my head to get him out – like children I'd seen playing at the seaside, whizzing tubes around their heads and making them flash and make a 'woo woo' noise. But then he might splat against a wall on exit. Stupid idea, Anna. Think. Quickly. (And less stupidly.)

My next thought was to go and get Mike. But I quickly dismissed that idea too. For one thing, there wasn't time: this was an every-moment-counts situation. For another, the thought of telling him I had lost a hamster up an oxygen tube was not at all attractive. Think, think.

I detached the tube from the machine and blew down it, hard. And hurrah! Out came a slightly damp, but none-the-worse-for-wear, Mr Jennings.

With outward calm, and inward waves of relief and exhilaration, I returned him to Amelia – now taking deep shuddering breaths in the waiting room under the supervision of her glamorous boiler-suited mother. A gorgeous Labrador puppy completed the party, wagging her tail rhythmically against the bench in innocent doggy pleasure at this unexpected family outing.

I was rewarded with a look of pure hero-worship from Amelia, an extravagant embrace from her mother – 'I'm Tamara Norton and you must be the new vet. So awfully embarrassing to meet like this, but thank you, darling, thank you, thank you.' – and a tight-lipped comment from Lois, who had just walked through the door. Avoiding all eye contact she declared on this our first meeting, before stalking off to her room, that, 'We'll have to tell Stanley he's got competition in the exotics department.'

After Tamara and her entourage had calmed down and headed off to restart their days, everything was quiet again. My racing heart stilled and I sat down to take stock. Plus points: I had survived my first consulting session. Perhaps veterinary surgery didn't need to be that difficult after all. Perhaps I might make it through on a combination of common sense and bravado. Minus points: I was an hour into my first day and already damp under the armpits and emotionally drained. In fact, I was feeling that post-adrenalin exhaustion that I associated with marathon training, or being shot at in the TA. Only, if this day was a marathon, I was only at mile three.

So, marathon-style, I gave myself water, a snack, and a pep talk. 'Come on Barrington, get on with it.'

Half an hour later, Mike emerged. 'Everything under control here, Anna?'

'Yes,' I smiled. 'Everything's under control.'

CHAPTER FOUR

The vet's ABC

'Let's get you happily settled in before we start sending you off on farm calls on your own,' beamed Stanley.

'Let's make sure you're vaguely competent before we let you loose on those poor farmers,' sighed Mike.

I'd been attracted to Mike and Stanley's practice in Ebbourne because it was a mixed one, where I would be able to work with both small animals (mostly pets) and large animals (mostly on farms). The mixed practice – now perhaps heading for extinction – was even then a dying breed, but it was exactly what I needed: I knew myself well enough to realise that if I didn't use all the skills I'd just spent five years learning, I would swiftly lose them.

Nevertheless, for my first few weeks in Ebbourne, as outside the drifting sea mists were thickening and the leaves were turning, I was kept pretty much confined to base, not using that broad array of hard-won skills, but working almost exclusively on dogs, cats and small furries.

I did pick up a few straightforward sessions to dehorn or castrate calves on farms that Mike and Stanley considered had reasonable handling facilities, and I attended my share of the out-of-hours calls – I had to, or Mike and Stanley would have been on their knees, sharing the nights between themselves – but other than that I was kept in the surgery, serving what I realised was a kind of unofficial veterinary apprenticeship. It was frustrating not to be able to pull my weight for the practice immediately, but I quickly realised that Mike and Stanley were both right. All those skills, all that knowledge, that I had spent so many years acquiring, would only take me so far. I needed to hone my skills. And there were some things they didn't teach you at vet school.

And so I worked hard through those first weeks to master my vet's ABC: which, of course, stands for anal glands, bites, and castrations. A great deal of my September was spent spaying and castrating: cats, dogs, rabbits, even the odd guinea pig. Thank God for all that practice with the RSPCA over the summer. And thank God for surgical glue – a fantastically useful alternative to stitching for rats and rabbits, because those small furries just loved to bite their stitches out. Even so, I was painfully slow at first, and there were many occasions when my hands shook or I just couldn't find that uterus. The old hands at the RSPCA could do a bitch spay in 20 minutes, from anaesthetic to stitch-up. At the beginning, I would take easily an hour and a half, not including my meticulous write-up ('Anna, we need a note, not an essay,' Stanley finally spluttered). Penny was almost as new as me, bless her – she turned out to be not 16 as I had first assumed, but 23, and like me she had come to her chosen profession relatively late. So we were pretty much learning together. I was relieved not to have some fierce old super-efficient nurse looking askance at my every incision, but with the partners often both out on farm calls it did mean I sometimes felt like I was operating without a safety net.

I knew all the arguments in favour of neutering and I believed in them strongly: castrated dogs and cats are less likely to run off in search of in-season animals and end up lost or splatted on the road, and are less aggressive; entire male rabbits that are kept together have been known to rip out each others' testicles fighting; early-spayed bitches are at less risk of breast cancer and infections of the womb; unwanted litters of kittens and puppies and baby rabbits are just too awful and a drain on the animal charities. Nonetheless, I was always very conscious that neutering was an elective procedure. Owners were trustingly handing over their perfectly healthy pets, sometimes with mixed feelings about whether they wanted their beloved Tibbs or Rover to be 'done' at all. They expected, rightly, to receive a perfectly healthy pet back again.

One busy late September morning, when I had got my cat spaying times down to a 45 minute average, a particularly fat tortie kitten, Queenie Black, came in to be 'done'. I probably should have sent her home to go on a diet – too much fat makes it more difficult for the vet and riskier for the patient and it is slightly harder to lose weight after neutering – but, perhaps because I did not want to seem a shirker and it was quiet, I went ahead with the procedure.

Penny and I had spent our first month together in constant good-natured tussles over the height of the operating table: at five foot and half an inch she was almost a full foot shorter than me which meant one of us would be stretching or leaning uncomfortably at all times when we were working together.

This time, we adjusted the table to a height that was somewhere in the middle (and therefore uncomfortable for both of us, in fact). Penny brought in the sleepy kitten who had already had a pre-med to take the edge off. I double-checked the anaesthetic dosage, then Penny hugged Queenie to her tenderly but firmly, and clamped the vein on her front leg with her thumb. That stopped the blood supply from flowing back to the heart, raising the vein up nice and proud for me to inject into. I clipped the area, swabbed with cotton wool and surgical spirit, then inserted the needle. I pulled back the plunger, to check I had hit the vein, and felt my stomach lurch as blood failed to spiral up into the syringe. I had missed. I tried again, and missed again. 'Third time lucky … ' Penny said, as though she were musing about something incredibly unimportant. It was sweet of Penny to try so hard to let me know she wasn't judging me, but my own inner voice was not so kind. I shouldn't need a third go, it hectored me. Finally I found the vein, injected the liquid and Queenie fell quickly into a peaceful sleep. We popped a tube into her airway and connected her to the anaesthetic circuit. Penny set to clipping Queenie's fur with meticulous care, while I scrubbed up, sorted my kit out, and clipped my sterile drapes onto the flank of the motionless mog. I winced as I attached one to the delicate skin – they did pinch rather.

I made my incision and had a gentle feel around with a pair of blunt forceps. Queenie was six months old so I was looking for an ovary the size of a plump grain of rice, and a uterus the size of a pencil lead. Nothing. I thought about my diligent former clerking partner, Mary. In all the time we had shared rotas together she had never seemed to encounter any difficulty in finding these structures. How I wished I had had Mary's focus in anatomy class.

With her quick understanding of what was needed, Penny raised the table up to my comfort-level, and raised her arms above her head to continue to monitor the anaesthetic. I muddled around a bit more: still no ovary, no uterus. My jaw tightened, my stomach seized. I looked over the table at Penny. She offered quietly, 'Maybe make a bigger incision?' I shook my head. That wasn't it. Penny tried again, tender but firm, just as she had been with Queenie. 'Remember the time you thought you were in but you weren't? Could you have done that again?' I had in fact made that mistake more than once – not cutting through the peritoneum before starting to search around – and it was easy to do with overweight animals because they had a deceptive layer of fat between the skin and the peritoneum. I felt a flush of anger that I was in this situation. Anger at Mrs Black, for expecting me to operate on an overweight kitten, then, quickly, an anger redirected at myself for my inexperience and ineptitude. Unwilling to ask the partners for help with what should have been a straightforward operation, I took a breath to steady myself and enlarged my initial incision again. Penny and I both smiled widely as I cut through the thin, shiny peritoneum, entered the abdominal cavity and exposed another layer of fat. She'd been right. Hands now shaking, I looked around. I still couldn't find anything. I spent a further 15 minutes in a determined search and there, finally, were the tiny sex organs.

I carefully removed them, tying off each blood vessel so that Queenie wouldn't simply bleed out. I used the standard technique involving clamping off and then tying with cat-gut, left ovary first. My first tie was too tight; the cat-gut snapped; and the air in the operating room went blue. I over-compensated with my second tie, leaving it so loose that when I made my cut, blood simply oozed straight through my knot. I wasn't taking any chances on my third attempt, and tied a triple-ligature. I managed the right ovary and the solid, more meaty cervix at my first attempt – tiny triumphs.

Now all I had to do was check there was no bleeding; check again just to be sure, with Penny looking on patiently; and stitch up the original incision, layer by layer. I knew from vet school that the skin healed beautifully without external stitches if there were good underlying intradermal stitches just under the surface, but Mike had his own reasons, borne of some 20 years' practice, for insisting on them. 'Stitches are like an appointment-reminder system. Half the owners wouldn't bring them back for their check-ups if they didn't need their stitches taking out.'

I stitched Queenie up especially prettily and Penny lovingly settled her into the kennels for the day. I couldn't believe what a meal I had made of the simplest of procedures but I had done it. There was just time for a celebratory cup of tea and a croissant before the next one.

Most days, though, there wasn't enough neutering to keep even someone as new and slow as me busy. So I would be given other treats to deal with.

For example, I saw a lot of cats with abscesses, from being bitten in fights. Cats' canines are like long needles and when they bite they are essentially administering a bacteria injection. The pus-filled abscesses that then form under the skin can be intensely painful. They will tend to be on the head and neck of brave cats who go head to head, or on the bottom of cats that have been running away. Or on the hand of naive and inexperienced vets.

The day after my adventure with Queenie, in the middle of a quiet, drizzly late September afternoon, I was brought an old tabby cat having difficulty peeing. This can be an emergency for a cat, so Penny had asked his owner to wait in reception, admitted him straight away, and popped him up onto the table in my consulting room. Squeezing the bladder gently, I could feel that it was massive and I was not able to manually empty it with gentle pressure.

I was going to have to proceed to unblock it immediately. Penny hurried off to prep the operating theatre. As I continued my gentle examination, the tom, who up until this point had given every appearance of being a docile old gent struggling quietly through his pain, suddenly became incredibly agitated, squirmed around, and bit me right through my thumb. I felt his teeth slice through my skin and crunch down to bone. Then I felt a very hot, searing sensation and saw blood running from my thumb and pooling on the floor.

I reacted with admirable calm and professionalism, screaming 'You f*cker' and jumping up and down. When I regained my composure I applied a makeshift bandage and went out to talk to the owner. Judith directed me with a raised eyebrow and almost-suppressed smile towards the large elderly lady, head nodding over a magazine in a corner of the waiting room. I explained the emergency situation and noted casually that the tom was pretty feisty. 'Oh yes,' she nodded slowly, as she hoisted herself to her feet, 'it's a semi-feral. We can never get near him normally. It was only because he was so sick that we managed to catch him for you.' Thanks so much for the warning, I thought. My hand was swelling before my eyes and my very own medical appointment beckoned.

The other really big treat, for really lucky days, was a dog with an impacted anal gland. The anal glands are at four o'clock and eight o'clock of dogs' and cats' bottoms. They can be full of very smelly matter and their role, other than making vets' rooms whiffy, is disputed. An impacted anal gland – which is a fairly common problem in small dogs – has to be manually squeezed, like a nasty pus-filled spot. And sometimes, these glands, on being squeezed, simply explode. Lovely.

We had one regular patient who came to get his anal glands squeezed once a month the way some ladies have their nails done. He was a very game little short-haired Dachshund named Horace whose owner, the white-haired and dapper Mr De Lacey, lived in the finest of Ebbourne's many manor houses.

Horace and Mr De Lacey would always roar up to the practice in Mr De Lacey's buffed up silver Jaguar, with Horace sitting up smartly in the passenger seat.

The first time I met them was later on the afternoon of my unfortunate encounter with the semi-feral tom. Penny and Judith rushed out, alerted by Horace's barking and the Jaguar's engine. Penny greeted Horace, picked him up and started stroking him. Judith – to my surprise, because I had her down as an intensely practical woman – started stroking the Jaguar.

I introduced myself and read through Horace's notes. Horace had been having his glands squeezed once a month for over three years: an unpleasant business for Horace and the vet, and a costly one for Mr De Lacey. I pictured poor Horace scooting on his bottom all day, along the thick carpets and tiled floors of the De Lacey manor house, trying to relieve the pressure. 'Have you

considered removing Horace's anal glands altogether?'
I asked.

Mr De Lacey coloured. He took off his glasses and wiped
them carefully. 'Miss Barrington,' he said. 'I am afraid that
that is something I simply will not countenance.'

I was confused. Mr De Lacey appeared to dote on
Horace. I tried again. 'This problem isn't going to improve
on its own. And I see from his notes that you've tried
bran and he has firm motions yet he still suffers with this
problem. You and Horace will be here every month for the
rest of his life. We could fix this with a surgical procedure.'

Mr De Lacey raised his eyes to the ceiling as though
in silent prayer. Then he put a kindly arm on mine. 'Miss
Barrington,' said Mr De Lacey wearily. 'I do welcome you to
Ebbourne. I would be so very grateful if you would please
squeeze Horace's glands for me today. And then, you might
find it instructive to consult Mr Dalyrimple.'

I obliged, of course.

'Ah yes,' deadpanned Stanley up in the vets' room later
that day. 'That was my handiwork.' Stanley recalled that he
had operated some years ago on Horace's father, Stephan,
to remove his troublesome anal glands. 'Well, as you know
Anna, faecal incontinence is a potential complication of
anal gland surgery. This was sadly the case for little Stephan,
although it only occured when he barked.'

'Ah', I said. 'Because of the increased abdominal pressure.'

Stanley nodded. He was pursing his lips together now,
trying and failing to suppress a smile and look mournful
and guilt-ridden. 'And every time he was in Mr De Lacey's

sports car, he would go ballistic barking.' He nodded again at my open-mouthed realisation. 'Yup. Everytime. All over the windows.'

The next afternoon, a Saturday, I happened to be on duty when Mrs Black rang to report that she had a very lethargic kitten with a big bloated tummy. With sinking heart I agreed to meet her immediately at the practice. I examined Queenie and her enlarged abdomen, popped a needle and syringe in, and to my horror, a yellow liquid filled the tube. 'That looks like urine,' I thought to myself and went to ring Mike, who was on 'second call' that weekend. I felt bad: Mike was a dedicated family man, always making the effort to get back in time for a bedtime story, and today was an especially precious weekend because it was his mother's 80th birthday party. But he came promptly and uncomplainingly, expertly tying on his gown whilst moving at pace into the operating room where I had settled Queenie. I felt a mixture of disappointment in myself and intense relief that Queenie was now in safe hands. Together Mike and I opened her up again, this time from underneath, between her nipples. We found a ruptured ureter. I must have somehow damaged this tube connecting the kidney to the bladder when I had been searching through all the fat trying to find her uterus. So now this poor little kitten was piddling straight into her abdomen. 'So Anna,' said Mike, with only a quick rubbing of his eyes under his glasses betraying any disappointment he might be feeling in me, 'what are our options? We are where we are, now you have to keep it together so you can fix it.'

I ran through the options. Reconstruction of the tiny ureter was a specialist job. We could refer Queenie on to a specialist, but that would mean more time and another, very difficult, operation.

'Or,' said Mike, 'don't forget, animals have two kidneys and can survive on one. We can be thankful it wasn't heart surgery.' We tied off the ruptured ureter and stitched Queenie back together.

I enquired after Queenie's health regularly for the next few months, and even after that. I can still make my stomach turn when I think of what that little bundle went through.

Some days through that early autumn I would do several neuterings in a row. My hands became raw and chapped from the constant scrubbing up. You're supposed to scrub for five minutes, and of course I diligently watched the clock as I removed the top layer of skin with anti-bacterial wash and a brush. It was also terrible for my back because of the positioning of the operating table – until Judith had the brainwave of giving Penny an orange box to stand on during procedures. I never pranged another ureter, and little by little my times came down so that by the middle of October I was averaging 35 minutes for a cat spay. I had also become a fairly competent anal gland squeezer. By mid-October I could now not only find the impacted gland, but nine times out of ten I could empty it without an explosion. And, as my hands roughened up, my client patter, complete with a pre-emptive line about where I was from, to head off the inevitable wary 'you're not from around here', became slicker.

I had felt reasonably comfortable from the start in my handling of another common complaint: dogs with skin conditions. Straight out of college, I knew that you weren't supposed to give steroids and antibiotics together, because then there was no way of knowing which one was working. For six weeks, I followed the protocol to the letter, asking owners to try one first and then the other. Finally Judith pointed out to me over a cup of tea that the owners were patiently listening to my earnest lectures then coming back to see Mike, who pragmatically handed out both.

My cups of tea with Judith often came with a filthy joke and some useful piece of information attached. Once it was a friendly warning that it had come to her attention that I had been driving too fast along the top road. 'You're not in the big anonymous city now, Anna, my dear. There's only one white Land Rover in Ebbourne, so you have to understand, everyone's going to know where you've been, at what speed and,' she gave me a wink at this point 'with whom.' Another time it was a quiet heads-up that my next client had shocking body odour and wandering hands. A third time I had saved up several pieces of local dialect that were baffling me, for Judith to translate. I thought of these chats as my little induction sessions and would have taken a pen and paper with me if I didn't think it would have looked strange.

A cup of tea one gloomy afternoon in the middle of October saw me regaling Judith with what I thought was a funny story about Mr Hathaway and his red setter, Monty. Monty had been brought in with a terribly itchy patch of eczema, which he had made worse by tearing at it in discomfort and frustration. I had treated the poor old boy with steroids *and* antibiotics (I was a practical old-hand by now) plus an Elizabethan collar to stop him from traumatizing himself any more. 'But oh Judith, Monty had terrible teeth and the most appalling breath, but I couldn't mention it, it really would have been so embarrassing, because Mr Hathaway's breath was worse, and he's only got about three teeth left in his entire mouth.' I waited for Judith to laugh that hearty laugh of hers. Instead, always smiling her warm, kind smile, she broke off from mopping the floor and said, 'Anna, how can you let a dog walk out of here with a sore mouth?'

The following morning, Judith gave me one of her looks, as an obese Labrador, Sandy, was brought into my consulting room by her equally obese owner, Mrs O'Mara, for her vaccinations. A vaccination is a good opportunity for a general health check so I ran through the usual nose to tail examination. 'Any concerns, Mrs O'Mara, everything okay? Yes, Sandy, you're a good girl, what a good girl,' I said as I did a full examination: lifted her lip, checked her teeth, pressed her gum, looked at her head, ran my hands down her neck, body, underneath, checking for any asymmetries or lumps, lifted her tail and ran my hands down it, looked through her coat for any signs of scurf or parasites, had a

74

listen to her heart. She was, other than the excess pounds she was carrying, a beautiful healthy specimen. Then, feeling the heat rise in my cheeks, and staring mostly at the floor, I stumbled my way through a lecture on diet and the risks to Sandy of carrying all that extra weight – the arthritis, the heart disease, the diabetes. An increasingly red-faced Mrs O'Mara nodded at everything I said and left as soon as she could. I was doubtful my lecture would have any impact, especially when I saw Stanley looking curiously at the appointment book later that day. 'Judith,' he asked, 'why has Mrs O'Mara booked to come and see me later when she saw Anna this morning?'

'I couldn't say.' Judith shrugged. Then she speared Stanley with another of her looks. 'But if you don't tell her Sandy has to lose 15 kilos, I'll put you on Anna's castrate list for tomorrow.'

When prisoners are being prepared for life 'on the out', they are occasionally sent out on day release. When children are growing up there comes a time when their parents decide they can walk to the corner shop on their own. As the days shortened and October drew to a close, Mike and Stanley occasionally sent me out on a house call.

These were often welfare visits for the owner as much as the animal, and the partners would sometimes make me log them as 'passing calls' – which were much cheaper because they didn't involve a special journey – when they were nothing of the sort. Mike liked to pretend he disapproved of this, as poor business practice.

These were the times I loved: ripping through the autumn glow of the countryside in the Land Rover, windows down, cool air rushing in, thinking: 'I'm being paid for this.'

And gradually, the blur of patient names and owner names and acronyms and drug names started to form patterns. I knew where everything was kept. I worked out the computer system. Not every patient and every client coming through my door was a new and unknown quantity.

At the end of each day's excitement I would head back to my little room in Mike's house. I felt a little awkward imposing on him and his family for weeks on end and tried to find ways to keep out of their way.

If I wasn't on call, or staying late writing up notes, I played squash at a local Bridport club or went swimming at the local pool. For my birthday, Judith bought me swimming soap for getting the chlorine out, and the thoughtfulness of the gesture from my new colleague touched me hugely. 'Can't have that barnet going green, can we?' she joked, as if it was really nothing. I'd often take convoluted routes there and back, practicing finding my way around the narrow roads and trying to commit to memory the peculiar-shaped oak that marked the entrance to a particular farm, or the succession of turnings that took me deep into the valley to another. I arrived home after the family supper, and warmed up the plate that had been left for me before retreating to Mike's study and the telephone.

Mobile phones were really used for emergencies only back then, and the charges meant that no one would use one to make a normal call where there was a landline available. So if Mike was not on duty I tied up the home phone talking to Sally and Lena and Athena.

Lena was locuming in Shetland, up at the end of the world, where if an animal fell ill in the night and there were no ferries running to that particular island, there was nothing she could physically do about it. Athena was thriving academically but indulging her taste for awful men and falling for the entirely unsuitable resident of neurology at the Royal College. Sally was working too hard in her small animal practice in London. Though I missed my spaniel, Nellie, terribly, I was pleased I had left her with Sally. Nellie couldn't have moved into this lively, dog-filled family home with me – she was a typically game springer spaniel, but also somewhat anxious, and had a nervous tic of peeing on the floor whenever she met someone new. And I knew Nellie would take care of Sally. It was to Sally that I picked up the phone most often: partly to get a fix of Nellie-news, and partly because I felt that of all my friends, she was the one who needed these new-vets-support-club conversations the most.

I often thought about Mary and other vetting con- temporaries too: people whom I had come to know over five fairly intense years. Mary popped into my thoughts whenever I was doing something practical we had learnt together, like taking and examining a skin scrape. In fact several procedures would each bring to mind particular

CALL THE VET

people. But it turned out I had parted ways with Mary and most of the others without exchanging numbers (this was way before the wonders of Facebook or even e-mail) so that was that.

Sally, Lena, Athena all understood – because they were doing it too – that under the serene professional exterior I was trying to show to the world, I lurched wildly, often on a minute-to-minute basis, between the triumph of getting something right and the terror of making a mistake; and between intense gratitude at my wonderful life and a nagging sense of there being something missing. Late into the night we would swap horror stories, confirm diagnoses, comfort each other over our inadequacies, counsel each other on our love lives, and compete over who had suffered the worst indignities in pursuit of our chosen profession.

Recalling my latest humiliation, dinner with my grandmother might have gone better if I'd brushed the anal gland pus out of my hair first.

CHAPTER FIVE

Letting my hair down

It was a Monday morning in early November, and Penny was not looking quite as clear-eyed and pink-cheeked as usual. 'You alright, Pen?' I asked, taking in her tousled hair and creased nursing uniform.

'Yup, fine. Just sleep-deprived. Den and me had a wicked weekend in Newquay. Young Farmers convention by the sea. Well, more of a beer festival really. You know, the usual.' I didn't know: I hadn't grown up around Young Farmers. This was yet another aspect of country life that was a mystery to me. The ensuing description, starting with a tug-of-war, and moving on to a surf in the freezing Atlantic, then a young farmer chained to a lamp post in nothing but wellies and a riding hat, and finally a disco in a barn, had me in stitches but left me quite glad that the upper age limit of 26 meant Young Farmers were forever off limits for me. Penny's laughter tailed off rather suddenly, and she bit her lip.

'You know its November the 5th on Wednesday?'

I nodded. Of course. November the 5th is a big date in the veterinary calendar. Remembering gunpowder, treason and plot is a bit of fun for most people, but for dogs and their owners it can be traumatic. In fact, I had already looked at the medicine cupboard, wondering what we had in our arsenal for the occasion. 'Well, Young Farmers are organising a bonfire and fireworks display. In fact, I've organised the whole thing, but I can't take Jazz, and I can't leave her either. It's been bad enough with the shooting season this year. One bang and she starts shaking and hides under the table. Have you got anything to help?'

Jasmine, or Jazz, was Penny's young collie – a slim, fit border collie from a working line. I explained that drugs probably weren't the answer. 'A friend was put on diazepam for anxiety, and she said she was still aware of what was happening around her, she just couldn't do anything about it. That must be pretty scary for an animal.' There were desensitising tapes and CDs, that slowly exposed a dog to the sounds and sights of fireworks and suggested rewarding them with treats when they didn't react. 'But you haven't got time for that now. You'll have to skip the display, stay in with Jazz, shut out as much of the noise as you can, and not react to her scared behaviour.' Penny nodded. Poor Jasmine. Bonfire Night was a miserable time for many dogs, and it seemed like Guy Fawkes was remembered for nights on end these days.

There was one date, though, that seemed to loom even larger for most of the town than November 5th. From October onwards, all talk in Ebbourne was of the

Farmers' Harvest Supper, traditionally held on the second Friday in November.

All the farmers and their partners were going, and everyone who worked with the farmers – the vets, the feed merchants, the National Farmers' Union reps, the local agricultural engineer – and their partners. Mike was going with Natasha, and Stanley was taking his lovely and very entertaining wife Vanessa (handily, a brilliant horse vet.) Penny was going with her long-term boyfriend, Den, a wiry young countryside contractor who spent his year outside, hedge-trimming, ditching, fencing, cutting, raking and baling. 'You must go, Anna, it's an Ebbourne institution, the social event of the year,' insisted Penny.

When I asked who would be on call, Stanley just laughed, and even Mike raised a wry smile. It seemed that it was the one night of the year when the farmers let their hair down – and the vets did too. 'Last year,' said Mike, 'I got called to a caesarean. We were all rather merry. I turned up at the farm in my black tie, the farmer was still in his black tie, we both just pulled our jackets off and put on our calving gowns and got on with the job.'

I didn't need much more persuading, even though I knew I would feel a bit awkward as the only single girl there.

The night of the supper, all the farmers were scrubbed up and in their dinner jackets. They looked so smart and polished, and completely different out of their boiler suits or old worn jeans: I couldn't place half of them. 'Oh, it's Anna,' one of them grunted in surprise when he worked out who I was. 'You scrub up alright.' I was wearing one of the few 'nice' outfits I owned – a three-quarter length tight black skirt and a cream silk blouse with billowy arms that wrapped over and tied at the front, and tights, and even heels – they didn't know I'd worn it again and again. My hair was down, and clean: no pus, no placenta, no straw. I even had a touch of mascara on (I'd given up wearing any make-up at all when I was working – it just forever seemed to be finding its way halfway down my cheek after I'd got a dose of something or other in the face). I did feel quite elegant.

The Memorial Hall with its tattered Union Jack flying from a rusty flagpole had been scrubbed up too: the rest of the year it was just a plain old town hall, used for play groups and book groups and ballroom dancing societies, but tonight it had been decked out with intricately-woven corn dolly affairs and sheaves of wheat and corn on the windowsills, and red and white checked tablecloths over the trestle tables set up in three festive rows plus a top table on a little stage at one end.

There were freshly baked plaited loaves on the tables, and dressed plates of newly churned butter. On a buffet table manned by a band of farmers' wives were great bowls full of coleslaw and potato salad, and tureens of delicious-smelling casserole. My mouth started watering: I had developed an enthusiastic taste for fresh local produce since my arrival in this corner of the world. At another table was a free bar offering ale or wine. There was a lot of farming talk, a lot of loud bawdy laughter.

Stanley, who looked like he had arrived promptly and

made heroic inroads into the ale already, greeted me warmly. 'Anna, you know my wife, don't you? Vanessa? She's a modern woman like you: didn't take my name. For some reason she didn't want to go from VE to VD.' Raucous laugh.

Vanessa smiled a forbearing smile – she must have heard that one many times before. 'And you know why Stanley never uses his middle initial when he signs his papers, don't you?' she asked me and the throng of farmers gathered around. 'I guess sexually transmitted diseases weren't such an issue when they christened you Stanley Thomas Dalyrimple.' One farmer nearly choked on his beer. The two of them made a great double act.

Looking round, I noticed Michael Porritt on the edge of the circle surrounding the Stanley and Vanessa show. Michael was the eldest son of a local dairy farmer. He was a hard-working young man with a kind face and huge hands from working outside in the cold all the time. No matter how hard I tried, they always made me think of plates of meat. I really didn't know Michael very well, but as I caught sight of him some unexpected thoughts came to the surface of my mind. What would it be like having a relationship with a farmer? Could I withstand it? They worked so hard and had to get up early every day of the year. On the other hand, Michael's farm was in a beautiful spot, so quiet and unspoilt – a bit like him.

'Shall we sit down?' said Penny, coming up to me and including Michael in her question. Her eyes were twinkling with mischief. So down I sat, with Michael, and Penny and

Den, a couple of Young Farmers friends of Penny's, and two farmers and their partners I knew a little from on-call visits. Mike was at the top table with the chairman of the local National Farmers' Union, Mr De Lacey, their wives, and some other local bigwigs I didn't recognise.

I liked Den: he didn't talk much, but he sat there and smiled with lovely creasy eyes, and clearly enjoyed listening to Penny doing all the talking for the two of them. Michael, well-built and fair, seemed like a nice, sweet young man too.

In the early part of the evening, the conversation revolved around many of the topics I had found mildly baffling at my job interview: the prohibitive cost of rural housing, the possible closure of Ebbourne's post office, rural crime. I found I had developed views on these matters.

As we tucked into the casserole, Michael and Den made a brief foray into the world of vintage tractors: Michael was happy with his Czech Zeta while Den extolled the virtues of the home-grown Massey Ferguson. Tractors and sheep, I noticed, were the two topics that did bring Den's conversation alive.

Between the main course and dessert – beautiful apple tarts, with thick clotted cream or custard – the chairman of the local National Farmers' Union gave a talk about the current situation with BSE or mad cow disease. I had had a couple of glasses of wine by this point and, childishly, found his failed attempts to pronounce 'encephalopathy' quite amusing.

Over dessert, we turned to every farmer's favourite topic: the weather. This was a relief to me because it meant

I probably wasn't going to put my foot in it and mention something I shouldn't. I'd noticed already that farmers could be pretty cagey about their enterprises: on the whole they liked to keep any new ideas, or any difficulties, under their hats. They expected similar discretion from their vets, and I found this unofficial Hippocratic oath made for awkward conversational silences: I would want to enquire after a particular calf or sheep, open my mouth to ask the question, and then stop myself just in time, mouth hanging open, expectant looks trained upon me.

As I was heading up to the dessert table for a second helping, Paul Rivers, wife on arm, intercepted me. He was a very experienced farm manager and I'd been called out to his farm one night a couple of weeks previously for what had turned out to be a straightforward calving. (Sometimes, no matter how experienced they were, the farmers just didn't feel they should be putting their hands in those places: they felt it was a clinical thing they needed a vet for.) 'Anna, this is my wife, Greta. Greta, this is the vet I told you about.' Greta nodded and smiled: I wasn't sure she had any idea what Paul was talking about. 'I want you to know, Anna, that I said to Greta when I spoke to you on the phone that evening you came out to my calving, "Oh no, not a bloody young woman coming up, she won't have a clue what to do," didn't I, Greta?' Greta nodded again, now looking slightly worried at the way the conversation seemed to be going. 'But actually, Anna, you were perfectly alright.'

'Ach, Paul, you are zuch a pig,' said Greta. Spotting the accent (it reminded me of my mother's) I asked her in

German how she came to be living in Ebbourne and soon she was pressing her phone number on me and inviting me to visit any time for *spätzeli und rotkraut* – and conversation.

I sat back down and looked around me at the heaving hall. I realised that I knew, or at least recognised, most of the people there. And it struck me that I didn't feel like an outsider looking in, an observer of someone else's arcane harvest-time ritual. This felt like my ritual, my community. I was becoming a part of it.

Farmers have to get up early every day, big night or not, so by eleven o'clock the night was coming to its conclusion. Standing on the narrow pavement outside the Memorial Hall, Michael said he had to get up early to milk, but could he see me home? I felt like the whole of Ebbourne was watching me. Feeling giddy from too much wine, I was tempted to take him up on the offer and was about to say so when Penny pulled me away. 'Come on, Anna, Den's going to bed too, I want to go and dance.'

Penny had the coming weekend off work, and somehow she persuaded me to go on to the locally legendary nightclub in Crewkerne where we danced for a solid hour before I sloped off to be sick on my shoes. In the taxi home my head was spinning away and Penny was leaning on me and giggling, and then suddenly crying. 'I don't mind if he doesn't want to come out, I don't mind if he doesn't want to dance, I just love him sooooooo much, Anna.'

I had had a great evening.

*

Crawling into work the next morning, a Saturday, I was grateful for the fierce rain raging in off the sea. It felt bracing: just what I needed to blow the cobwebs of my hangover away.

I found the surgery deserted although there was a note from Lois, who had drawn the short straw and was covering reception that morning, that she had just popped out to buy milk. My relief that Judith had had the sense to keep the appointments book clear was punctured by an hysterical phone call. 'It's Mrs Stafford. I need Mike, or Stanley. It's my mare, she's struggling to foal.' I phoned Stanley who was on second call. No answer at home or on his mobile – it was either not with him (quite likely) or out of signal (also very likely). He was probably somewhere en route to the practice but could be picking up a farm call. I ran down the road to Mike's house but just as when I had left it ten minutes previously, the curtains were drawn and all was silent. It was Mike's weekend off and the boys were at granny's; I was loathe to wake him. So, adrenalin acting as an instant hangover cure, I set off for the Stafford farm. I had never even seen a foaling let alone done one, but I knew if I didn't get there quickly we could lose the mare and the foal. My mind went completely blank as I raced over in the Land Rover. It was like someone had just taken the chapter of my mind marked 'horses' and rubbed it all out. There was nothing there. I tried to breathe, slow down, focus. 'You can do this, Anna, you can do this.'

The Stafford farm was an interesting set up. It wasn't really a farm at all, more of a secluded house with some barns and stables built in the local style, and some acres given over to equestrian activities, right in the middle of nowhere and surrounded on all sides by woods. It was one of those farms that I wouldn't have wanted to be visiting on my own at night.

Mrs Stafford, a well-dressed, well-spoken lady in her early 40s, met me at her gate and half-walked, half-ran with me to the stables where I counted six horses peering out at me with varying degrees of interest. There was no sign of a husband, or any children, apart from the large tree house and a forlorn set of cricket stumps. I dimly recalled from one of Judith's little induction sessions, with their fine blend of important information and gossip, that Mr Stafford worked in London during the week, the kids were away at boarding school, and the horses were Mrs Stafford's hobby.

'What is her name, Mrs Stafford?' I asked.

'Josie. In full, Josephine of Marleaze. She is very well-bred. And turned to a top class stallion.'

Great, I groaned inwardly to myself, no pressure then.

The mare – about 16 hands, I guessed; a bay, with a beautiful white blaze down her nose band – was in a sweat, pacing around in her box. Mrs Stafford was in a similar state, and out of breath.

'Hey Josie, hey girl, come and say hello,' I said quietly, looking her up and down from the stable door. Then I tried to get a history out of Mrs Stafford – when had she first noticed a problem and so on – but she wasn't making much sense. Some horse-owners are pretty clued up and will diagnose the problem before you even get there. That was not what I was dealing with here. So I slipped a head collar on the horse, asked Mrs Stafford to hold her, and had a look at what was going on.

There was no sign of any foetal fluids, and no foetal membranes presented. On initial examination, it was clear even to me that this mare was not foaling. Relief flooded through me that I wasn't going to have to deliver a foal; closely followed by dismay that I was going to have to make a diagnosis.

'Well, the good news is that your mare isn't foaling, Mrs Stafford.'

'But she's looking at her flanks,' Mrs Stafford insisted. She was, and that could have been because she was in the beginning stages of foaling, and contracting, except that this mare couldn't possibly be foaling.

'Your mare isn't pregnant, Mrs Stafford.'

I began to repeat my work-up, working slowly partly out of inexperience and partly to give me time to think, over the incessant torrent of anxious questions from Mrs Stafford:

'How can she not be pregnant? I paid £3,000 for the stud. Are you absolutely sure? Can I get my money back, do you think?'

As I lifted up this bay mare's soft, velvety lip to check the colour of the mucus membranes, looking at her gums, she whickered quietly. 'You can sometimes get a second go for free if you don't get pregnant the first time,' I said.

'If Josie's not pregnant, what *is* wrong with her?'

I pressed the membranes to see how healthy her circulation was, and said, 'That's what I'm going to find out, Mrs Stafford. Hey lovey, let's get a heart rate, shall we?'

'What's caused it?'

I checked the mare's pulse by feeling the artery that runs just underneath the mandible. Oh, if only Mrs Stafford would be quiet and let me think. Josie fidgeted from foot to foot.

'Could it be cancer? Is she in a lot of pain? Is it catching? Could my other horses catch it?'

I put the stethoscope in my ears and listened to the mare's heartbeat. She stamped a front foot rather too close to my own.

'What are you doing now?' asked Mrs Stafford, her anxiety constricting her throat.

'It's just a standard work-up, I'm just checking everything out.'

I listened along her flanks to hear what was going on in her guts. They seemed to be constantly on the move, as though someone was flushing a toilet in there over and over: classic spasmodic colic, I thought. Horses have enormous intestines, poorly adapted for our husbandry systems. They are designed for a life of roaming and constant poor-quality grazing and we box them up and feed them rocket-fuel so it's no surprise that they frequently suffer from colic. The most common kind is a spasmodic colic, where the muscles that usually contract in nice smooth rhythmical movements to push the food along go into painful overdrive – constricting and relaxing, constricting and relaxing.

'What are you doing now? And now?'

I realised at this point that Mrs Stafford wasn't really listening to my answers: she was just one of those people who expresses her every thought as a question. Every answer I gave was met with 'mmmm, mmmm, mmmm' and then a far-off look as she started thinking about her next question. She probably loved Mike's more brusque manner, his 'it's going to be fine, leave it to me'. That would have reassured her. My witterings just seemed to lead to more and more questions.

Just as I was concluding my work-up, with my hand inside the mare's rectum checking for any blockages, my pager went off. 'Beep, beep, beep, beep, beep.' The mare and I both started: I was extremely lucky to avoid a hefty kick, and she was lucky to avoid a torn rectum.

These were the times when I thought longingly of James Herriot. If James Herriot had been on a farm with his hand up a horse's bottom, he would simply have been unreachable. There were no mobile phones in those days, not even brick-sized ones with no reception. There were no pagers. Most people didn't even have home phones. He would have taken all the time he needed over his work-up, and done the job in peace, and then he would probably have been invited into the farmhouse for a spot of dinner.

I removed myself from the mare, removed the pager from my pocket, and left it on the front seat of the Land

Rover. Whatever it was, it would just have to wait. I went into my kit in the back of the vehicle and drew up the right quantity of Buscopan – an anti-spasmodic and painkilling injection – into a syringe.

Back at the stables, I stuck the stethoscope back in my ears, and listened to her flanks again, really just to buy myself some more thinking time. With a client like Mrs Stafford I wanted to be absolutely sure of my diagnosis. I deemed obstructive colic less likely after the rectal – no impactions or narrowings of the gut were palpable. And surgical colic was not high up the list – the heart rate was too low for that. Finally:

'Mrs Stafford, your mare has spasmodic colic. Tummy ache. She is in pain, but I can give her an injection that will make her feel better very quickly.'

More questions: 'Are there any side effects? What should I do if it doesn't get better? How long will it take to work?' I answered them all, injected the mare – swab the side of her neck; raise a vein by putting my thumb over the jugular groove halfway down her neck – it comes up like a beautiful hosepipe; pop the needle in; draw it back; blood comes into the yellow fluid and I know I am in the vein; gently inject and pull back, inject and pull back over the course of 20 seconds; pull out; cap the needle and put it in my pocket – and finished up as quickly as I could.

Back at the Land Rover, I cracked open my emergency biscuit supplies and checked the pager. It had been the practice paging me and, delighted to have reception, I dialled the number. Immediately, an unhappy and tense

Lois picked up the phone. 'Anna, at last, thank God. I'm the only one here. Tamara's brought that idiotic Labrador Sophie in. She's eaten something stupid again, we think. Her stomach is really swollen up. You need to get back here now.'

I drove as fast as I dared back to the surgery, running through scenarios. Almost certainly Stanley would have arrived by the time I got back, or perhaps Lois would have called Judith, who had a little nursing experience. If not, maybe I could wait to operate until one of them did get there.

But when I got back to the surgery, it was still just Lois. And when I saw Sophie, I realised I couldn't wait for reinforcements. Her abdomen was huge, she was having trouble walking, and she was clearly in great discomfort. 'She broke into the larder and found her food bag,' wailed Tamara. 'And then Amelia gave her breakfast and she ate that too. Can you believe it?' Sophie started to turn purple. 'Come on, Lois,' I said, 'you're going to be nurse.'

I was worried about gastric dilatation volvulus or GDV. It happens to deep-chested dogs like setters or Irish wolfhounds. The stomach blows up with gas and then twists, stopping gas escaping and cutting off the blood supply. The dog goes into shock and can become toxic, and if the stomach isn't deflated quickly the tissue can die, or the stomach can even rupture. And yet … Sophie's stomach didn't seem to be full of air. I flicked it, listening in with my stethoscope: it didn't ping and it felt rigid.

On X-ray Sophie's stomach was not full of gas, and did not need decompressing; it was chock full of something solid – presumably food.

'Lois, I hate to ask. But even if I ring Penny or Judith they're half an hour away. Sophie's colour is getting worse, she's deteriorating. I have to put her on fluids and put her under and open her up. You have to help me with the anaesthetic: we'll run it light, and you'll just need to help me get her under and tell me what her eyes are doing.'

Lois closed her eyes slowly, drew herself up and nodded.

I talked Lois through how to bring a vein up for me to catheterise to put on a drip. She did a brilliant job; I got the needle in first time, hooked up a bag of fluids, injected the anaesthetic agent and an already-floppy and accommodating Sophie went out like a light. Now we had to tube her.

'Okay Lois, can you hold the head up, and I'll pull the lower jaw down.'

Lois gasped at how heavy a lolling Labrador head was. I pulled Sophie's tongue out and inserted the tube down through her larynx.

'Okay, you can lie her down now.'

I fumbled with the anaesthetic machine and got the oxygen and anaesthetic flowing into Sophie's inert, swollen body. I watched her eyes going down, down, down.

'Lois, you need to watch her eyes. If they come up, tell me.'

We manoeuvred poor Sophie into a plastic cradle so that she was lying on her back, belly up to keep her in the right position on the operating table. I showed Lois how to clip her and clean her, and how to pass me the surgical kit to keep both me and it sterile. Apart from tutting about the mess and donning a plastic apron she did a good job of it all.

Once I was inside, I found two kilos of dry biscuit expanding in Sophie's stomach. Fluid was being drawn into it and it was stretching her stomach like food being poured into an overfilled bin bag. Awful, painful, life-threatening.

'Anna, the eyes are coming up. They're coming up.'

'Okay, that either means she's too light, or she's too deep. I need you to check her reflexes. If you pinch her toes does she pull down her foot?'

To my astonishment and dismay, at this point, Sophie half woke up, paddling all four feet. With her abdomen open on the operating table, she half raised her head as if to see what was going on.

'Turn up the gas, Lois, turn it up.' But Lois was frozen in horror.

And then the dog that would eat anything clocked the anaesthetic tube in her mouth, and started chomping on it. My still-sluggish mind immediately focused. If Sophie managed to bite through her tube, I would have a complete disaster on my hands: the anaesthetic would stop flowing altogether, and she would wake up properly, entirely unstitched. I moved over to turn up the gas then stuck my hand into Sophie's mouth to try to stop her chewing. She bit me, right through my gloves. As blood seeped through the bite-wounds in my gloves (now definitely not sterile), I wrestled a mask over Sophie that delivered the anaesthetic gas that knocked her out again. Once she was out for the count, I re-tubed her, shaking and dripping blood, and stitched her back together.

Good old Sophie recovered beautifully, with nurse Lois by her side stroking her and talking to her until she came around. Within an hour she was wagging her tail and looking for food. Lois went back to her desk. Putting on the kettle, I wondered whether the experience might bring me and Lois closer together. 'I can't wait to tell Judith and the others, Lois: you were a hero.'

'I wasn't a hero and nor were you. I was scared, and you were stupid, and Sophie nearly died. I don't want to talk about it and I don't want you to talk about it, ever again.'

At the end of morning surgery I checked Sophie, now gently snoring in her kennel, and headed out on a couple of farm calls. It was two o'clock by the time I had finished those and checked on my hospitalised patient once more. With my car stash of food depleted by the Stafford scenario earlier, I suddenly felt light-headed and empty-bellied. Lunch would be waiting for me at Mike's house, but instead of driving that well-worn 80 yard stretch, I took off, on a whim, in the opposite direction, driving up out of Ebbourne and over to the Marshwood Vale. Coming across a large wooden crate and a cardboard sign reading 'apples', I pulled over. I dropped a few coins into the honesty jar and picked up the biggest, reddest apple I could find.

Leaning against the warm bonnet of the Defender I took a bite and savoured the moment. The apple was tartly delicious; the apple trees in full turn as a riot of orange and red leaves littered the ground; the views through the light rain deeply restful. It was nearly three months, I reflected, since I had arrived in Ebbourne. Autumn would soon turn to winter. And, lack of lunch and a slight headache notwithstanding, it had been a pretty good day. Mike's house, and the surgery, had been a comfortable cocoon. It had been lovely having delicious hearty meals cooked for me, and reassuring to be able to consult Mike when an emergency call came in for me in the evening. But I wanted to unpack and arrange all my belongings, use the phone when I liked, play Bon Jovi at top volume any time of day, and not worry about the grey colour of my once-white bras hanging above someone else's Aga. And, now that I was managing challenges on my own that back in September would have had me wringing my hands and on the phone for advice, I desperately wanted to make more of a contribution to the practice. Looking out over this wide vista, I felt the need to unfurl my wings, dry the delicate membranes, and fly.

PART TWO

Winter

CHAPTER SIX

Testing, testing

On the first day of December, I finally moved out of Mike's home and into my own.

My new cottage was perched on a hill, halfway along a dirt track in the tiny picturesque village of Redcombe two miles out of Ebbourne. Hillside Cottage: my very own home. It had just one neighbour – owned by a retired high-ranking civil servant and his wife who came up for the weekend sometimes – and fabulous views in three directions of rolling fields threaded with oaks, ash and beech trees. In the distance I could just about make out the area's grandest country house, surrounded by its manicured grounds. When they held a fireworks display (which happened surprisingly often), I could watch from my bedroom window.

I felt overwhelmingly and undeservedly lucky to be working in this beautiful corner of the world, with my very own home, my own car, a decent income, and kind, supportive colleagues.

And yet … and yet. This gentle lifestyle was a long way from the university social life I had just left behind. My cottage – even once the wonderful Cauli had done his magic and installed floors, a kitchen and running water – was isolated, exposed and difficult to heat (the floor was concrete screed over earth, the single-glazed windows rattled in their frames, and the only heating was night storage heaters which were at their peak when I was at work or a 'proper fire' which I could never get going properly until I was nearly ready for bed). The dark valleys with their overgrown hedgerows and tree tunnels, and the villages with their high stone walls, that had at first seemed so pretty and charming, were, at times, starting to hem me in. Most of all, returning to my silent cottage each evening, or going for solitary walks at the weekends, I felt a bit lonely. I would put the radio on or play loud music (I did not own a television) but somehow it was still quiet. Some weekends when I was on call, I found myself hoping for an emergency so I could go out and treat someone's animal and have a conversation. I remembered, slightly ruefully, the advice of my mentor from vet school – advice I had ignored. 'The most important thing for a vet's first job is to be near friends and family.'

I could usually gain a sense of perspective by phoning one of my old friends. Sally, in London, was working back-breaking hours for a man who humiliated her in front of the nurses. I could hear the sounds of traffic and sirens outside the window of her tiny one-room flat whenever we spoke. Lena, on the other hand, was still in Shetland, dreaming of escaping to Africa or India or Bali – anywhere warm and mountainous would do. My isolation was nothing compared with what she was going through. Talking to either one of them reminded me of all the reasons I was happy to be where I was.

This particular mid-winter morning, though, my spirits needed no extra lifting.

December the 6th was always a good day in the Barrington calendar. My ever-thoughtful mother never failed to celebrate an anniversary, a rite of passage or a seasonal festivity (and being an Anglo-German household we had two countries' celebrations to open a bottle of bubbly for).

Saint Nikolaus Day was on the 6th of December: he visits German children who leave their shoes out to greet him. If you have been a good child they are filled with fruit, nuts, marzipan and little toys, maybe a book. If, however, you have been bad then his more demonic accomplice will fill your footwear with coal. Somehow, to date, St Nikolaus' parcels had always found me, wherever I happened to be. I was most relieved to see that he had come early to this large child in West Dorset, now adult and earning but very happy to still celebrate traditions: a sizeable highly-sellotaped jiffy bag with Mum's familiar looping script had arrived and the postie had shoved it through the cat-flap. At home the arrival of these goodies was always announced with a loud, slow knock at the door, but when we looked there was never anyone there. My sister still shrieks in joyful terror at the sound!

Breaking into the Fort Knox of my parcel would have to wait though because – hurrah – I had my first scheduled farm visit to attend to.

Perhaps I had earned their trust. Or maybe it was just the cold weather drawing in. Whatever their reasons, as autumn turned to winter, Stanley and Mike seemed keener to send me out to the farms to tend to the large animals. I was delighted. The only large animals I had attended so far had been emergencies, when I had been on call in the evenings or at the weekends – prolapsed uteruses, milk fevers, colicky horses – or occasional basic disbudding or castrating of calves. Now I was going to get a chance to work with the farmers and their animals in more relaxed circumstances. Plus, spending a couple of hours on a farm was more companionable than seeing a succession of people for ten-minute appointments.

My assignment on this frosty December morning was a routine fertility visit to a Farmer Fairchild. (Economically, it's important for farmers that they get each cow in calf once a year: a routine fertility visit will involve checking any cow who doesn't seem to be getting pregnant, and trying to work out what's going on with her.)

As I rifled through the practice clothes bin, Goldilocks-style, for a boiler suit that would fit me (Stanley was so tall the crotches of his boiler suits reached my knees; Mike was so short that his boiler suits left me with frozen exposed ankles – ah! This one was just right) I hummed contentedly to myself. As I did up the poppers I sighed deeply in pleasurable anticipation. I, Anna Barrington, was a real vet (or at least I looked like one), about to take my kitted-up Land Rover out on a routine farm visit.

'I'm off to see the Fairchilds,' I shouted happily to no one in particular as I walked out to the courtyard. Judith was bantering on the phone with a farmer, but hearing this she broke off the conversation with: 'Right, I can't waste my time winding you up this morning, I've got things to do.' Under pretence of making sure I had taken a sandwich with me (of course I had: a big doorstep cheese and pickle sandwich and a lardy cake in fact) she quickly told me what she thought I needed to know. 'Lizzie Fairchild's been on the land all her life, so she looks 70 but she's probably 40. She loves her cows, she's really kind to them, keeps the older girls even when they aren't milking. She looks a bit eccentric, but don't be misled by all that. She's nobody's fool. Oh and she runs the farm herself – husband's gone.' My joy undented, I set off.

The route took me climbing up out of the bowl in which Ebbourne sat, through a patchwork of fields in winter shades of yellow and green and past a hopeful llama farm. (I imagined I might be seeing some of those llamas one day. There was a new venture in the area using them as companions on guided walks; they carried the baggage and the picnic lunch and sometimes trekked the footpath right outside my cottage.) The countryside looked beautiful to me once more, with the morning frost still clinging to the hedgerows and the now-bare branches of the trees. A flock of birds – plover perhaps, I wasn't really an expert – flew ahead of me, as if they had decided to be my escort for the day. I turned off the road and the low winter sun tried feebly to dazzle me as I rattled up a steep rutted path to the exposed farmyard.

Lizzie was waiting for me by her gate. I leapt out, beamed a smile and held out a hand to her as a raw wind whipped right through my boiler suit. She nodded back neutrally – not hostile, just someone whose smiles I would have to earn, I thought – and her gnarly dry hand in mine made me feel like a child being clutched by their grandma. Her face was like leather, her eyes were blue and intelligent, and she was practically dressed for the cold in an ancient aran sweater, a well-worn once-waxed jacket, a woolly hat and fingerless gloves, which she had accessorised with a striking, unusual necklace.

Lizzie had five cows lined up for me in her artificial insemination stalls – not because I was going to be doing any of that, just because that was the best place on her farm to present cows for examination. Her cows were lovely-looking old-style Friesians – black and white with fleshy frames – and they didn't seem at all put out with the way their morning was going so far.

'These are my girls that aren't bulling, Anna.'

Most cows will show you when they're bulling (or actively in oestrus, ready to be mated), which ought to be every 21 days or so. When they're ready to be served they tend to get more frisky, more active – a bulling animal can cover three to four times its normal distance – and sometimes they mount other cows or get mounted themselves. These days farmers are quite high tech about it. They may even use satellite GPS so they can tell when they're moving about. Back then, the farmers I dealt with relied on simple observation or something to detect pressure on the rump area.

I felt Lizzie's quiet gaze as I started my investigations.

The diagnostic method for working out a cow's reproductive cycle, which was what I needed to establish first, is fairly simple. I had to rectal each cow – literally stick my hand up their bottoms to feel the reproductive organs that lie just underneath the rectum.

But making the diagnosis is less simple. Working by touch, very gently, because rectal tissue is delicate, I had to work out whether I had an early developing foetus, or ripe follicles on the ovaries (meaning ovulation was about to happen), or a corpus luteum (meaning ovulation had taken place but the cycle was possibly stalled at this point).

And the trouble was, one of the injections to kick-start a stalled cycle could also abort a pregnant cow.

I pulled on my gloves and made a start. Rectalling a cow is not an unpleasant task. Dairy cows in particular are used to being handled twice a day and usually from the hindquarters so they are pretty compliant and don't tend to make a fuss. On a cold day like this it was actually pretty agreeable: as I entered cow number one I felt a warm, squishy sensation around my chilly hand and arm and thought, 'people pay good money at the spa for this experience'. It was quite soothing. There was too much poo in this cow though for me to be able to feel anything useful. I hoicked that all out (not sure people would pay up for that experience), and started again. Feeling up and down and around, through two layers (my gloves and her rectal tissue, the thickness of an inner tube), after what felt like half an hour but was probably five minutes, I thought I could detect something spherical and firm the size of a walnut: an ovary, probably. And on the probable ovary, a little firm bump, like a pea sitting on the walnut: a follicle, probably. (I find most of my sizes are food-related. Lumps on animals are often satsumas or plums.) She was probably stuck in this phase and needed to be kick-started to grow the follicle further and release an egg. I injected her with FSH or follicle stimulating hormone.

Same thing for cow number two. Again I knew I was taking too long: five minutes is a long time when you are inside a cow. Again I couldn't be sure. Again I decided to inject with FSH.

Cow number three was a young heifer: unlike the other cows I was examining, this one had never had a calf. She should have just now been starting to cycle. I gloved up freshly and went in, and … nothing. I couldn't find the uterus, I couldn't find the cervix. My spirits sank. And then I caught sight of the vulva and noticed how hairy it was. 'Was this heifer a twin?' I asked Lizzie.

'She was a twin.'

'And was her twin a bull calf?'

'He was,' said Lizzie. And then: 'Oh, of course. She's a Freemartin.'

This was what I suspected. When a cow is carrying twins,

108

they share a blood supply. If the twins are male/female, and too much male hormone from the male twin passes across to the female twin, she will be born sterile. I confirmed my diagnosis by establishing that this cow's vagina was short.

'Mrs Fairchild,' I began.

'Please call me Lizzie,' she said, offering me my first smile of the visit.

'Okay, Lizzie. She is, as you rightly say, a Freemartin. She will never get in calf because she doesn't have the full female reproductive tract. I am sorry but I guess you will have to fatten her and send her on.' Sending her on did not sound as harsh as saying sending her to the abattoir or slaughterhouse but still, Lizzie was no longer smiling.

'Poor beast,' she said. 'Won't get much for her, will I?' Indeed a pure-bred dairy Freisian, even of the older variety with the slightly bulkier frame, would never be meaty enough to make steaks. Pies perhaps. On many dairy farms the pure-bred dairy male calves – who would obviously never be any good for producing milk – were shot, as fattening them just did not make economic sense. I had once illuminated Henry, my vegetarian sister, with this difficult fact and suffered the wrath of my mother when Henry's next trip home had been under a vegan banner. I admired her principles until she became ill on it.

A heavy rain blew in and within two minutes Lizzie and I were soaked. As suddenly as it had started, it stopped, leaving me drenched and miserably cold.

Cow number four 'had the whites': a white trickle of pus was evident. She had a case of metritis, a uterine infection. I felt happy dealing with this as I inserted a long plastic straw into the vagina, gently manipulated it through the bumps and folds of her cervix and into the uterus and injected an antibiotic down the straw and into the infected organ.

Only one cow to do before I could head back to the practice and warm up. But I had more trouble with this final cow. With my hand in her rectum, I could see Lizzie out of the corner of my eye, unsmiling, self-assured, wet, waiting for me. 'I'm not sure,' I said, tentatively. I thought I saw Lizzie suppressing a tetchy sigh. What to do? I knew the partners wouldn't really mind coming to give a second opinion, but I also knew that Lizzie was a busy farmer and it would be another morning's disruption for her. I'd already dithered over the first two cows; I felt I ought to be able to handle this; Stanley and Mike wanted me to handle this; I was desperate to give a diagnosis. Okay, I thought, that's the ovary, and I think I can feel a corpus luteum, the remains of an old follicle. So she's not in calf, and I need to bring her on from this phase. I injected the cow with Prostaglandin.

'While you're here,' said Lizzie, as she walked me back to the gate, 'would you have a look at those two as well?' I had now gone beyond the point where I thought I might ever be warm again, and my lardy cake was calling to me from the Land Rover. 'Fertility test two more?' I quavered.

'Those girls must be 20 years old, they're not going to be calving,' said Lizzie fondly. 'You could hoof them for me though if you've time: I've got the cheese wire ready.'

Wow. I was intrigued just to see a 20-year-old cow: most dairy cows only lived to five or six years and then they either got so knackered they became infertile and stopped calving, or they became lame. Either way, most farmers would send them to the abattoir at this point. We headed down to the yard and Lizzie introduced me. 'This is Katie, and this is Hollyhock.'

Katie and Hollyhock were impressive to behold. Instead of being horizontal, their backs dipped down in the middle, bowed with age. Rather than standing on their toes as young cows do, they were sunken back as though they were rocking on their heels – which explained why their toes had grown. Their udders dangled beneath them, shrivelled and useless. But they still had those beautiful cow faces that I loved, with huge dark eyes and starlet eyelashes. Katie and Hollyhock ambled over to say hello to Lizzie, nuzzling her as she snuck some concentrate out of her jacket pocket and fed them like you would a horse – from her palm.

'Should we move them to the stalls then?' I asked.

'No, they will stand for you, believe me.'

I rolled up my sleeves again and gave these two old ladies their pedicure, trimming away the overgrown pieces of hoof at the toes, forming a slipper of each of their weary feet. That's quite an achievement, I thought: these dainty little feet bearing that enormous weight for twenty years. As I straightened up, gathering up the debris from the procedure from the frozen ground, Lizzie held out her hand. Puzzled, I handed over the doorstop-sized blocks of sawn-off hoof, and she looked at them and beamed me a crinkle-eyed smile. 'Thank you Anna, there's enough here to start a new necklace.'

With blue lips and white fingers, I headed back to the practice. Going over the morning's work as I drove back, I felt pretty pleased with myself. As I drove down into the market square I saw that someone had put up the Christmas decorations while I had been out with Lizzie. White lights twinkled and a Christmas tree stood proudly by the butter-cross. Yes, this had been a good day.

My second scheduled farm visit, the following Monday, was a less routine scenario – but sadly becoming more routine. Soon after I had arrived in Ebbourne, there had been a tuberculosis outbreak around the Emersham parish. Stanley and Mike – and now me too – were having to go out to every farm to test every member of every herd.

TB was a difficult situation for the farmer. Because of the dire consequences for the herd, because there is no cure for bovine TB, because it is potentially infectious to man, and also, I guessed, to guard the export market, there were strict, time-consuming, bureaucratic and burdensome governmental procedures that swung into action as soon as a single case was reported. Vets at least got paid by the Ministry of Agriculture, Fisheries and Food or MAFF, as it was then, to do the testing work, but the farmers just had extra work getting their animals in and through the cattle handling system to be clipped up and injected; and the strain of watching helplessly knowing they might have to destroy members of their herd.

So, despite the happy evening Michael and I had spent at the Harvest Supper, and despite my success in having saved their cow with a vaginal tear the previous week – the night of the cling film incident – I didn't expect to be given a hero's welcome as I arrived on the Porritt farm dressed in my warmest clothes and biggest woolliest hat. Old Simon was there, and Michael, grim-faced, and the other two Porritt children, a younger brother and a sister, all gathered for this sombre task.

The Porritts had 200 dairy cows, all of whom I was going to have to test today.

The dry cows, so-called as they were within about two months of calving but not currently milking, were in the first group, penned in the collecting yard. Michael manoeuvred the first cow into the crush. I clipped two areas the size of a ten pence piece on her neck and gave her two little injections with the specially-designed T-shaped TB 'gun': one injection to test for the presence or exposure to bovine TB and one designed to test similarly for avian TB. She mooed loudly throughout, and crapped comprehensively once at the beginning and once at the end.

A TB test is trying to detect an animal that has TB. The area of the injection comes up in a lump in the presence of TB. But the tests aren't terribly accurate. If a cow has been exposed to the avian TB strain, which is extremely common, and not at all harmful, then the test for the harmful, bovine strain will come up positive even if the cow doesn't have bovine TB. So we inject tests for both avian *and* bovine TB – avian at the top and bovine at the bottom – and then compare the lumps. If the top lump is bigger than the bottom lump, that's fine: the reaction is due to avian TB. If the bottom lump is significantly bigger than the top lump, or there is only a bottom lump, it's not fine. This means the reaction is more likely to be due to bovine TB. The cow is removed from the herd for slaughter and post-mortem, and the whole herd must be re-tested 60 days later.

Michael moved the first cow out and got the second cow in. I clipped twice, measured the skin thickness twice, injected twice. She mooed and crapped. We did this 198 more times.

Michael attempted to make conversation a couple of times, shouting to be heard over the noise of the clanging gates, metal on metal, and the din of the cows. Michael's conversational gambits were mostly about the absurdities, iniquities and dangers of the TB-testing regime. 'TB can't spread from cows to humans anyway if we pasteurise the milk, isn't that right, Anna?' bellowed Michael. And then, 'We should educate our customers. Spend government money on promoting our product, not torturing us. Don't you think, Anna?' And then, 'Take care, Anna. I heard of one vet who was killed by a bull during a routine TB test.'

But, although I didn't entirely disagree with him, and rather enjoyed his concern, I struggled to keep up my end of the conversation: I really needed to concentrate on getting the avian and bovine injections the right way round; and on avoiding getting my fingers caught between the crush and a cow throwing her weight around at the sound of scissors near her ear; and on preventing the 'gun' from slipping and slicing my knuckles. By the end I was wonderingly grateful to Mike who had insisted on me heading to Bridport the previous weekend to buy neoprene fishing gloves. 'Just cut off the tips of the index fingers,' he'd said 'for pulling the gun when you're injecting.' Despite the gloves, I had quickly lost much of the feeling in my fingers (which was, in a way, lucky, because it meant I couldn't feel the pain in my crushed and sliced knuckles). Without them I wouldn't have managed at all.

At the end of all this the Porritts invited me into the farmhouse for some dinner. I was hungry and dog-tired but I said no. It wasn't like in James Herriot's day when each job could be followed by a hearty meal, or a drinking session, or at the very least a cup of tea in the farm kitchen: our time was portioned out and we could rarely afford to stop for such things. And anyway, I felt I had imposed on them enough for one day.

Three days later I returned. Each of the 200 cows had, once more, to be rounded up and put in the crush for me to examine their necks. It was a difficult moment for me and for Simon and Michael when anything walked into the crush with a lump. I would measure the top lump and the bottom lump with my metal callipers, and remeasure, with the Porritts looking on anxiously. More often than not there was no reaction at all but 30 times there was a top lump which was bigger than the bottom lump. Then, at cow number 113, the bottom lump was bigger than the top lump. I double, triple checked before breaking the news.

Michael turned his back on me and walked away. I watched him punch a wall, twice. Then he came back and talked quietly with Simon, his dad. I busied myself with the paperwork I was now going to have to prepare. A whole set of activities would now be set in train. I had to fill out a movement restriction license so that nothing could leave the farm except direct to the abattoir; check and sign the medicine book; and fax the paperwork to the Ministry. Within a few days a valuer would arrive to assess the amount of compensation Simon and Michael would receive for cow 113. The valuers were fair, but there were things that couldn't be compensated for, like suckler calves left motherless, or the loss of bloodlines that had been years in building. I suspected in the Porritts' case that losing the income stream from selling young stock at market, combined with having to absorb the costs of feeding, bedding-down and housing more animals than usual, could sorely test their reserves, both financial and emotional. MAFF didn't offer compensation to farms whose cash flows were not robust enough to cope with these shocks, and it was not unheard of for farms to go under just because of one positive reactor. And quite often the poor beast was not even positive at post mortem.

We continued with the rest of the cows in silence. The rest were all clear, but we all knew it didn't matter. Cow 113 would be destroyed, and the farm shut down. The Porritts' Christmas was likely to be a muted affair.

I searched desperately for something to say to break the silence. What could I say to make it better? Nothing.

As I left, I felt I had to say something. 'Happy Christmas. I'll be back again in 60 days to re-test the herd.' Ugh. Nice one, Anna. Why hadn't I just wished them a better New Year?

Simon nodded, and Michael nodded, and then they turned and walked towards the farmhouse.

Mike seemed happy to provide cover over Christmas time, and I was going to have a whole four days off. Judith and Penny had put up a Christmas tree in the corner of the reception area, and organised a little Christmas party for the afternoon of December 23rd: crackers, party hats, white wine in plastic cups, and a secret Santa. When Mike stood on a chair, ready to make a speech, I realised Penny was missing. 'I think she might be over in the kennels, Anna. Could you go and check?' asked Stanley. In the middle of the courtyard was a huge cardboard box, on which someone had drawn a smiley face and a Santa hat. The box was squealing. I looked inside and there was Penny, jumping up and down ineffectually, arms pinned to her side by the sides of the box.

'You're a very naughty man,' shouted Penny, slapping Stanley on the arm as, liberated, she joined the party. Stanley mimed innocence and confusion. 'Stanley, I know it was you,' protested Penny. 'Who else would sneak up while a girl's sweeping the yard and stick a blinking box over her?'

'It's Judith's fault,' countered a twinkle-eyed Stanley. 'She gave me the box and told me to get rid of it out the back.

And it's your fault. If you weren't so very short, I wouldn't have been able to just reach up and stick a box over your head. Honestly, I don't think anyone could have resisted that temptation.'

The phone rang. 'Hello! Ebbourne's favourite super-vets!' answered Judith exuberantly. Then she held her finger up to quieten us all down. I didn't like the look on her face. She passed the receiver over to Stanley. Now I didn't like the look on his face.

Stanley finished the call and took me to one side. Still wearing the green paper crown from his cracker, he gave me the news. 'That was Lizzie. The cow you injected? She's just aborted.'

Acid washed through my stomach. I thought back to that fifth cow and knew immediately what I had done. What I had felt hadn't been an ovary. It had been a cotyledon – one of those mushy buttons on the inside of a pregnant uterus that attaches to the placenta. I had seen them so clearly only a couple of days before visiting Lizzie's farm, when replacing that prolapsed uterus in the middle of the night.

Everyone had gathered round by now, and Penny had turned off the Christmas music.

'We all make those mistakes when we first start practicing, Anna,' said Stanley. 'I did it myself.'

'It's unavoidable, you're learning,' said Judith, sitting me down and finding my plastic cup of white wine.

'That's why I'd never let a junior doctor anywhere near me,' said Mike grimly. I knew it was the kindest thing he could bring himself to say, which cut me harder than it would have done if he had bawled me out. My throat tightened and for an awful moment I thought I might burst into tears.

Everyone tried to be kind. Even Lois pointed out that my insurance would pay out to Lizzie. But I was furious with myself, and appalled for Lizzie and her cow. I pictured Lizzie finding a dead foetus in the barn, or perhaps stumbling across her cow with the placenta hanging out. I made some calculations: the foetus would have been the size of a small dog, hairless, curled up, eyes unopened. That poor calf that I brought into the world too early. I wanted to crawl into a hole.

I had been looking forward to spending some relaxed down time with my colleagues but now I wasn't in the mood. I wished everyone a happy Christmas and headed back to my cottage, where I sat on my bed and had a good cry.

The next morning, Christmas Eve, I took the wheel cover off the back of the Land Rover so no one would know where I was from and drove the four hours up to my parents in Leicestershire. I spent the journey trying to persuade myself to forget about my veterinary failings for a few days, enjoy the holidays, and make a fresh start in the New Year.

I felt better as soon as my mother, resplendent in red and green, opened the front door, and the smell of pine and baking wafted out. Christmas in my family was a very German affair – my mother's second-favourite holiday, after Easter – and every year she would bake *plätzchen* for weeks and then decorate the entire house according to her chosen theme. As I walked into the house I saw that, as usual, it was completely bedecked (the theme this year appeared to be red apples). There were several Christmas trees: a massive real one in the conservatory, smaller artificial trees in the living room, even a miniature one on the chest of drawers in my bedroom. Amongst the red apples of course were interspersed the kitschy decorations my sister and I had made as children. On my bed was a red bath towel and a green hand towel. The heating was on full-blast and within a few minutes I was properly warm for the first time in weeks.

My sister Henry was already installed on the sofa, and my father, and Oma, my lovely German grandmother. I sat with her and listened to her news: news delivered in German and punctuated with frequent 'Oh Gott im Himmel's and 'Donner und Blitzen's. A lot of her news was about which of her friends had died but she remained her usual delightful smiley self. It put my worries in perspective.

At six o'clock, the festivities began. There was comfort in the rituals. The children (that's me and Henry, aged 29 and 28) were banished upstairs. We washed, dressed smartly, brushed our hair. A little bell tinkled and down the stairs we came. My father played the piano and we sang 'O Tannenbaum' before toasting each other with champagne. We opened our presents, then sat down for a delicious meal. There was no set menu for this meal, it just had to be special, and this year Dad had requested lobster and chips with an endive salad. There were profiteroles and Irish coffees to follow.

The next day there were no stockings and no more presents but – good multi-cultural family that we were – we did do the English thing and sit down to a full turkey dinner topped off with Christmas pud. This year for the first time, after nine years of being a student, I was telling my parents about what I had been doing at work, not what I was learning at college. I had even bought all my own presents with my own money.

I worked a few days between Christmas and New Year, but to my great delight I was free from the afternoon of New Year's Eve until the evening of New Year's Day. One of my closest friends from university, Lexi, was having a house party only about an hour away from Ebbourne: a wig and beard party. I turned up straight off two 13-hour days and walked into a room full of happy people shouting over the Nirvana CD being blasted out from the player in the corner. I was so exhausted that the wigs and beards completely threw me and I struggled to recognise anyone. Then my heart did a little somersault as I caught sight of a tall figure with long pianist's fingers. Even in that huge mop of ridiculous curls and matching Cossack's beard, I recognised Allen – my big love from university days – from the laughing dark eyes and flashing white smile. I had wondered whether he might be here. Suddenly rejuvenated, I went upstairs to change into my Cleopatra wig, came back down, and was thrown again: everyone had swapped wigs and beards so again I didn't know who anybody was, and Allen was nowhere to be seen.

I amused myself by displaying the deep scratch marks a cat had given me earlier that day and convincing my friends I was now working with tigers. (Only my astute friend Lexi, whose mother owned my favourite cat in the world, a Burmese cross called Kiska, wasn't taken in. 'My mum's got exactly the same scratches on her hand from her horrid new Russian Blue,' scoffed Lexi. You could always rely on Lexi for the truth.)

Wandering outside for some fresh air, I found Allen, still sporting the Cossack's beard, now topped with a rather fetching blonde bob. We had broken up amicably and there was a great fondness there. We found there was a lot to catch up on that evening.

I drove home to Ebbourne on New Year's Day with a most excellent hangover and a nasty stubble rash. It had been wonderful to be back in the warm embrace of my family and friends for a few days, but I was excited to be returning to my own home and my own life. I wondered what 1998 would bring. I didn't know why, but I had a good feeling.

CHAPTER SEVEN

The cat woman of Ebbourne

One weekend in early January, my sister Henry – half an inch shorter than me, with legs three inches longer, and straight blonde hair rather than my unruly brown frizz – decided she would come to visit me.

I wasn't keen, not because I didn't want to spend time with my little sister but because I knew what she was like around animals: she was utterly soppy and gooey.

The previous year, when I'd still been at vet school, she had phoned me at midnight in a state. Her cat had been run over by a car and completely squashed. I talked her through all the signs to look for and she relayed back to me what was going on down the phone. 'I'm so sorry, Henry,' I said finally, 'but from what you're telling me Samson has got to be dead.' Even so, she insisted on calling out the vet in the middle of the night to double check. She walked through his door wailing, 'Save him, please save him'.

Henry has always been like this.

When I was eight and she was seven, we'd found an abandoned and sparsely-feathered baby bird in the garden. Knowing the cat was around I had scooped it up and climbed up onto the flat roof of our garage and left it there, hoping its mother would see it and rescue it. I wasn't religious at all at the time but I remember praying that evening that this small bird would survive. The next day we went back up on the garage roof. I climbed up first and saw that it was still there, not moving, and I knew it was dead. I was upset, but I could cope somehow. I knew Henry, though, would be distraught, and I felt I needed to shield her. So I put my eight-year-old foot over it and said, 'It's gone, it's gone. Its mother must have come and taken it back to the nest.'

When I had received a microscope for my tenth birthday I had been mesmerised looking at the pre-prepared slide with the dragonfly's wing on it. 'Look, Henry, it's amazing. It's transparent so you can see the entire structure. It looks like lots of little ladders.'

'Ugh, disgusting,' Henry had said, and she'd refused to look.

Her later vegetarianism came as no surprise, despite her love of bratwurst.

It wasn't so much that I disapproved of Henry's attitude – quite the opposite. It was more that being around her made it so much harder to maintain the aura of tough, objective professionalism I felt I needed.

But Henry – and perhaps our parents – had decided that I needed cheering up; so she was dropping her trendy

London set and heading out to the country, whether I liked it or not.

'Okay, but I'll be on call,' I eventually conceded.

'You're always on call, Anna,' complained Henry.

Sometimes it did feel like that, and I was tired, a lot of the time. But sometimes it was just a good excuse, and anyway, that was just the way it was in a small mixed practice, and always had been and always would be. There were three vets in the practice and between us we had to provide 24/7 cover. So one weekend in three I was on duty from Saturday morning until Monday morning; the next weekend in my rotation I would have off; and the third weekend I would be on duty on Friday night and be the second vet on call on Saturday morning. I would hope to finish by Saturday lunchtime, but that depended really on what happened. If there was a lot going on, we couldn't just walk out; we just carried on until it was finished. I got one afternoon off a week. And I covered one in three nights. Some nights nothing happened but often there was a call out. If Stanley or Mike went on holiday and we didn't get a locum, the rota changed from a 'one in three' to a 'one in two'.

Henry arrived on Friday evening and we spent a few hours discussing our parents' increasing eccentricity while we unpacked the last of my boxes and put up several posters that had accompanied me through my various house moves at university: a particularly large version of Michelangelo's 'Creation of Adam' and a couple of romantic pre-Raphaelite paintings by Waterhouse. On Saturday morning I packed Henry off to the market in Bridport while I did morning consults and then paid a 'passing call' to Mr Lockheart. Mr Lockheart was a lovely old gentleman with a passion for his greenhouse who had become quite infirm and couldn't get himself or his elderly tom cat into the surgery any more. Tom had an abscess on his rump – a running-away-from-a-fight abscess as Tom was getting too old to defend his territory – and at that time the longest-acting antibiotics lasted 48 hours so I had been visiting every other day to inject him and check the abscess was healing nicely. When I arrived, Tom seemed much recovered, as demonstrated by his energetic wriggling and yowling as I gave him one last injection. Mr Lockheart was delighted, and he had a surprise for me. He tottered off to his greenhouse and indicated I should follow him: 'Come on, young lady, this way.' Once inside this jungle paradise he selected a beautiful specimen with long leaves and a purple-y flower at the end of a long stalk. 'This is for you, Anna,' he said. 'It's a streptocarpus. It will do just fine on a windowsill.' Mr Lockheart couldn't have known it, but this was my first-ever gift from a client. I was so thrilled, it was all I could do not to kiss him.

Henry had always been quite the shopper and when I arrived home I found she had bought me a boot-full of handmade local pots and beautiful plants at the market to brighten up my cottage, as well as a new wallet made from the softest calfskin leather I had ever felt, and embossed with a wild primrose. But none of these lovely items made me so happy as my streptocarpus.

That afternoon I was determined to drag Henry out for a walk before the winter evening closed in. I knew Henry wouldn't have brought – or owned – any suitable footwear but I was now an appropriately well-shod country girl with a good range of outdoor footwear. (Nor had she brought appropriate clothing with her: she dropped clanging hints about how cold my cottage was all weekend, despite me having warned her in advance about its temperamental heating systems.)

I took Henry on a walk around my glorious little village of Redcombe. I wanted to show her what I saw, I wanted her to experience the pleasure of the fabulous undulating views right outside my cottage, or of tramping along the little river, the silence disturbed only by our footsteps, the bird calls, and the magical sound of running water. I showed Henry the beautifully restored old mill house, the grand houses with wild flowers tumbling out of their stone walls even in January. I dragged her around the 13th century church with its tumbledown graveyard that always filled me with such peace.

Down by the river we stopped to watch a couple of young spaniels behaving like excitable toddlers, throwing themselves over and over into the cold running water. It was such a happy scene that I threw a couple of sticks for them, though I knew I shouldn't. (I'd seen and tried to remove broken bits of stick impaled in soft palates caused by dogs mis-timing their joyful jump onto an upright stick.) Standing there, hugging our arms to ourselves to keep warm, Henry and I were joined by a tired-looking Lucy, with her own spaniel, my heart patient, Charlie, plodding along beside her like a very well-behaved gentleman dog. Lucy and Charlie stopped to take in the scene too. Charlie dutifully gave Henry his paw, much to her delight. 'That was my Charlie as a young dog,' said Lucy with a wistful smile, as she watched the young dogs gambolling about. 'He loved the water. Such a water spaniel, weren't you, Charlie boy?'

'How's he doing?' I asked, fondling his silky ears and thinking wistfully about Nellie, my springer spaniel I had left behind with Sally. Nellie would have absolutely loved this walk: I could just imagine her now, nose down, tail up and constantly wagging.

Lucy turned away from him, as though she didn't want him to hear. 'Not so well the last couple of weeks. He's slowed right down, and he has a coughing fit every morning.'

It sounded to me like his heart condition could be deteriorating.

'Why don't you give him one of those extra water tablets a day over the weekend, and come and see me on Monday.'

That evening Henry and I were just setting off for dinner at the Admiral pub not far from Lizzie's farm when my pager went. It was Mrs Hall, one of Ebbourne's cat women. You get these characters in every practice. The cliché is quite true: they are often single, and their lives revolve around their cats. And I take my hat off to them because they rescue lots of waifs and strays who would otherwise be homeless. But they often can't say no to yet another one, so there will be twenty cats in the house, all giving each other the snivels and the snots.

This particular cat woman on this particular evening had a very elderly cat that was on its last legs and she had decided it did need putting to sleep. 'Fergus here has decided it's time for him to go to heaven. Could you come and help him along please, vet?'

Henry teared up when I told her what we had to go and do on our way out to dinner. I told her she'd have to wait outside in the Landy while I went in: I couldn't have her crying all over the place and making things worse.

The house was a proper old farm worker's cottage on a smart street in Ebbourne: the cottages weren't large and the ceilings were low, but every house had a freshly-painted exterior and well-tended pots of flowers in its tiny front garden.

Mrs Hall opened the door to me in slippers and a housecoat, cradling Fergus in her arms. The pungent smell of cat pee hit me immediately. As I followed Mrs Hall to her back living room I started to make an inventory. There were cats here in at least double figures. In the hallway, on the kitchen table, in the inglenook fireplace, on the arms of every available comfy chair and sofa. There were litter trays in equal numbers, and bowls of half-eaten food and biscuit and water bowls in every room. Under the kitchen table I spotted a couple of kittens who both looked like they had cat flu. It was terribly dark which added to the sense of slightly eerie gloom. I noted too the many photos of happy family scenes on the walls (unusual for a cat lady);

and on a little side table by the chair into which she now lowered herself, still cradling Fergus, the *Times* crossword, nearly completed, and a big cut-glass decanter full of some luscious-looking amber liquid.

These houses full of unhealthy cats, unvaccinated and stressed out by being amongst too many other cats, made me cross. I decided I needed to say something to this obviously intelligent woman and thought I'd break the ice with some small talk.

'Are these your children in these pictures, Mrs Hall?' I asked tentatively.

'They are. All grown up now.' Her curt tone wasn't quite the warm maternal one I had been expecting. In fact, I sensed I might have stumbled onto difficult ground. But I couldn't just drop it now, so I ploughed on.

'And are these your grandchildren? You must be very proud of them.'

'I am. I never see them.' Mrs Hall's watery eyes dared me to pursue the conversation further. The little spidery burst blood vessels on her cheeks seemed to fuse as Mrs Hall flushed. The small talk gambit hadn't worked so I decided to retreat and just go for it.

'You know, Mrs Hall, cats are solitary creatures in the wild,' I said in my most professional voice.

Mrs Hall's chin jutted out. 'I know what you want to say, why don't you come out and say it? I shouldn't have lots of cats, is that it? Well, all my cats are absolutely fine. They're company for each other. Look – those two are sitting on the sofa together.'

There were two fierce-looking cats on the sofa: one on one end, one on the other end. They were avoiding all eye contact with each other. I wasn't convinced.

'Okay, Mrs Hall,' I said, giving in for now, and switching again to my most sympathetic tone of voice, 'well, let's have a look at Fergus.'

Mrs Hall was right about this poor old Fergus. He was an elderly cat and had grown very scrawny. He was in the last stages of kidney failure. I could feel every bony process of his backbone and his skin stayed tented up when I picked it up. Really, he should have gone some time ago. Or if I'd been called earlier I might have been able to do something about it. I considered having that conversation with Mrs Hall:

'You know, Mrs Hall ... '

But Mrs Hall wasn't in a state to listen now. Tears were starting to form in her bloodshot eyes. She was wholly focused on Fergus and his last moments.

I felt desperately sorry for her, and for Fergus: I knew that he would have been uncomfortable and nauseous without let up for some time. I could at least take that pain away now.

'I want you to do it on my lap,' she said. 'I want to be holding him at the end.'

It made it trickier, but I found a towel and an old pillow and slipped them under the pitiful little curled-up bundle. Trying not to stab myself in the half-light, I sedated Fergus with an injection into the muscle. He was so emaciated and weak he hardly seemed to feel it. Then I drew up the barbiturate into my syringe.

'I'm going to bury him in my back garden, with his friends,' said Mrs Hall, breaking off her rhythmic stroking of Fergus to take a large slug straight from the decanter.

I gulped and drew up some more barbiturate: if I was going to leave Fergus here, I needed to make absolutely sure he had gone. Into Fergus's kidney I injected enough blue juice to make a Labrador sleep forever. I listened to his heart, checked his corneal reflex, and then said my own silent goodbye to Fergus.

I let myself out.

Back at the Land Rover, Henry was in tears. 'I don't know how you do this,' she snuffled. I didn't say anything. It was hard, and I can't pretend it didn't get to me some-times, but it was also a privilege to be able to take away suffering so gently: to end animals' lives at the right time and with dignity.

An hour and a half later, Henry and I were just about to tuck into our steak and kidney pies when my pager went off again. For once I cursed the slow pace of life down in Dorset: in London, we could have eaten three courses and be halfway home by now. I borrowed the landlord's phone and Mrs Hall came back on the line.

'Cat's not dead,' she slurred. 'It's still alive, it's moving.'

My mouth went dry, my chest tight, my cheeks were suddenly burning hot. Henry and I abandoned our fragrant pies, tumbled into the Land Rover and sped off, Henry keeping up a steady stream of reproach: 'How could you do that? That's terrible, you're terrible, Anna. Are you sure you want to be a vet? Oh, the poor cat, the poor woman.

Oh my God, oh my God.' Nothing she said could make me feel worse about myself than I did already.

I rushed in, apologies on my lips. Mrs Hall and Fergus were sitting where I'd left them. As my eyes adjusted to the gloom, I saw that the top button of Mrs Hall's housecoat had come undone, her collar was skewed, and the decanter was now half-empty.

Drunk as a skunk, poor Mrs Hall had hold of Fergus's head in her right hand, and was waving it around like a sock puppet. 'Look,' she slurred. 'He's moving. He's alive, he's alive.' Even before I examined him, I could tell that old Fergus was already happily curled up in front of God's Aga.

That night Henry and I sat up talking. Henry, who usually moaned about the lack of eligible men in London, seemed rather smitten with a new chap currently doing his accountancy exams. She also filled me in on our 'brother' Angus's latest exploits. (The family had kind of informally adopted Angus when he'd been about 15 and although he was still in touch with his own parents, and loved them, he called my parents mum and dad. Angus probably saw more of my parents now than I did.) Angus was a Royal Marine, and making the most of the new regulations allowing women to serve at sea.

'What about you, Anna?'

'Ummmm. There was a farmer's son, Michael, but the TB test has shut things down in more ways than one. Allen intermittently raises my hopes. I haven't got the time or energy anyway, Henry.'

I thought that would be the end of it, but I had underestimated my sister.

'Anna,' said Henry, as she was leaving for London the next day. 'Do you know what you need?'

Many thoughts flashed through my mind. What did I need? What would Henry think I needed? A break? A boyfriend? Comprehensive re-training? Central heating?

'Anna, you need a dog. Something that can guard the cottage as well as keep you company.'

As soon as she said it, I knew she was right.

In fact, I got a cat *and* a dog.

The next weekend was my weekend off, and I took the train up to London for a return visit with Henry. The real purpose of the trip though was to pick up Kiska, my favourite cat in the world, from Lexi's mother. I had been in love with Kiska (Russian for pussy cat) since she had been a beautiful little black kitten. Lexi's parents had bought Kiska to keep Lexi company when she moved back home for a year after university, but she was quite an independent thing and not really what Lexi wanted in a cat at all: Lexi wanted someone to curl up on her lap, or sleep on her bed, and Kiska just did her own thing. So when Lexi had left her parents' home, Kiska had stayed. And now Lexi's mother had decided on a whim to get a Russian Blue, 'because they are such beautiful creatures,' and – Lexi had told me despairingly on the phone that week – the Russian Blue had started beating up Kiska.

'My mother is pulling her hair out about it,' said Lexi. 'Kiska's started peeing in the house – do you think that could be from stress?' (Yes, it could.) 'Now she's started licking herself obsessively.' (This was also a sign of stress in a cat.) 'Mum thinks she's going to have to re-home her.'

'No, no, no.' I was actually jumping up and down at this point. 'Don't give her away. I've got the perfect home for her here in the middle of the countryside. There are no other cats, nothing to stress her, it's perfect.'

When I turned up at Lexi's flat, the designated handover point, I was horrified. Kiska's back legs were like plucked chicken legs – she had licked all her fur off. She looked absolutely awful. Lexi's mother said she didn't have a cat basket, and I hadn't thought to bring one. She did have a Fortnum and Mason's hamper though, and we both thought that would do just fine.

The Sunday train was cancelled and there was, instead, a replacement bus service – in fact, a series of replacement buses. The bus for the final leg of my journey was completely packed so I couldn't put my hamper on the seat next to me. Instead it went on the luggage rack. After ten minutes up there, my hamper started to howl. This dreadful racket continued to emit from the pile of suitcases above our heads for the entire forty-minute journey. What could I do? I pretended it wasn't mine. I looked around pointedly, as puzzled as everyone else about what on earth that noise could be.

Kiska settled in quickly and slept on my bed from the first night I had her home. She couldn't come for walks with me though, or bark loudly when anyone strange approached the cottage: I definitely needed a dog too.

I had thought hard about asking Sally to let me have Nellie back. But I felt that Sally needed her more than I did; I couldn't quite work it all out from our regular late-night phone calls but she seemed to be in an emotionally fragile state. Sad as I was to have lost my dog, I couldn't take Nellie away from Sally.

Instead, I rang the local Labrador rescue set-up. I assumed that, being a vet, they would offer me all manner of dogs, no problem, and was shocked when they firmly said that they would come out to see me to check my suitability. (Later I would realise how right they were. With the hours we work, vets are not necessarily ideal dog-owners.) So a rather officious, short, plump plummy lady in a blue quilted jacket and a headscarf came to see me. I obviously passed her test because a week later she rang me and said she had a dog for me. I felt like someone had told me I was having a baby: excited, nervous about the responsibility I was about to take on, and with a long list of shopping to get through. I also felt a wistful tugging at my heart. Would Nellie forgive me for getting another dog? Would she understand? Would she care?

I never managed to establish the whole story behind Rocky: the rescue centre couldn't, or wouldn't, tell me. He was an entire Lab-Collie cross: a big, solid 35-kilo dog, about two years old. He was all muscle, no fat at all – in fact a bit ribby – and had big teeth that he wasn't afraid to show me. Such a very handsome boy though: all black except for a white diamond on his chest. He had belonged to a man, and was used to being outside a lot, and had lived with cats, that's all they would divulge. I had a slight alarm bell at some of this – sometimes a man's dog will always respond better to a man, and at two years old he could well be bursting with teenage energy – but I silenced it. I couldn't wait to get my new companion home.

The introduction between Rocky and Kiska went fine, to my great relief. (The previous week I had stitched up a kitten who had been almost eaten by the family dog.) Initially I had Rocky on a lead and Kiska free-ranging. She had lived with a black Lab before and seemed totally unfazed by this new addition to 'Hillside Cottage'. She rubbed against him, marking him with her scent glands, and helped herself to his food. Rocky for his part had a little sniff of this small furry resident and was not at all fussed about having to share his bowl of biscuits. I went to bed feeling optimistic about my new happy family.

When I woke up in the morning, Rocky had evacuated his decidedly liquid bowels in three places on the kitchen floor.

Oh, dear. During the night I had ignored a few whines, because I had thought he was just seeking attention and was determined that I should be a good owner from the outset and not reinforce bad behaviours. But now I realised that the poor dog must have been feeling anxious about messing in the house – for surely his previous house-training would have told him that that was wrong – and had only been trying to tell me that he needed to go outside. The stress of the travel, new home and new food had obviously had this all-too-common effect on his gastrointestinal function. It rather affected mine too as I cleared the foul-smelling liquid off the new lino.

I hated the thought that Rocky was feeling bad about himself after his first night with his new owner. I sat on the bottom stair and talked gently to him. He cocked his head, turning his clever eyes on me. When, after a few minutes of sweet nothings, he nudged me with his wet nose, I felt forgiven. 'Come on Rocky, we'll go to the butcher's and buy a nice chicken breast to share. That will settle your tum.'

For her part, ruddy Kiska had eaten my prized strepto-carpus and was now sitting nonchalantly on the windowsill, surrounded by fragments of long green leaf and a chewed up purple flower. There had been no side effects to her gut function, I noted, much as the wretched beast deserved it.

CHAPTER EIGHT

To walk in another's shoes

Kiska thrived in my little cottage at Redcombe. The night storage heaters that failed to keep the cottage warm when I was there in the evenings and at night actually did a pretty good job during the day, and I'd usually arrive home from work to find her curled up happily on my bed. Often I would join her for a while: it was soothing just to sit and stroke her, and sometimes even to tell her about my day. I did a full dermatological work-up on Kiska but I couldn't find anything underlying that could have caused her coat to fall out or to make her over-groom herself, physically removing her own hair. Once she was settled and happy, her glossy black hair all grew back beautifully, apart from one little patch on her tummy that she continued to lick, and her feisty Burmese-moggy cross character came back out. She liked to jump on me and pretend to attack me, but that was just: 'do something with me, I'm bored.' I found her a really good companion.

Rocky on the other hand was turning out to be a right little hooligan. Right from the start he was always a bit skittish.

I didn't know his history and I didn't know whether to trust him or not. Every now and again he would put his mouth around my wrist. He always took his teeth off, but he'd let me know what he could do – given me a little warning.

And I soon discovered for myself why he had been re-homed: he ran off. All the time. If he came within sniffing distance of anything chase-able – a deer, a sheep, another dog – he would run off. It didn't matter how much I shouted and screamed and lowered my voice to make it sound like a man's, he was just gone. It drove me nuts.

There were a few berries left in the hedgerows as I set off down my track for a lunchtime walk with Rocky by my side one chilly day in late January. I breathed in the damp air, enjoying having a good reason to get out and about. What were those berries, I wondered. Rosehips? Hawthorn? Could I make an interesting – and edible – tea from them? My musings were interrupted by a high-pitched bark from my four-legged companion, who shot off, ears pricked, after a white tail in the distance. The deer bounded easily out of sight but so did my dog: again. I spent the rest of my lunch hour in a now-familiar activity – calling and tramping for miles – before returning to the cottage hungry and despondent.

I was in the Land Rover, engine running, ready to drive back for the afternoon's surgery, when Rocky appeared, covered in mud and tongue lolling hugely. Half of me wanted to shout at him but the other half was just relieved to see him. I ruffled his filthy ears and bundled him into the Defender.

That night I set my alarm extra-early with the aim of giving Rocky an extra-exhausting walk before work. Outside my bathroom window the next morning, the dark was punctured only by the distant lights of an early car sweeping along the opposite side of my little valley. As I brushed my teeth, my feet turned to stone by the bathroom floor and my whole body rigid with cold, I thought of Lena. The previous week I had received a letter from her, telling me of her latest adventures under the African sun with the rare Ethiopian wolf. I felt a wistful tugging. It felt like it had been a long winter already and I envied Lena the light, the warmth, the change of scene. Dorset was lovely, as were my colleagues, and most of the clients. But was I ready to settle down? Forever? My thoughts started to wander to a life of six months in Dorset, six months abroad. People did it. But not, I thought, reluctantly coming back to reality, people with pets. And especially not people with badly-behaving rescue dogs. I had responsibilities now. And one of those responsibilities needed to be taken for a walk. I had a quick cup of tea and then, as the first of the sun's rays were breaking through a somewhat murky dawn, I picked up Rocky's lead and we headed out to the woods.

Thirty minutes later, I returned, dejected, frustrated, and alone again.

The woods around my cottage had been deliberately planted to provide cover for shooting and they were full of game. Ten minutes into our walk, Rocky had smelt something, and that was the last I had seen of him. I sat down, hungry and irritated, for a hasty bowl of muesli, only to be interrupted by a loud rapping at the door. It was the local gamekeeper – who, to make things more awkward, was a client of the practice – and he was not happy. He stood on my doorstep, dirty dog on the end of a piece of baler twine in one hand, floppy dead pheasant in the other and a list of expletives in the air. It was his job to protect these birds, even if they were only later to be shot from the skies. I looked at him sheepishly and took the twine thrust angrily towards me.

'Keep your bloody dog under control, miss,' he glowered darkly.

That lunch break I bought Rocky a long extendable lead so that I could take him for a walk on the estate without incident, but it didn't seem much fun for him, and it meant he couldn't burn up all that teenager energy.

'Have you thought about dog training?' asked Judith, when I was moaning to her about Rocky's latest antics that afternoon. Judith herself owned two beautifully well-behaved Labradors whom she loved like children and who would sometimes accompany her to work and lie blissfully under her desk while she took calls or tapped away at the primitive computer. 'I know Penny took her little Jazz and it worked a treat for her. Maybe not in Ebbourne though: you don't want to be there with all your clients reciting their doggy ailments at you all evening.'

And so I found myself in Crewkerne with Rocky every Tuesday evening. It wasn't that I would have minded my clients seeking my advice. It was more that I was embarrassed at the thought of them seeing how badly behaved the vet's dog was, and how awful their vet was at dog training. Rocky was pretty much the worst-behaved dog in the class, right from the very first day when we walked into the hall and he immediately peed on a chair.

Oh, and also, my poor big handsome boy had separation anxiety. I found this out from one of my clients, who lived just up the road from my cottage. About ten days after Rocky had moved in, she brought her own dog in to be treated and commented meaningfully, 'You know, your dog doesn't like it when you leave. I hear him howling in the morning when you've gone to work.' I hadn't realised, and I felt awful.

So then, of course, Rocky came to work with me every day, which was another nightmare. He didn't like being cooped up in the kennels or a locked room – in fact, he chewed through the freezer room doorframe in protest one day and I had to patch it up without Stanley or Mike finding out. But he was also a complete liability on a farm: he barked incessantly at any cattle and I couldn't contemplate letting him out anywhere near any sheep. It wasn't a good situation.

'Oh, Anna, I can't seem to locate my foot trimmer. Would you mind checking in your large-animal foot box?' asked Stanley vaguely one bright late-January morning. Stanley, though hugely capable at anything veterinary,

143

was hopelessly disorganised, and constantly losing things. His car kit was always a complete pickle. I headed to the courtyard, where all our Land Rovers were parked up in a row. I opened the back of my Defender, reached in and hauled over the heavy foot box. I lifted its lid and immediately something long, thin, pale and fast shot out, took a flying leap at my shoulder, dug its claws in, leapt down onto the ground, and started scurrying happily around and around the courtyard.

After a brief squeal I got a hold of myself and took stock of the situation: what I had here was a ferret on the loose. The small furry running circuits at my feet had a collar, I noticed, so I fetched a dog lead from the kennels and managed to scoop up the little creature and secure the lead to my new friend as it passed me on its next lap. Ferret under control, I went back to my Land Rover, musing to myself that didn't Stanley keep ferrets?

'Here you go,' I said to Stanley, handing over the foot trimmer. He was standing in reception with an expectant smile on his face and his eyebrows raised up to his hairline, the effect only slightly diminished by the smear of poo on his glasses. Judith, Penny and Lois had gathered to witness my entrance too. I could just imagine Stanley, like a complete child, running round the practice telling them all, 'Guess what I've done!'

'Oh, and I believe this might belong to you,' I added, looking down at the ferret trotting docilely at my feet, as nonchalant as I could manage. 'Is that cowshit on your glasses, by the way?'

'Terrific!' Stanley beamed. 'Good girl.' I wasn't sure at this point whether he was talking to me or the ferret, who he now gathered up in his arms like a newborn baby.

'Frightened the life out of me actually, Stanley,' I admitted with a rueful shake of my head.

'Be careful: his next trick is asking you to look in the dead animal freezer then pushing you in,' smiled Penny.

'It's true. He's done that to both of us,' said Judith, heading back to reception and sitting down heavily. 'He only does it to people he really likes though – it's a compliment.'

'Yup. You're fitting right in,' noted Lois sourly, jaw set, lips thin. She swished her sharp blonde bob and stalked off to her office.

'There was actually a reason I brought young Ferdie in today, other than to amuse us all,' said Stanley now. 'Anna, please enlighten us all on why we vasectomise ferrets.'

I scrabbled around in my mind: this was information I hadn't had to access since my examinations several months ago.

'Erm. The female ferret, or Jill, is an induced ovulator, or a constant summer cycler if not mated. That means if she isn't mated she comes into oestrus again and again. The high level of oestrogen in her blood affects the production of red blood cells in her bone marrow and she can become anaemic and die. So, you need to mate your Jills. And if you don't want to keep having lots of baby ferrets, you have to mate them with a vasectomised male, or Hob.'

'Textbook answer, thank you Anna. For extra marks: you can, as an alternative, inject the Jill to stop her being in season, but you have to keep re-injecting and it gets expensive. If you've got one vasectomised ferret you can just pop him in and he has a nice time. Job done. So, young Ferdie is here today so that he can become the lucky Hob and so that you can vasectomise your very first ferret.'

Mike passed through at that moment and winced. Why is it, I wondered then, and wonder still, that men will always do that wincing thing at any mention of vasectomy, which is a pretty minor op? I've never seen anyone blanch at talk of a female ovario-hysterectomy, which is pretty major surgery.

A ferret vasectomy is done by micro-surgery. Stanley and I both scrubbed up. 'Okay, Anna, this is a "see one/do one" situation.' He went first, and then supervised me as I found the tube that carries the sperm out of the testicle, cut it, and tied it off. 'Cut out a decent segment, Anna. If you don't, the two ends can sort of find their way back together again and recanalise. Then you'll have lots of baby ferrets and an extremely angry owner on your hands – in this case, me … Nice, neat work, Anna. Lovely job.'

It seemed that by taking the whole ferret episode on the chin I had passed some kind of rite of passage. I was one of them now. Plus, my cat spayings were down to 32 minutes, I was no longer having to look up every drug dose, and my consults were more often than not taking only the required ten minutes. And so it was that two days later, Stanley announced gleefully, 'I think it's time we let you loose on the branch surgery.'

*

The branch surgery was eight miles down the road from Ebbourne, in Peighton Lubbock. Peighton Lubbock boasted two pubs; a baker's that made excellent Chelsea buns; a travelling fishmonger's; and an excellent village shop with its own deli counter that doubled up as the post office.

Surgery was quite a grand name for what was in fact a small reception area selling dog leads and flea products, plus a single consulting room, in a cold leaky Portakabin, in a car park, offering appointments with a vet three afternoons a week. Nevertheless I came to enjoy my afternoon surgeries there, as well as the friendship I formed with the quietly confident Peighton Lubbock receptionist, Deloris, a young mother from the village married to Frank, a burly Fijian with a most infectious and ready belly laugh. He and Deloris were generous (and frequent) entertainers who cooked sumptuously and who only owned wine glasses that held half a bottle of wine and always had to be full! I spent several happy, hazy evenings (and occasional impromptu nights) in their cosy home with its terrace overhanging the river.

It was a beautiful drive over the top road. First the road out of Ebbourne wound and wound, up and up out of the valley, past farms that each now meant something to me: here I had performed my first TB test, here I had carried out that tricky calving. Constricting tree tunnels and high hedgerows were left behind and instead, hitting the long, relatively straight top road, the entire valley opened up below me. Through the bare branches of the oaks and beech trees lining the way I had expansive views to the north and south of steeply-banked agricultural land – field upon field, every shade of green and gold, dotted with farm buildings and massive oaks – and sometimes, on a clear day, I could see as far as the coast, where the blue of the sky was separated by a faint line from the blue of the sea. No matter how cold it was, I opened the windows, put my foot to the floor, and breathed deeply. Then the road fell again, and twisted its way back down onto the valley floor and into Peighton Lubbock. Rocky enjoyed these journeys too: he was a super travel companion, sitting up straight in the side seat, or, if he was feeling sleepy, slumping down and putting his head on my lap.

It was also a bit more responsibility, being out at the branch on my own. Penny wasn't there to suggest tactfully that sometimes Mike does this or that. Mike and Stanley weren't there to give a second opinion or come and rescue me from some kind of bodge.

And the branch surgery introduced me to a wide range of what Judith fondly called 'proper rural folk'.

I wasn't sure what Judith meant by this at first. When I asked, she was oddly cryptic. 'Well, Anna, I know you're a competent vet now. But when you know a lot about something, you forget what other people do and don't know. Plus, you're not from around here. Sometimes good vetting is about being able to put yourself in someone else's shoes. It can save a lot of mess.'

That didn't make things much clearer.

On my very first day at the branch, in came Mrs Doris Dobbs ('a very rural lady' said Judith later). Mrs Dobbs was small and bird-like, with straight grey hair that she had possibly cut herself. I thought she was probably in her mid-sixties. She brought me her cat, Minnie. 'I think she might have broken her little leg,' suggested Mrs Dobbs. I had a look, and a gentle feel. Minnie let out a deep growl and hissed. Minnie wasn't putting any weight at all on her front right leg, and it was very swollen over the middle of the radius and ulna. There was too much swelling for me to be able to feel much underneath it, and it was too painful for me to be able to manipulate the leg very much – something I knew because my examination was accompanied by a constant low, threatening throaty rumble. Inspecting her paws I also noticed that Minnie's nails were scuffed.

'Could Minnie have been in a car accident, Mrs Dobbs?'

'Oh my dear. Oh, my poor Minnie. I don't think so. She's a house cat, aren't you my Minnie?'

'It's just that her nails are scuffed. That can often happen if a cat's been involved in a road traffic accident: the cat gets bowled over and puts its claws out to stop it going further down the road, and its nails get completely shredded on the tarmac. That could explain how she came to hurt herself, why her leg's so swollen.'

'Well dear, if you say so.' I wished that Mike or Stanley were there so I could ask them to have a quick look and a feel. In their absence, I felt I had to be cautious.

'We'll need to X-ray to be sure whether it's a fracture

though, and we don't have facilities for radiography here. We couldn't operate here either. Could you take her over to Ebbourne? I'll ring through and make sure Mike sees you this afternoon.'

'Oh my dear,' quavered Mrs Dobbs in her strong Dorset accent. 'How do I get there?'

I was taken aback. Was she serious? 'Well, it's just along the top road here.'

'Towards Crewkerne?'

'Yes, and then you drop left down the hill.'

'Oh. I've never been there.' She gave a small nervous smile that put me in mind of my grandmother.

I realised she was totally serious. Mrs Dobbs had never in her life been eight miles across the valley to Ebbourne. I tried to put myself in her shoes. She presumably didn't drive. Asking her to come to Ebbourne for radiography was like someone asking me to pop over to the Amazon basin for a quick blood work-up.

'I tell you what Mrs Dobbs, I have to go back over to Ebbourne myself after surgery, I can take Minnie.' But, reluctant as she was to stray out of Peighton Lubbock, Mrs Dobbs was even less keen to be parted from her cat. 'Well, Mrs Dobbs, if you can wait for half an hour until I've finished here, we can go across together.'

I drove Doris and Minnie back over the top road at the end of the afternoon. Minnie travelled in a cat basket on Doris's lap: Rocky, nose most definitely out of joint, was consigned to the back and spent the entire journey slouched in a dejected heap on the floor. Driving west, into the setting winter sun, small flocks of sheep quietly grazing on the steep pastures to our left and right, and buzzards circling on the thermals overhead, the top road provided as magnificent a vista as ever. I wondered whether Mrs Dobbs had noticed: she breathed shallow silent breaths, repelled all attempts at conversation, and clutched the cat basket to her stomach. (This was actually quite a common reaction to my driving.) Minnie gave the occasional growl from within her basket and when we arrived, we found that she had been sick. (This was also quite a common reaction to my driving.)

Penny had prepared everything for the X-ray by the time we arrived. Judith prised Minnie's basket from a bewildered-looking Mrs Dobbs, and chaperoned her to the accounts office. 'Come on, my love, let's have a cup of tea and a chat and let the vet do her job. How's your troublesome brother doing? And that lovely nephew of yours?' Judith had been born and raised in Peighton Lubbock and really did know everyone for miles around.

Penny and I worked together, weighing Minnie, drawing up the right amount of sedative for a 3.8 kilo cat, and then injecting it into her vein. I took several X-rays of her leg. Just to be sure, I did a cat-o-gram as well: if she had been in a car accident I wanted to make sure her chest and abdomen, diaphragm and bladder were intact. Penny popped up to put the plates through the wet X-ray chemicals and was back down with them within five minutes. There was no sign of a fracture. I had a good feel while Minnie was still sedated and I couldn't feel any crepitation, which is when two ends of broken bone rub on each other. Neither were there any puncture marks indicating a bite and an abscess.

'Mrs Dobbs,' I said. 'There's no fracture and no break in the skin. It's just badly bruised and swollen. I'll give Minnie some painkillers and she can come home with you tonight: she just needs plenty of rest.' I wondered: if I had had more experience, would I have put her and Minnie to all this trouble and expense?

'Oh my dear, well that's wonderful, but how am I going to keep her rested?' wondered Mrs Dobbs. 'She likes to leap up and down on the furniture does Minnie.'

Penny seemed to have already anticipated this, because she was at this moment struggling into reception, her tiny frame completely eclipsed by the big fold-up crate she was carrying. 'Here you go, Mrs Dobbs. Keep Minnie in here for a few days, with her litter tray and food, and she'll get a lovely rest.' Mrs Dobbs looked doubtful. 'Anna will set it up for you,' added Penny. Mrs Dobbs smiled.

I ferried Mrs Dobbs and Minnie home again. It was dark by now but, relieved about Minnie and delighted at her own adventure, Mrs Dobbs was suddenly super-chatty, talking non-stop about the 'view from up here' and how she must take her nephew up on his offer to take her over to Bridport one day, she'd always said no before but now she thought it might be rather fun, and how she was going to tell her good friend Betty Taylor all about it. 'You feel like you're on top of the world up here, don't you Anna?' I couldn't have agreed more.

After dropping Doris home I took the top road west again but dropped north rather than south to go and see

Mary, my friend from vet school. Sally had tracked her down and told me she was working in a small animal practice near Yeovil, not that far from me.

Mary was a sweet but shy and studious girl; we had not been close friends, but we had worked closely together at college, through the rotation system when students would be placed in small groups to study different disciplines. Mary and I had car-shared on a fortnight at Bristol PDSA where her dermatology knowledge had proved awe-inspiring, and had manned the ICU (intensive care unit) during a particularly testing week with many middle-of-the-night checks on sick animals. All whilst lectures and marathon training continued. That bonds people regardless of how much or little they seem to have in common.

I followed Mary's directions and found the house that her practice provided for her on an anonymous Yeovil estate. No panoramic views, just small boxy properties, mostly with unkempt gardens and satellite dishes. Inside was pretty depressing too: deck chairs to sit on, no wall decorations and a dejected Mary. 'A cat I was spaying last week died under the anaesthetic,' she told me unhappily. As we ate chocolate biscuits and drank tea, I tried to cheer her up with tales of my recent similar near misses and the assurance that it did not sound like it was her fault – that sometimes animals have unlucky idiosyncratic reactions. Mary shook her head. She couldn't see it that way. I tried again, reminding her of her excellent anatomical knowledge and telling her how often my thoughts turned to her when I was rummaging around in a cat's abdomen. She shook her head again. She wouldn't accept the compliment.

It seemed all wrong. Mary had been such an excellent and promising student. And yet, as we went out into the world and put our learning into practice, the responsibility and freedom that I was finding so energising seemed to weigh heavily on Mary's shoulders.

I left feeling glum for Mary and her situation and jolly glad to be returning to mine. I wouldn't have wanted to be in her shoes.

I was soon to meet Doris Dobbs's good friend Betty Taylor myself. She brought her dog in the next time I was at the branch in Peighton Lubbock. 'Doris told me how sweet you were my dear, so I've brought you my Lolly.'

Mrs Taylor set off describing Lolly's symptoms but I barely took in the detailed history she was giving me, so distracted was I by her eccentric get-up. This woman in her late sixties was wearing very mucky sturdy walking boots but had matched her lipstick shade, and her eyeshadow shade, exactly, to the vibrant orange of her blouse. How clever, I thought. I wonder if she does that with every outfit … Mmmm – she couldn't possibly with, say, a green blouse … I wonder if she only wears pink and orange and red blouses …

Lost in this reverie, I came round to hear Mrs Taylor saying, 'So that's about it, really. What do you think, doctor?'

Oh no. It wasn't the first time I had become so wrapped up in what a client was doing or wearing, or in what some poor animal was doing, or even, on a farm, in some particularly interesting vernacular building, that I had completely missed a history. It was quite naughty and I really had to stop it. 'Sorry Mrs Taylor,' I said. 'Did you say she had been sick?'

'Other end, dear.'

Lolly Taylor, a lovely black and white mottled collie dog with a shaggy coat, had colitis. Basically, loose and urgent diarrhoea caused by inflammation of the colon. I prescribed sulphasalazine, an anti-inflammatory, and, with some effort, made sure Mrs Taylor understood that it was to be given 30 minutes before food. It was better absorbed that way. 'And please, Mrs Taylor, bring Lolly back in a week so I can check her progress.' I wanted to make sure Lolly didn't develop kerato-conjunctivitis sicca, or dry eye, a possible side effect of the medication. I was probably being over-cautious, but it was a possibility.

'In a week? Oh yes, okay dear.'

A week later, Mrs Taylor and Lolly were back, Mrs Taylor glorious in a magenta blouse-lipstick-and-eye-shadow combination.

Lolly gamely jumped up on the table and gave my face a good wash. With some trepidation – Lolly seemed a sweet-natured dog but I was never sure whether a collie was going to snap – I checked Lolly's tear production with a Schirmer tear test. I took a special stick of paper with a measure along its side and placed it in the lower conjunctival sack of Lolly's eye. Lolly blinked a couple of times but stood remarkably still. The tears wicked up into the paper and drove a tide of blue dye across it. I noticed Lolly had odd eyes – one brown, one hazel – but was determined not to be distracted today.

'Well Mrs Taylor, there's 20 millimetres of tear production in each eye: no sign of dry eye, which is excellent. What about the colitis? Is the medication helping do you think?'

'I think so dear, but it has been very difficult to give it to her.'

'Difficult?'

'It keeps popping out again, my dear.'

'I'm sorry – popping out? What do you mean, exactly?' Mrs Taylor had my full attention now, magenta get-up notwithstanding.

'Well,' she blurted out, 'you stick it up her arse and it comes straight out again.'

I don't know whether it was the visual image of Mrs Taylor administering the drugs (did she wear Marigolds to do it? Did she match her eyeshadow to them?), or the sound of the word 'arse' coming out of the very correct mouth of a beautifully turned out 60-something woman that made the giggles start to rise up. The dog's got colitis, I thought, it probably will shoot out again. But, thinking of Judith, I tried to put myself in Mrs Taylor's shoes. How was she to know?

Developing a sudden cough to cover up my loss of composure, I made a mental note: the next time I prescribe this, make sure to specify the medicine is to be given by mouth. It would save a lot of mess.

CHAPTER NINE

The dog's bollocks

Whether because I was keen to share the country gem I had discovered, or because I needed the company, I set about enticing any friend I could to visit me in my rural idyll.

In February – the loneliest month, I think, with Christmas long gone but the days still cold and short and dark – we had a student shadowing me for a couple of weeks.

Monica was in fact an old friend of the family and I had helped to set up the placement for her. Her mother and my mother had been at school together in Germany and we had known each other since childhood. Monica was five years younger than me, which had been a fair old chasm in childhood. But unlike me she had gone straight to veterinary college from school, so professionally she was only one year younger than me now, and in her final year of vet school in Berlin. Monica looked like a Viking: slim and tall with flat cheekbones, thick blonde hair, and an open, straightforward face that clearly signaled whatever feelings she might be experiencing.

'Why on earth would you have her shadowing me?' I asked Stanley and Mike when they told me the plan. 'She'll learn ten times as much if she shadows one of you two.' The truth was, I still felt like a student myself much of the time. I felt I was robbing the clients when my consult cost the same £16.50 as Mike or Stanley's.

'Anna, it will be great this way. You realise how much you know once you start having to explain to someone else what you're doing. And it's the youngsters who have all the new knowledge: we're utterly outdated,' urged Stanley.

'Yup,' intoned Mike. 'You'll feel like an oracle and a dinosaur all at once. Welcome to my world. And you never know, it's possible you might learn something from your student. It's been known to happen.'

My nerves turned to excitement as soon as Monica arrived. Who better, as my first student, than Monica: smiley, easy-going, eager to learn, and some much-needed young female company for me.

Judith had prepared us a light schedule of small animal consults that first morning. Thank God for Judith. Because everything I did, Monica questioned it. Not rudely – in fact she was thoroughly charming – it was just that she took absolutely nothing on trust, and was determined to learn as much as she possibly could.

So when a local farmer brought in his working dog, limping, and when I found a pain reaction in her foot, I swiftly jumped to the (natural, sensible) conclusion that she had probably trodden on something and developed a painful infection.

'How do you know this is the problem, Anna? Do you not perform a differential diagnosis? Could it not be a fracture, or a congenital problem?' asked Monica, with a wide-eyed smile.

She was absolutely right, it could be. Only there had been a small raised red area underneath the spaniel's foot where a foreign body could have entered. 'Feel this area here Monica, just in front of Molly's shoulder, what can you feel? Compare it to the other side.'

'Ah yes. So the lymph node is bigger on the painful leg.'

Even so, I re-examined the leg from shoulder to toe and gave farmer Musgrove the full set of options: 'I suspect Molly does have a thorn or similar in her foot. There is evidence of a puncture mark and the draining lymph node that filters the blood is reacting to a possible infection. We could poultice it to try and draw it out. We could put her on antibiotics for the infection but if any foreign body is still in there it is likely to flare up again after the course. We could admit her to sedate and X-ray and rule out possible fractures, dislocations, explore the foot, that sort of thing but we can still do that later if we need to.' Mr Musgrove did not hesitate to go for a poultice. ''Tis the cheaper way, eh?' (Thankfully when Molly returned for her poultice removal the red mark had come to a head and on squeezing, a half-inch wicked-looking blackthorn popped out.)

Every consult that morning proceeded along these lines. I began to feel slightly chastened. I'd started taking shortcuts based on my limited, but nevertheless real, experience. Monica sent me rushing back to the books,

CALL THE VET

and jogged me back into being a 'proper' vet again. But consultations were ten-minute slots and all this took time. Even with a light schedule we were soon running behind, and we had a farm visit booked for the afternoon.

The last consult of the morning was Flynn, an unforgettably beautiful liver-and-white pointer. Though I was delighted at the prospect of seeing him, I knew he was not going to help get us back on track with our timekeeping: Flynn had been flummoxing me for some time. When I had first met him for a routine vaccination, back in October, Flynn had been, like most pointers, a graceful, glossy-coated, alert bundle of energy. I'd found him so beautiful – his muscling, his gait, his movement – that it had made me consider getting a pointer myself.

'Think carefully, Miss Barrington,' his owner, a local retired accountant called Mr Spend (of all things) had warned, keeping a firm grip on him. 'This one is a complete handful. He's always on the go. He doesn't stop. He needs constant attention and constant exercise.'

The next time Mr Spend had brought Flynn to me, several weeks ago now, it had been a different story.

'He's just not himself, sick a couple of times this week, lost his get up and go,' said Mr Spend.

Even off colour, he was still such a handsome dog. There was something about that gun dog physique with its lean, defined contours, and something about Flynn's quirky gun dog face – regal and aloof, but slightly goofy too, with that crumpled mouth, one lip stuck furled above his incisors as if he had been smiling in the wind. But Mr Spend was right:

160

his usual four-year-old antics were curtailed and there was no pulling on the lead. I liked Flynn very much and didn't like seeing him so out of sorts.

On examination, all had appeared normal. I had run some blood tests and nothing remarkable showed up: sodium a little low; all else within the normal range including the complete blood count; nothing to suggest any organ failure.

Over the course of the next few weeks Flynn had presented with vague, non-specific signs and sometimes was better for no apparent reason. I had tried all kinds of things. A course of antibiotics had made no difference. A shot of steroid had perked him up but only temporarily. Two weeks ago he had seemed so flat and a little dehydrated with now a mild anaemia that we put him on fluids too – that had perked him up but then he went back down again.

Now, before we called Flynn and Mr Spend in, I explained the history to Monica – stopping several times to answer eager questions.

In came Flynn and Mr Spend. The perking up effect of the steroid had clearly only been temporary. Flynn was pitifully lethargic: it was awful to see him brought so low. I had to admit to Mr Spend that I was at the end of my resources and completely stumped. 'I think you will need to refer him to a specialist, no?' said Monica. She was right. But I didn't even know what kind of specialist: something medical, I guessed. I sent Mr Spend and Flynn away promising to consult my more experienced colleagues and then phone with a suggested course of action.

It was a dispiriting end to the morning consults, but as ever duty called.

'Come on Monica, we need to get straight on to the farm visit.'

'You start so early and you do not have a lunch break?' That was another thing I didn't question. It was what everyone did: it was part of the job.

'Not always: not if things get busy. Come on, we can eat in the car.'

I collected Rocky from his bed in the freezer room and the three of us jumped into the Land Rover, Rocky sandwiched in the middle and showing great interest in the food being consumed on either side of him. I stuffed down my sandwich as with my free hand I guided the Land Rover at pace down some particularly narrow, particularly winding roads towards Barbara Blunt's farm. Sandwich finished, I became a tour guide, pointing out the route to a local wildlife reserve that apparently had orchids; the farm that was under severe TB restrictions, unable to sell the calves it normally sold on for fattening and now bursting with livestock, the farmer, Mr Porritt, anxious about running out of food for this unprecedented number of housed animals; and the stream running alongside the road that would eventually lead us right into the Blunt farm at the base of the valley. On this dank February afternoon, as we drove deeper and deeper into the bottom of the world, with the tree tunnels heavy with rain and the track reduced to a gravelly mudslide, it was hard to imagine that this darkly-wooded spot ever got any sun. As I pulled up at our destination, Monica (whose graceful face was, I suddenly noticed, looking white and peaky) wound down her window and puked down the side of the door.

'Anna, I am so sorry. I don't know what happened. I'm absolutely fine now. I'm okay. Let me get some water to clear it up.'

Poor girl, she was blushing furiously – quite a feat given how white she had been a moment earlier. And it was my fault entirely. 'No, I'm really sorry, Monica. I did drive hellishly fast round some of those bends.'

Although I tempered my speed and tried to be gentle on the bends, my driving continued to make poor Monica sick throughout her two-week placement. Come wind come rain, she travelled with her window down and her head brushing the hedgerows, breathing slowly and deeply. That aside she proved to have a pretty strong stomach, which was good because she got a full whack of blood, guts and gore.

Here at the Blunt farm, Barbara came out of the old slate-roofed farmhouse to welcome us.

'Is she on her own here?' Monica asked me in German. I didn't know and I didn't like to ask, but looking around I guessed she was. The whole farm had a tired, rundown look about it, and Barbara looked done in.

'Hello, Anna is it?'

'Yes, hello Mrs Blunt. And this is a student, Monica.'

'Monica, hello, yes, welcome. Yes, well, one of my cows is lame and I'd like you to have a look at her. They can be a bit wild so I'm glad there's two of you come.'

'Are you on your own here?' asked Monica.

'I am today,' said Barbara, in a way that stopped even Monica from asking further questions. But Monica took me to one side.

'That crush is very rusty and old. It doesn't look safe. I think you will refuse to treat the cow?'

The thought had crossed my mind, but I'd dismissed it. The crush – the metal handling contraption for immobilising the cow and allowing us to treat it – did look completely knackered. In particular, the yoke for putting around the cow's neck looked very rusty and corroded, and the bar that should have run along one side was completely missing. The whole thing could well give way under a cow's weight. I could then be crushed under a cow, or Monica or Barbara could. Could I refuse? Probably, yes. But then what would happen? Mike or Stanley would come out and do the job with the same rusty old crush. Sometimes this was a dangerous business and it just did not seem practical to refuse to do things like this.

'I'm going to do it, Monica. Just stay well out of the way.'

'What about negligence?' asked Monica. 'The farmer could sue you if you mess it up.' That had never really occurred to me but Monica was right. Potentially a farmer who got injured because of her own broken machinery or un-handleable animal could try to claim that I hadn't been controlling her cow properly. I looked at Barbara's exhausted, honest face as she patiently waited for her two vets to finish conferring.

'Come on Mrs Blunt, let's go and bring in that cow.'

The three of us formed a funnel into the gates leading to the crush and chaperoned a large Limousin cow into the handling system. I tightened the yoke around her neck. The poor old girl couldn't put her foot to the floor at all and once I got a good look at her it was obvious why. She had a great big nail in her foot.

'Those things get washed down in the stream sometimes. The water runs through the farm and the cows cross it all the time,' said Barbara.

We tied the foot to the side of the crush and with a pair of pliers I pulled out a three-inch rusty nail. Fortunately it had not been too deeply embedded, nor had it been in an area where it would damage important underlying structures. I pared away the surrounding hoof to let it drain.

Looking at Barbara Blunt's drawn anxious face, I made another judgement call. I could have bandaged the foot and left Mrs Blunt with antibiotics to administer. That would have meant a lot of extra work for her, for something that by rights ought to come good on its own. 'Keep her in for a couple of days, on dry straw, Mrs Blunt. Once she's putting full weight on the foot, she can go back out with the rest. I don't think there's any need for antibiotics.' Mrs Blunt blew out her cheeks as she exhaled deeply. As she nodded her assent at me, I thought her shoulders lifted slightly.

At home that evening, while Monica was making the meatballs, I turned to Rocky for some advice about Flynn Spend. 'Woof,' he suggested, when I talked him through

Flynn's blood picture. Hmm. Rocky was usually an excellent listener but he seemed distracted today for some reason. Certainly his suggestion wasn't very helpful.

Casting around, I had one last thought: my friend from vet school, Athena. She was a mad dog-lover and a brilliant diagnostician. I dialled her number.

'Okay,' Athena said after I had painstakingly gone through the history. 'Sodium is low, potassium is at the high end of normal. And eosinophils are normal despite physiological stress. Have you thought about Addison's?'

Like a bolt from the blue it hit me. Why hadn't I thought of that? Rocky, why didn't you think of that? Addison's disease is when the adrenal glands are not producing enough of the body's own steroid and mineralocorticoids (hormones to regulate sodium and potassium levels). It causes all kinds of imbalances. That's why Flynn had perked up when I had given him a shot of steroid. The fluids had worked because they had sodium in them. And he had been dehydrated due partly to chronic fluid loss through the kidneys and from vomiting. This had to be it. I would ring Mr Spend first thing in the morning.

I felt a bit like Monica's questioning attitude was waking me from a happy slumber. I couldn't decide whether I was right to have gone along with the way things were – after all, it's easy to ask challenging questions of everyone if you are disappearing back to Germany in two weeks' time – or whether I was slightly embarrassed to have to be prompted by my student. These feelings were never stronger than on the day of our visit to a Powerstock farm.

'Anna, Monica: Powerstock have just rung through. They've got a cow with red water. It's probably babesiosis. Could you get down there and check it out?'

I headed out to the Land Rover. Monica jumped in beside me, textbook in hand, and wound down her window. We stopped in a lay-by for me to have a quick flick through the textbook and for Monica to take some big sucks of air. Ah, yes. Babesiosis causes crashing, potentially fatal anaemia in a cow. It's caused by a blood-sucking tick that not only bites the kindly host and sucks its blood but at the same time injects a single-celled parasite into it. This organism finds and enters red blood cells, popping them as it does so. As the organism prospers and multiplies, it pops so many red blood cells that the cow becomes severely anaemic. Classic symptoms to look out for are pale or yellowy mucus membranes and dark red pee that looks like port: the disease is often known as red water.

Monica had lots of questions. If the area was infested, why were any cows grazing there at all? Why had only one cow succumbed and not all of them? What was port?

I enlightened Monica on the answer to her third question and we quickly found out the answers to the first two. The farmers were well aware of the ticks, and generally managed the situation themselves. They knew the early signs to look for, but they also only allowed cows to graze there that had already developed immunity, either through having already had the disease, or through having had immunity passed to them through their mother's placenta and milk.

'This one that's off colour,' said the farmer as he led me through the fields to my patient, moving around his animals in the calm, assured fashion of an experienced stocksman, 'she's not from this herd originally. She was orphaned, and we had a girt cow here who had lost her calf, so we put the two of them together and she sucked the cow.' He wasn't panicked – that wasn't his way; too much hustle and bustle spooks the cattle – but there was no small talk. We didn't even introduce ourselves. 'We thought she'd get enough cover from that, guess not. She's been a bit quiet a couple of days but started pissin' red-brown this mornin'.'

Cattle aren't energetic at the best of times, but there was something about the immobility of this beast when we came upon her that brought my spirits low. She was breathing hard and barely moving, and the look in her eyes said that she was past caring. She didn't protest as I peeled her vulva back to check the colour inside. 'That's the easiest place to look on a cow – to look inside her mouth I would have had to restrain her head,' I explained to Monica.

'She in't movin',' said the farmer.

I stared disbelievingly at what I saw, and rocked back on my heels as I thought. 'Look,' I said, 'the membranes are the colour of paper. That's wrong. You want them to be a pinky-orange. I can inject her with Imazol and that will kill the plasmids that are very likely causing this,' I went on. 'But I'm worried that this cow has had so much blood destruction, she might die before she can get better.

What I'd like to do is run some quick tests, to check how anaemic she is, and then if it's as bad as I think, I'd like to do a blood transfusion.' It was unusual, but if this was a dog or a human she would likely get a blood transfusion, so why not a cow?

The farmer manoeuvred our sick beast, and her healthy foster mother, into the crush and I took blood samples from both of them. 'Keep them nearby,' I said. 'We'll need them in there again soon.'

We raced back to the practice, and ran the tests. As I suspected, my sick patient had an extremely low red cell volume and would almost certainly die in the next day or two without a transfusion. 'It's a shot to nothing, Monica: if we don't act, she'll definitely die.' Mike came and helped dig out some old chemicals and equipment long-confined to a dusty shelf and I sloshed as much anticoagulant as I could find into a Winchester – a huge brown glass jar – before we headed back out to Powerstock.

Patient and foster mother were lined back up in the crush. 'You have done this operation how many times?' asked Monica, as I popped a big catheter into the healthy cow's neck.

'I've never done it before,' I said.

'We should call Stanley, no? Or Mike?'

'I don't like to call them if I can help it. I feel like I'm here to take a third of the workload and that can't happen if I'm always asking for help. I try my hardest just to get on with it. I don't like to make a nuisance of myself.'

'But how will you learn if they are not here to teach you?'

'Mmmm,' I said, non-committally. 'It's not that technical, and it's not something they will have commonly done either.' I also thought to myself 'how will I learn to do it myself unless I do it myself?' Yes, I found cattle surgery daunting, but I tried to fight my inclination to shy away from it.

'But Anna, what if something goes wrong? What about litigation?'

'I don't think this farmer is going to sue me, Monica, for trying my best.'

I honestly believe my generation of vets was the last who were prepared as a matter of course to go out on our own, and handle most things on our own, without wanting to check back a lot, make middle-of-the-night phone calls, ask people to come out. The following generations were more cautious and more demanding (and their mobile phones worked better). Much of this was born of the emerging litigation culture. Perhaps these new generation vets make fewer mistakes at the beginning, but perhaps not fewer overall. At some point, you'll have something's guts hanging out or something bleeding in front of you, and no one to call, and you have to make that decision or perform that C-section or whatever. The cow standing before me now, desperately needing the blood transfusion I had never performed before, was just such a case.

I opened the valve and drained about five litres of blood from the healthy cow into my Winchester. 'Monica, could you keep swilling the bottle to stop clots from forming, please.' Then I put a big needle into the sick cow's vein and reversed the process, running the fresh healthy blood into my sick cow. Wow, I thought. It was fairly basic, it wasn't as sterile as you would get through the NHS Blood Transfusion Service, but it was still pretty amazing.

And then my weakened, 300-kilo patient collapsed against the side of the crush. Her entire weight fell sideways, cushioned from the metal sides of the crush only by my arm, still holding the needle that was feeding blood into her vein. I was totally trapped, and in sudden and incredible pain. Although she was only a half-grown animal my right elbow was being squeezed and twisted into an angle it had never experienced before. I felt intense, unbearable pressure on the joint, while an acute wave of pain washed down my arm.

Monica was standing holding the Winchester, swilling it dutifully and plying the farmer with questions. Neither of them was looking in my direction.

'Could somebody please help me,' I politely requested, not wanting to make a big fuss. As Monica and the farmer went on with their chatting, oblivious to the little drama playing out behind them, I waited for the sound of breaking bone.

'HELP!! HELP!!' Okay, I conceded, with the part of my mind that was now observing the scene from outside, this is one of those times I *do* need to ask for help.

At my cries, the farmer and Monica turned around and sized up the situation immediately. Monica put down the Winchester, and then the two of them worked together to heave at the top line of the heifer, managing to shift her weight just enough for me to remove my arm. Unable to move it, I used my left arm to pull my right arm clear.

'Sit down,' urged Monica, as the cow collapsed back against the side of the crush. But I had to finish the procedure. The farmer and Monica heaved some more and managed to get our patient into a more upright position. With my one good arm I ran the rest of the blood into her, with Monica and the farmer braced against her in case of another sideways collapse. But there was no more collapse: she seemed more stable now. Which was more than could be said for me.

Relieved the job was done, Monica and I headed back to the surgery, me steering with my left arm, Monica managing the gears.

As it turned out, I escaped with only a badly bruised arm – and a keen awareness of my own vulnerability. The next day I plied Mike and Stanley with questions of my own. It turned out they both had payment protection insurance that would help them pay their mortgages and so on if they themselves were injured at work. I didn't have a mortgage, but I had a cat and a dog who relied on me. I made some calls and took out some insurance pronto. The experience had shaken me up, and I wanted to be sure I was prepared for every dangerous eventuality.

On Monica's last day we were scheduled to go back down to Barbara Blunt's farm, right at the bottom of the valley. Two six-month-old calves were going to be running with their sisters so she needed them castrated. Back down the windy narrow road we went, heading ever deeper into the wetland, Monica's head in its usual position. I imagined there would be a refreshing verdant wetness to the place in the summer but now, in February, the damp was a cold one that clung to the skin and penetrated the bones.

I did one calf as a teaching case, then Monica did the other one.

'We'll use an open castrate technique because there's no risk of flies this time of year, and it's more reliable,' I said, 'so long as they have plenty of clean straw to lie on.' Barbara Blunt nodded. I cleaned the skin and injected local anaesthetic into the testicle. Judging by the kick I received this was the most painful part of the procedure. Five minutes later, I made an incision and popped out the testicle. 'Twist with tension, then twist and pull, twist and pull,' I said to myself as much as Monica. 'We leave the incision open to drain. Right, now it's your turn.'

As Monica slowly and carefully worked her way through the procedure I had just demonstrated, Rocky started howling from the Land Rover, as if in sympathy. When Monica approached the calf with her needle, Rocky turned up the volume. As she was twisting and pulling, he was getting so overwrought I was worried he was going to chew the steering wheel or do some other damage to my vehicle.

'Maybe Anna if we let him out for a minute?' suggested Monica, looking slightly flustered. So, against my better judgement, I let him out. He sprinted over to the crush and immediately snaffled up one of the snipped spherical items lying on the ground. The howling stopped and the tail started up a rhythmic wag as Rocky savoured his offaly treat. Barbara pretended not to notice. Oh, this dog was such an embarrassment.

We drove back in silence. Rocky was digesting his snack; Monica was breathing; and I was calculating just how much local anaesthetic Rocky had ingested.

When we got back we'd had a couple of cancellations. 'Your kitten vaccination and your itchy dog have cancelled, Anna. You've got a free hour. Maybe write up that post mortem report … or take Rocky out, he looks like he could do with it,' said Judith.

I eyeballed Rocky. He had only eaten the one ball and breakfast had been hours ago so his stomach would be fairly empty … and he was frisking happily and looking for trouble. I had a better idea.

'Right, you old bugger. You know what? Today's the day. Monica, scrub up, you're going to help me castrate a dog.'

Afterwards, surveying my handiwork and comparing it to a beginner's, I realised that Stanley and Mike had been right, as usual. Monica, with all those questions, had taught me a lot. Not only that, but, just as they had predicted, with her inexperience and her newfangled attitudes, she had made me feel more learned, experienced and old-fashioned all at once.

'Can we dissect the testicles together? It would be good for my anatomical revision,' asked Monica with her usual enthusiasm, pulling me out of my reverie. I admired her studiousness, and was quite keen to perform a bit of dissection myself, so I readily agreed. But the day got away from us. We had Rocky's post-operative protocol to carry out – mostly cuddles – and then we got called out to an aborting sheep.

'I tell you what,' I suggested. 'We'll go to the sheep, then do the dissection after supper.' Monica and I had planned to have a celebratory meal together at my cottage on her last night in Dorset. I put the testicles in a pot of formalin – an alcohol-like preservative – and put the pot in my favourite cloth shopping bag to take home. I thought we could do the dissection on the chopping board in my kitchen.

The sheep belonged to Robert Carraway and his brother, who farmed some of the incredibly steep land that lined the top road between Ebbourne and Peighton Lubbock. It was pretty un-farmable land – machinery couldn't work it – and the Carraways kept it close to nature, with only their hardy flock of sheep keeping the gorse under control. They were fine stockmen and only called out a vet when they were really stumped or desperate. I couldn't diagnose the cause of the abortion – the fifth one in a week – on the spot, but with spring and lambing season approaching it was important we got to the bottom of what was going on. I advised on hygiene to try to limit the spread of whatever it was, and sent one of the brothers to the Veterinary Investigation Centre near Langford with the poor dead lamb and its placenta, for further tests.

We returned for afternoon and evening consults. By the time we had finished it was 10 hours since Monica and I had set off for the Blunt farm that morning. We drove back to my cottage, had supper, got a bit tipsy, and forgot all about the testicles.

That weekend, my friend Sally came to stay, with her younger brother Max and my springer spaniel Nellie. At the allotted time I looked out of my window to see a dark blue, high-powered, low-slung sports car bumping carefully up my steep drive. An ashen-faced Max jumped out and pulled a large branch from underneath the car.

I bounced out to meet my friends. I gave Sally a long hug, Nellie an even longer embrace as she jumped up to give my face a thorough lick, and Max a kiss. Max went in for a second one: very continental and sophisticated, I thought.

'Hello! Exhaust still attached? Sorry, it's not a very car-friendly track,' I jabbered, excited to see them.

Max attempted a smile, 'If I'd known you lived in the middle of nowhere I would have brought the Range Rover.'

Rocky bounded out of the door now, even more excited than me. After 24 hours of rest and recovery it was difficult to believe that he had just been stripped of his manhood. I did however try to be a good owner and restrain him from leaping up and stretching the incision site and my sutures. The usual canine etiquette dictated that Nellie and Rocky sniffed each other's bottoms; even that did not concern my patient. They circled a couple of times, decided that there was no mutual threat, and then largely ignored each other, each being more interested in the two-legged friends. Phew.

I explained about Rocky's 'little op' and Max did that male wince thing before giving a brotherly look of concern and kneeling down beside Rocky to give him a long and much-appreciated chest rub. There seemed to be some male bonding going on. How sweet, I thought.

I'd prepared some local delicacies for lunch – cheese and ham and fresh bread – and then had a walking itinerary planned for the afternoon. I knew Nellie would love the area. We had trained together for the London Marathon, running the length and breadth of the Mendips. She had been a brilliant companion, always keen to come on a run, whatever the weather. In fact I would often get home and collapse but find Nellie raring to head out again after five minutes' recovery. Sally had also been a champion supporter of the cause. A self-confessed couch potato she would plan routes, take timings, read the running magazines and meet me at regular points on long runs to refuel and rehydrate me and (more importantly I guessed) check Nellie's feet. Sally had even come to London with Nellie on the big day and met me on the course. Sadly dogs are not allowed to run the race but Sally battled the crowds and made sure we met up. She was a star.

While Nellie may have been up for the adventures I had planned, it was sadly too soon after the op for Rocky to join us. Max volunteered to stay behind and keep Rocky company – the two seemed to be becoming fast friends – but I reasoned that Rocky would curl up and sleep again on his own, and I urged Max to come and see the spectacular views.

The conversation as we picked our way over the hills was mostly a continuation of the long phone calls Sally and I had been making over the last few months. We were both working long hours in our first jobs, both drained by the broken nights and the learning curve. We were doing the same job, I thought, but in such different environments. My lovely friend Sally had a boss who made her feel inadequate and a cramped flat in Shepherd's Bush, above a noisy practice in the middle of a shopping centre. I had supportive bosses and was working amongst peace and beauty. It probably wouldn't have been right for Sally, who did love the city, but the conversation served to remind me how right it was for me. I berated myself for complaining about the hours, and for not appreciating what I had.

As the three of us tramped with Nellie around my favourite spots and then huddled round my fire back at the cottage, the thought crossed my mind that Sally might be trying to set Max and me up. I'd always thought of Max as my friend's younger brother, but now I made an effort of will to look at him in this new light. When we had greeted each other earlier, I now remembered, I'd had to reach up: and he had been pleasingly stubbly. I found myself enjoying his easy sibling banter with Sally, and wanting to be drawn into its sardonic warmth. I noticed, too, that he was laughing at my weak attempts at jokes. Perhaps we were on the same wavelength. And Rocky's endorsement of him earned him extra brownie points in my book.

I'd planned chilli con carne for supper: easy, delicious, and the beef came from a good local farm. Dessert would be my mother's Christmas present of Rumtopf with ice cream. Rumtopf (literal translation, rum pot) is a completely delicious traditional German dish made by pouring rum over a layer of fruit; then adding another layer of fruit and more rum; another layer and more rum; and so on, over a period of weeks or months. You just keep adding to it, and the mixture matures until by Christmas-time you have a vat of highly alcoholic, highly tasty fruit.

I set Sally to laying the table, and Max to cutting up the onions for the chilli. While he chopped, I noticed how well he wore his jeans. That smile was rather attractive too, I thought, as he turned to ask me how many onions to chop. His straight dark hair was styled a bit long and swept-over for my tastes and it was a shame about his slightly podgy fingers. Oh, but he'd brought his own wellies. That definitely scored points.

Then Max started to talk about his terrific job as a management consultant and all its perks – the company car, the nights out on the town, the bonuses. I wondered: was Max possibly a bit much for me? Why would he have any interest in me and my life? What did we have in common?

As the chilli bubbled away, and Max kept on talking, I realised I had run out of rice. You've got to have rice with chilli con carne. The shop in Ebbourne would still be open if we hurried. 'I'll be right back,' I said as I grabbed my wallet and picked up my favourite shopping bag. It was still lying where I had dropped it in the hall when I had come in with Monica the previous day.

'Anna, I'll come,' said Max. 'In fact, let me drive. You

navigate. Sally can watch the pots. And the dogs.'

I'm sure it was a lovely car – I liked the shiny badge and the beige leather seats – but I barely noticed whatever it was I was supposed to be appreciating. What did come to my attention was an eye-watering smell. It seemed to be coming from my bag. I took a peek and remembered, with a jolt, Rocky's testicles. There they were, bobbing happily in their leaking pot of formalin. I didn't want the formalin to leak all over my lovely bag or, worse still, my prized soft new leather wallet, so I removed the pot, screwed the top on properly, and put it upright on the rubberised mat in the footwell. I would take it back into the cottage when we got home, and dispose of it properly at the surgery on Monday.

We had a great evening. The chilli was a huge success; I managed, for the first time ever in my life, not to overcook the rice; and the Rumtopf was particularly fine. We drank quite a lot of wine too, and stumbled blearily off to bed in the early hours, having had a wonderful time.

It was two weeks later that I realised. I was searching at the bottom of my shopping bag for a tomato that had gone astray and I caught a faint whiff of formalin. The smell jolted me right back to the night Sally and Max had come to stay. Oh God! I'd forgotten about the dog's bollocks for a second time.

Which meant that when Max and Sally had clattered down my drive in his sporty little number that Sunday afternoon, and then roared off up the road back to civilisation, those gory little gonads had still been floating happily in their formalin jar in the footwell.

Perhaps that explained why Max never rang me.

CHAPTER TEN

Just another day at the office

As the winter dragged on I started to yearn for some warmth and light. I couldn't decide which I found hardest: getting up in the cold and dark, or going to bed in the cold and dark. Or perhaps, more than either of those, it was working on an exposed windswept farm in the middle of the night in the cold and dark.

This particular February morning it felt like it had been raining forever. It had rained all day yesterday, and all day the day before. The sound of the rain lashing my roof had entered my dreams overnight. Driving to work, the windscreen wipers at full blast fought a losing battle with the sheets of water that were falling from the sky. Did there come a point, I wondered, when all the rain had been rained and there was nothing left?

On days like this, a schedule of small animal consults was a mixed blessing. On the one hand, I was warm and dry, inside a centrally-heated building, with access to a kettle and a box of biscuits. On the other hand, I am not a huge fan of the smell of wet steaming dog.

The consults whizzed by me in their dizzying ten-minute slots, an endless succession of names and faces. Penny and I worked like a well-oiled machine now, each anticipating what the other might need – Penny had a range of eyebrow movements that I had come to know, love and value, whose meaning ranged from 'Oooh, be careful, this cat's a feisty one,' to 'Are you sure you want to do that?' She also had an uncanny knack of knowing when I needed a quick look at the textbook.

Here was Tamara, with Sophie, in for a nail clipping and ear clean. 'It's your favourite greedy patient,' chirped Tamara, and she was right, I was very fond of this daft dog with her indomitable and indiscriminate appetite.

Here was Olive, the owner of possibly the yeastiest, doggiest-smelling basset hound I had ever come across. He just needed his annual booster vaccination, but his five-minute visit to my consulting room would have me starting every subsequent consultation with an apology for the smell.

Here was old Mr Michaels, straight off his farm from the look of his boots, and worried about a lump he had found on his beloved eight-year-old golden retriever, Muffin. Without a command or gesture from Mr Michaels, Muffin padded into the consulting room – her feet were as wet and muddy as Mr Michaels' boots, but for a farm dog her heavy golden fur was remarkably clean – and sat beside him. When she raised her head and gazed up at him with big soft eyes, she revealed a pink nylon collar with embossed silver bones, and a swelling under her jaw.

I had met Mr Michaels only once, at the Harvest Supper. He hadn't mentioned what kind of farm he ran (although, from the refreshingly clean smell of the disinfecting solution that now perfused the room, I guessed he had dairy cattle). Instead this bowed old farmer had told me all about Muffin, his wife's golden retriever. On their Golden Wedding anniversary, Mr Michaels had recounted eagerly, his eyes shining, he had presented his wife Sarah with 'a real piece of gold'. 'I handed her a box, wrapped with a bow and inside was Muffin, eight weeks old she was.' With Sarah now sadly passed away, Mr Michaels had then confided, Muffin and he were companions for each other: he spoiled her as much as Sarah had ever done. 'She gets the best seat in the house in front of the Aga, and I know I shouldn't, Vet, but I feed her whatever I'm having.'

I felt the lump and started to narrow down a possible cause, finally alighting on the likelihood of some kind of inflammation, or else neoplasia – a growth. It was a firm-feeling lump that moved freely under the skin; it was where the right lymph node – or gland – under the jaw was normally found, and the left side also felt a little larger and more firm than average. There was no history of any recent damage. The rest of the clinical examination was unremarkable, except a moderate amount of tartar on her molars, but it seemed unlikely that that would cause such a reaction; all other lymph nodes seemed normal.

I barely knew Mr Michaels and I'd never treated his animals before so I had to make a quick judgement about the best way to approach this discussion. I decided to be fairly clinical and matter-of-fact about the situation. 'The most likely explanation,' I began, trying to steer a path between teaching my grandfather to suck eggs and giving him all the information he might want, 'is that this is simply a swollen lymph node or what you may know as a lymph gland. They act as filters for the lymph which is an important part of the body's defence. However, other than some slightly dirty teeth I cannot see why they are reacting; there is no sign of obvious infection today. It might be, though, that she had a sore throat a while ago. The only way to be sure is to take a sample.' Mr Michaels seemed to be with me so I carried on. 'To do that, I'd either take a needle aspirate biopsy where I take a few cells and smear them on a slide; or we can anaesthetise Muffin and take a slice of the lump out for analysis. Though if we're going to do that we may as well simply remove the whole thing. If we take a needle biopsy there is nothing to lose except the cost of the lab fees for the specialists to look at the cells, about £30, and we can make a decision from there.'

At this point, I realised that I had misjudged it. Mr Michaels' eyes had glazed over. Either he hadn't understood anything I'd said, he was thinking hard about something else, or he was about to throw up.

'Or,' I went on hastily, trying hard to read the situation, 'we could try a course of antibiotics, or we can just monitor it. I can measure it today, and you can bring Muffin back in two weeks for me to measure again, and we can see how we go.'

Mr Michaels stroked the top of Muffin's head with a weather-beaten hand. Muffin pushed her wet black nose against his leg. 'I don't like the idea of biopsies and operations.'

'Okay,' I said, and I measured the lump and noted it down. It was about the size of a walnut.

Next came a young couple with a dog with diarrhoea. There's not always much you can do for a dog with diarrhoea, I explained: like with humans, it's very common, and like with humans, the best cure is simply to eat bland food in small amounts several times a day and sit it out.

'Can't you do something for her? We thought perhaps antibiotics?' asked the young woman.

The dog probably didn't need antibiotics. In fact they could make the situation last longer because they would knock out the normal good gut bugs that were in there fighting the baddies.

But it's quite difficult to do a consult and give people nothing to take away with them. People have paid their consultation fee, and they expect something for it: some tablets, or a paste; preferably antibiotics. Plus, I reminded myself, humans with diarrhoea don't crap on the carpet. I sent the young couple away with a probiotic paste, and three tins of chicken and rice with instructions to feed a dessertspoon full every two hours.

'Nice patter, Anna,' said Stanley, poking his head around my door after this encounter. I was puzzled. Whatever could he mean? He nodded his head towards the small panel of window connecting my consult room to the empty one next door. The vent was open. 'I just happened to be in there looking for … something,' said Stanley, unconvincingly. I realised that he could have spent hours listening in to my consults to check I was doing the right thing, and cringed as I recalled various of my early splutterings and half-formed explanations.

But there was no time to worry about that now. My final consult of the morning was Flynn.

Two weeks before, the day after my phone call with Athena, I had called Mr Spend and Flynn back in, and injected Flynn with a hormone to test for Addison's. Since then, every day, two or three times a day, I had checked the fax machine and the post for his results. Then on Thursday afternoon, as I'd wandered through reception between consults, en route to the biscuit tin, Judith had quietly passed me a still-warm fax. 'YES! Athena, you genius,' I had shrieked, punching the air with delight. A smart lady in a Laura Ashley blouse had given me a bemused look, paid for her worming tablets, and left. I didn't care. Flynn was a confirmed Addisonian, which meant I could help him, I could treat him, I could return him to full health and nuttiness. Untreated, Addison's is very serious: the lack of hormones has so many effects on the body that the dog ultimately will collapse and die. But, once diagnosed, it is generally straightforward to treat.

That same day I had called in Mr Spend, prescribed synthetic adrenal steroid tablets and a pinch of salt to address Flynn's mineral levels, and asked them to come back in a week.

And now, into my office bounced the old 'let me at 'em' hyperactive Flynn. 'He's right back to normal, Anna, as you can see,' smiled Mr Spend ruefully as Flynn wagged his tail energetically and raised himself on his hind legs to give my face a big old lick. Thank you Athena, I thought. Thank you.

Flynn was a high point in an otherwise fairly routine morning. It was very naughty but my other personal high point was coming across Lois gagging helplessly in front of the fridge in the accounts room. We kept two fridges, precisely to avoid this kind of situation, but sadly sometimes people didn't follow the protocol: well, it was a long way to the upstairs refrigeration unit when reception was busy. That was how Lois came to open a tupperware container thinking it was going to be a delicious treat, only to find it full of cat vomit that some kind owner had brought us.

I was enjoying a rare long lunch break (a fresh Hommity Pie from the deli, perfect on a cold wet day) when Judith came up the stairs to the vets' room.

'It's your phantom pregnancy woman on the phone,' she said, slightly breathless. 'Mrs Stafford. She's asking for you. She thinks it's colic this time and it's her favourite mare.'

My heart joined the Hommity Pie in my mouth. In a moment, my gentle, boring, uneventful day of dog consults had disappeared and been replaced with an unasked-for adrenalin-pumping adventure. How attractive an afternoon of fragrant basset hounds suddenly seemed.

The truth was, I was not that keen on treating horses. I could admire them as splendid creatures. But I was not one of those people brought up around horses and I had never had that instinctive love and understanding of them that some vets have. In fact, they made me uncomfortable.

Yes, horses could be statuesque and athletic. Yes, their conformation was amazing, with those fine equine limbs and the muscling of their shoulders and hindquarters. Yes, I found it extraordinary that they could run so fast on their hooves, which I had learnt from comparative anatomy were essentially the tips of their middle fingers and toes. But personally I had always found cows' faces just as pretty, with their eyes like deep pools of peace framed by luxurious lashes. And whereas the average cow I saw was gentle, patient and down-to-earth, horses – especially the smart ones, the racing types that I thought of as the supermodels of the equine world – seemed quite often highly-strung creatures. I respected horses and had an aesthetic appreciation of them, but I was cautious and cagey around them. And of course, these sensitive animals sensed it, which made them more likely to bite and kick, which made me more tense.

I didn't understand all the terminology either – the snaffle bits and off side legs, the curry comb (vs a dandy brush!), the insistence on calling white horses 'grey'. My equine reticence was mostly born of ignorance.

But my main problem, my own stupid self-limiting problem, was not dealing with the horse, but dealing with its owner. The farmer who came with the cow was usually as down-to-earth and easy-going as his animal. In my admittedly very limited experience, further confirmed by my encounter the previous November with Mrs Stafford, the owner at the end of the horse's lead rope was often as highly strung as his companion. It was understandable. However fond a farmer might be of a favourite bull or ram or cow, as much as he might love his stock, this was different from the relationship owners formed with their horses, whom they might ride several times a week and muck out, feed and groom daily. And never dream of eating.

I knew it was wrong to run away from what I didn't know. I knew I should confront my fears, run towards them, and embrace this opportunity to grow.

'Send Mike,' I pleaded. 'He's the horse expert.' Mike was one of those vets who was a good all-rounder, could think laterally and would relish a chance to treat a horse.

'Mike's gone to a parents' evening.'

'In the middle of the day?'

'Yes – sorry. And they're completely sacrosanct.'

'Send Stanley?'

'He and Penny have Mark under anaesthetic for a full dermatological work-up.' Despite my early promise with hamsters, Stanley had remained our exotics expert. Mark, a bald mouse, belonged to the grungy-looking but very pleasant and enthusiastic young couple who owned the local pet shop, one of whom had knitted Mark a body stocking in Rasta colours to keep him warm. Although Mark, to my surprise, was quite happy to wear his little red gold and green outfit, and although he didn't seem to be in any distress, the couple wanted everything possible done to cure Mark of his baldness. He was currently under general anaesthetic having skin scrapes and biopsies taken. Stanley couldn't leave.

My journey over to the Stafford farm was a re-run in many ways of my first journey there, though mercifully without the dreadful hangover I'd had that morning after the Harvest Supper. The weather was similarly awful. I went into the same blind, heart-pumping panic; had that same awful feeling that I knew absolutely nothing about how to treat a horse. 'What do I do? What do I do? What do I do?' seemed to be the only thing in my head, beating out a useless rhythm with the windscreen wipers. Finally, I got a grip of myself. Thinking 'What do I do?' on a loop wasn't going to help anyone. I made myself take deep breaths; concentrated on conquering my heart rate; recited, out loud, the steps I was going to take.

By the time I arrived, although I was still mainly thinking, 'arrgggggghhhhh', I thought I probably at least appeared to be in control of myself and the situation.

Mrs Stafford ran-walked out from her house – a Spanish-style casa, I now noticed, how unusual – to greet me. Seeing that flushed face and strained smile, I remembered with dismay that I was going to have to manage her anxiety as well as mine and the poor horse's. I gave her hand a firm shake and smiled a reassuring smile. I was hoping that my 'calm and competent' act would convince us all.

Keeping up the act, I strode over to the stables with Mrs Stafford jogging along beside me.

'Last time I thought it was a foal and it was colic. Wouldn't it be funny if this time I thought it was colic and it was a foal?' said Mrs Stafford, nervously.

'It would,' I said. It really wouldn't, I thought. I was worried enough about treating one horse, let alone two.

The lights from the house shone out through the rain-drenched gloom, casting eerie late winter shadows as we walked. The assembled half dozen horses noted our arrival with tosses of the head and gentle whinnies, their breath steaming in the cold air. All except my patient, a very white Grey about fifteen hands high. She was being walked gently up and down on a lead rein by a small, lean, soaking wet man who looked about a hundred years old. The Grey's breath was making vapour trails too but despite the cold she was in a sweat, tail twitching, and too turned in on herself and her pain to notice her visitors. Not a hair was out of place though: she had been beautifully groomed.

'My "man who does" has been walking her up and down,' said Mrs Stafford.

'Reckon I've walked fifteen miles with Beauty today,' he said, looking done in. Sometimes a colicking horse would be trotted up and down to stop them rolling over in their pain and hurting themselves.

'This could indeed be colic. I'll do a full examination,' I said, attempting a slow, controlled voice. There were all kinds of colic, which is essentially a vet's word for abdominal pain, and the treatment varied, depending on what was causing it. 'Come on girl, we're going to get you better. Would one of you hold her for me?'

Beauty gave a little whicker, which put me a bit more at my ease. She looked like a nice gentle horse, but I could see she was agitated: her eyes were so wide I could see the whites. Perhaps my own act was fooling me, but I started to feel more positive.

I checked her mucus membranes and took her pulse. I listened to her heartbeat and took her temperature. I listened along her flanks for gut sounds. Having learnt my lesson the last time when I narrowly escaped a hearty kick, I carried out my rectal examination from a safe position behind the closed bottom stable-door.

In the meantime I tried to take a history. Mrs Stafford was in such a pickle that I wasn't counting on finding out anything useful from it. But a history had to be done.

'How long has she been like this?' I asked.

'Oh, it seems like hours. I don't know. Do you think she's in terrible pain?'

'She's certainly in discomfort, but no, her heart rate suggests she isn't in terrible pain. But she is all lathered up. You were right to call me. What has she eaten today?'

'I don't know. Just the normal. Could it be something she ate? Do you think she's got food poisoning? Do horses get food poisoning? Could it be cancer?'

'Have you wormed her recently?' I ventured.

'No. Yes. Is last week recently?'

'Have you seen her pass any droppings?'

'No. None. None at all. Is she constipated? Maybe Mr G has.'

The man-who-did hobbled over and quietly muttered in my ear. 'She's been like it for three hours, and she's eaten a scoop of oats with mix from the feed merchants and a hay net today but not passed a nugget.'

Her heart rate wasn't terribly high but it was faster than I would have liked, and her temperature was within normal limits and the mucus membranes were pink. I couldn't feel a rectal impaction or an obvious twist or bloating. My main concern was that I couldn't hear any normal gut sounds. In a healthy horse I would expect to hear some tinkling and flushing – the sounds of fluids sloshing around. The left side in particular was completely silent.

'What is going on with you then, my Beauty?' I murmured to the mare. Mrs Stafford and her man-who-did looked at me expectantly.

The best thing I could think to do was to keep this side of the stable door and keep my hand in the rectum and gently feel around – with time more structures became apparent and this time, on rectal examination, I felt something firm and solid on the left hand side of her abdomen. A foal? Could it be? But no, whatever it was had a doughy consistency. It wasn't a hard little head.

It was, though, extremely bad news from my point of view – because it meant this wasn't the kind of colic I was going to be able to fix with a quick dose of some medicine or other. This beautiful frightened beast almost certainly had a blockage that was preventing food from travelling further through her. And in the process of dislodging it, I was going to be presented with several opportunities to make a dire mistake.

'Mrs Stafford, I think she has a blockage. I'm going to need to clear it. I'll be right back.'

'A blockage? What could be blocking her? How are you going to get it out? Will she need an operation?'

Back at the Land Rover, Mrs Stafford's questions carrying to me on the wind from the stables, I rummaged around in my horse box for the long flexible tube I was going to have to pass down the fretful mare's throat and into her stomach. Then I pulled out the drugs box and prepared the sedative: I wasn't going to attempt this for the first time in practice with a fully conscious and rather nervous horse. Once I'd found everything else I needed, I double-checked the dose. Then I triple-checked it. Getting the dosage wrong was my first opportunity to go wrong, and quite a likely one given that this was in fact my first ever horse sedation. Then I forced myself to wait by the car and take ten deep breaths.

By the time I got back, the exhausted-looking man-who-did was resting on an upside-down bucket in a corner, and the horse and her owner had both worked themselves up into a terrible lather. I was quite keen to administer the sedative to Mrs Stafford.

'Mrs Stafford, I need you to keep calm because she's picking up on how you're feeling and it's making things worse.' That seemed to have an effect.

I injected the sedative into the jugular vein on the left side of Beauty's sweaty neck. Within a couple of minutes her head hung down and she seemed calm.

'What are you doing now?'

I remembered this was Mrs Stafford's favourite of all questions. 'Mrs Stafford, I need to dislodge the impaction with liquid paraffin. But I can't just ask a horse to drink liquid paraffin, so I'm going to have to pass the tube into Beauty's stomach and pour the paraffin into her.

Hopefully, that will lubricate everything up a bit and move the blockage. I need to ask you to keep quiet during this procedure, please, so that I can focus all my attention on the horse.'

With my back to the mare, and her now very heavy head on my shoulder, I passed the tube into her left nostril and beyond, being very careful to avoid tearing the blood-rich soft tissue that covered the wafer-thin bone inside her nostrils.

She swallowed, I pushed on further and saw the bump going down the left hand side of her neck. I could tell from the gurgling and bubbling that the tube had gone where I wanted – down her throat and into her stomach, not down the windpipe and into the lungs. Pouring any quantity of liquid paraffin into a horse's lungs is another pretty easy way to kill it.

I poured a cup of water down first, just to be extra-careful, and then, happy that the tube was definitely in the right place, I poured five litres of paraffin slowly into the funnel and down the tube and then carefully pulled the tube out. At the very last moment, as I was pulling the very last bit of the tube through her nostril, Beauty shook her head.

It was like a tap had been opened. Blood gushed. She bled and bled and bled. I grabbed a yellow water bucket, and she filled the bucket with blood.

'What have you done to her?' screamed Mrs Stafford.

'She nicked herself on the tube when she shook her head. Her nose is full of blood vessels and she must have bashed one of them open. It's like when children have nosebleeds.' It popped into my mind (oh why have such a useless thought at a time like this?) that this abundance of blood vessels so close to the surface of the skin was also the reason people snorted coke through their noses. It was the quickest way to get it into the blood supply. At least I managed not to say that out loud.

I tried to calculate how much blood a horse had in her, and what the capacity of the bucket was. Could it be 30 litres? How much blood could a horse lose?

'That's half a leg of blood in there, how long are you going to let her bleed,' panicked Mrs Stafford – and it had to be said, it was completely fair to be panicking at this point.

I tried to stem the flow with ad hoc cotton wool tampons. They made her sneeze and snort, which only created a yet-more dramatic spray effect.

'I'm sorry, I need your bucket,' I said to the poor old man-who-did, who was watching with silent alarm. He hauled himself up, I grabbed it, turned it upside down again and stood on it, my back to the horse, to try to hold her head up. I thought it might help. And at the very least if she swallowed some of the blood rather than spraying it everywhere it would look less awful and we might be able to stop and think.

It felt like it had been going on forever, and would never stop. The beautifully-groomed grey was so drenched with blood it looked like she had been murdered. Feeling as agitated as Mrs Stafford now, my thoughts became wilder and less ordered. Who could I ring? Stanley's wife Vanessa was an experienced horse vet and happy to give advice. Where was she, was she even in the county? How quickly could she get here? I remembered Mike telling me about a bullock he had castrated who had bled a lot from a blood vessel he hadn't been able to reach to clamp off: he had sedated the beast further to reduce the blood pressure. Would that be a good idea? Probably not. I was going to have to ring someone. I felt sick in the pit of my stomach and it was not from the sight of blood. Could I do a blood transfusion on a horse?

And then, just as I thought I couldn't physically hold Beauty's head up any longer, the gush started to slow and turn into a steady trickle rather than a gush. That was a good sign. It was beginning to clot. The trickle slowed and slowed until I could count drips, and finally, about an hour later, just after she successfully passed a lovely stool, it stopped completely.

It was dark, and still raining, by the time I left the Stafford farm.

Driving back to the practice, weak-legged and shaking with exhaustion, dog-tired in body and mind from the emotional and physical effort of the last two hours, I saw something shoot out from the verge and then, immediately and sickeningly, felt a bump under a wheel. It wasn't a pothole. I stopped the car on the side of the road, my already knotted guts twisting further. Had I run over someone's cat? Was I going to have another upset owner on my hands? Another emergency to deal with? I hauled myself out and shone my torch at the front of the car. The Land Rover had survived unscathed but just behind it on the road I could see a clearly dead, very squashed squirrel. I burst into tears.

I stood and stared at the poor creature, hot tears running down my cheeks and mingling with the rain. All I could think was, 'I'm supposed to be saving animals and now I've gone and killed one.'

It was a bad end to what had turned out to be a bad day.

Eventually, I got a grip and pulled myself together. I walked back into the surgery feeling rather wobbly – the adrenalin had worn off completely now and I was simply shattered – so it was nice that everyone made a fuss of me.

'Yes, I am quite shaken up actually, that was draining,' I said, as Judith rushed me an emergency cup of sugary tea and Penny started wiping me down and Stanley asked me over and over again what had happened.

It was only after five minutes of excitable flapping around that I realised I should explain that it was a horse's blood all over my face, and not my own.

PART THREE

Spring

CHAPTER ELEVEN

Down cow

I really don't know why, but for some reason I was feeling particularly jolly.

I always enjoyed the peace of my isolated cottage in the mornings and I usually washed and dressed in silence – and quickly, because the place was so cold. Only the sweet cacophony of the birds disturbed the absolute quiet. But this particular morning in early March, I had Radio 2 on loudly as I made sure I had everything I needed for my day. (I couldn't do Radio 1 any more – it was all R&B and rap and it didn't do it for me. It was Radio 4 or 2. I worried fleetingly that I might be turning into my parents.)

Perhaps the reason I was feeling so buoyant was that spring finally seemed to be pushing winter away. We'd now had several of those early spring days when it had been frosty in the morning, and chilly in the shade, but positively warm when my back was to the sun; those days when everyone was constantly taking off and putting on layers of clothes to try to get it right.

I walked outside with my mug of tea and took a moment. Glorious. I always enjoyed the view from my cottage but today it seemed particularly breathtaking. The sky was, at last, a vast expanse of clear sharp baby blue, rather than the heavy grey harbinger of doom it had been for the last few weeks. The biting wind had dropped to a gentle breeze.

Or perhaps my mood was down to the pleasantly idle weekend I had spent with my parents in their centrally-heated-to-within-an-inch-of-your-life home in Leicestershire. They'd laid on the full treatment: huge meals, good wine, lots of snoozing and reading the paper. I had even been spared the formerly mandatory Sunday constitutional. This bracing family tradition had been quietly dropped now that my father was entering his dotage and preferred to sit and read the paper from cover to cover. And I had returned with a food parcel that would see me through five or six hard winters.

I called for Rocky and he bounded up, eager as ever. There had been no change in his energy levels following his 'little op'. Nor had his poor behaviour noticeably improved. We were still bottom of the class at our weekly training sessions in Crewkerne; Rocky still ran off all the time, was still terrible on the recall, still howled if I left him on his own, still nipped and showed his teeth. The previous day he had disappeared on yet another deer chase, returning panting and proud two hours later. This time I had been really cross, first shouting at him and then ignoring him for the rest of the afternoon. Dogs hate being ignored: at least being shouted at is getting a reaction. But Rocky was a forgiving soul: this morning, he was still my best friend and keen to come to work with me. No grudges, just glossy-coated adoration.

Rocky and I drove the familiar two miles to the surgery in Ebbourne with the car radio on full blast. The air was light, the greens and yellows of the fields bright. Fluffy clouds cast shadows on the undulating fields that spread out endlessly on either side of me, and the fields fractured into a hundred different shades. I pulled up to the surgery and its pale stone walls looked splendid.

'Don't get comfortable,' said Mike the moment I walked in. 'I'd like you to head out to Kingcombe Meadows please. We've just had a call through from the Deputy Warden: he's found a down cow.'

I'd visited Kingcombe Meadows before. It was a wildlife reserve, owned and managed by the Dorset Wildlife Trust, and its wild pastures and meadows provided some of the beautiful top road views that gave me so much pleasure on my drives over to the branch surgery. The Trust had an education centre housed in a 17th century threshing barn from where it ran guided walks and courses on everything from painting the landscape to identifying insects. It also operated as a working farm, keeping organic herds of shaggy black-coated, white-belted Galloway and the more utilitarian white-faced Hereford-cross cows, and flocks of speckle-faced Beulah and goat-like dark-coated Soay sheep. These old breeds grazed the land, stopping it getting too overgrown and gorse-y, and naturally maintaining its wildlife character.

I had attended a couple of fairly straightforward

scenarios here, and I'd successfully treated a ringwomb on a sheep only the previous week.

The Warden, Phil, was an old school ex-postmaster. I'd had dealings with a couple of the younger chaps too, who helped check and manage the stock and the land. I'd never met the Deputy Warden though, who had phoned in this down cow.

I was delighted to be heading back out again on a day like today. I double-checked my kit, scrabbled around for overalls that kind of fitted, rounded up Rocky who had gone off in search of doggy treats from Penny, and headed out. Up, up out of the valley we climbed, Ebbourne now laying itself out below us: past higgledy-piggledy farm buildings, and fields and trees and high hedgerows suddenly bursting with white and yellow and purple flowers. We roared along, windows down, fresh spring air pouring in, before turning off onto a narrow rutted lane heading back down the side of another valley.

Coming up to the main entrance of the Nature Reserve, I spotted one of the lads in his lumberjack shirt and dealer boots, waving to me from the side of the road. He opened the gate leading directly onto the reserve and motioned to me to drive through. Down we bumped, past newborn lambs with purple identification numbers sprayed on their flanks (they really do skip), over the tussocky grasslands and then up again to the brow of the hill where a second lad wearing gaiters stood under a single majestic old oak tree in full, delicate, lime-green new leaf. He waved us to turn left. The land dropped away steeply here, and became boggy as we headed down. At the bottom, in the lee of a line of hazel bushes, the cow and the Deputy Warden were waiting.

I'd seen the reserve before, but never on a day like this. The pastures were teeming with every kind of life: birds, the first butterflies, wildflowers and the dark yellow gorse. I even spotted a rabbit scurrying about. Rocky spotted it too of course. He was beside himself, there was such an abundance of life to chase. He started barking excitely to be let out. 'Rocky,' I said, in what I hoped was a stern voice. 'If you want to be let out there is to be NO running off. Otherwise you will have to stay in the Land Rover. Do you understand?'

I jumped out from the Land Rover, turned round, and was confronted with a pair of amazing green eyes. I blinked and held them for a moment, before putting out my hand for a brisk vet-to-client handshake.

'Hi, I'm Anna.'

'Hello. Rob.'

While Rob started running through what was going on, and an unleashed Rocky took off blissfully in no particular direction, I took stock of my new client. The Deputy Warden had strong features in an open face that I guessed spent most of its time outdoors. I also took in a big thatch of thick yellow hair that looked like it had never met a comb, a green army NBC jacket (a Nuclear, Biological and Chemical warfare outfit which I recognised from my student army days on Salisbury Plain), recycled as a wildlife-friendly green camouflage top, and chainsaw wellies. He was probably about the same age as me, and was noticeably taller – I had to look up to meet those stunning green eyes.

I came round to find Rob midway through his exposition. I'd missed it and was going to have to busk it a bit. Great start, Anna.

'So she calved when, sorry?'

'She calved overnight.'

'And she's been down since when?'

'I found her an hour ago, but I think she's been down overnight.'

'And she's been on her side the whole time?'

'Well, I only found her an hour ago but she's been on her side since then.'

'Gosh. She looks pretty sick.' She was not just down but lying flat out on her side.

He was looking at me closely, like he thought I might be an idiot. As well he might. I resolved to focus and try to make at least a vaguely competent impression.

My patient's beautiful brown eyes were glazed over, her coat covered in dew and her breathing decidedly laboured. I examined her. She had a high temperature, a hard quarter and a mucky back end.

'Okay, well the first thing we have to do is to turn her. We don't want her weight on one side for too long. Come on girlie, come on my love.'

Turning a down cow is easier said than done. I started pushing and heaving, with little effect, conscious of Rob's eyes on me.

'Could you help me to rock her?' I asked. Rob and I stood

side by side with our hands on the upper part of the cow's flanks and started rocking her in a steady rhythm, gently at first and then building up more and more movement. But nothing happened, except that I was now in a sweat and out of breath and needed to remove a layer. While I was doing that, Rob carefully approached the cow and tucked her front legs underneath her. Then he slipped a halter around her head. He moved easily and confidently.

'Alright 157, let's get you moving,' he murmured softly.

We went back to rocking and this time, with her legs repositioned, and with Rob also pulling her head up, we managed to shift her great bulk over.

'Was it a large calf? Sometimes a large calf can cause nerve damage inside the pelvis as it comes out.'

'No, it wasn't, particularly. It was dead though.'

'Very dead? I mean, like days before?'

'Difficult to say. The crows had had a go and pecked its eyes out but it wasn't too blown.' I admired Rob's tone. He struck a note of concern without any hint of squeamishness.

'So you didn't put a hand in to calve her?'

'No, she pushed it out herself overnight. Apparently there was no sign that she was due to calve yesterday. This is my first day back on the reserve.'

'Okay. Right. Well, we're looking at mastitis and metritis – infections of the udder and the womb. If the calf was dead inside her for a while, that would explain the womb infection. She may also have some nerve damage from calving, and she's quite possibly low in minerals. That's less common in beef cows but as she's down its possible.'

Okay, so I wasn't looking my hottest in my full Mole Valley PVC gear – a blue plastic smock top and matching over-trousers that rustled when I walked – but I hoped I was at least making a fairly competent impression now.

'Minerals – milk fever then?' asked Rob.

'Exactly, low calcium. Milk fever, maybe even a touch of low magnesium or phosphorus.' I nodded at him, impressed by how quickly he'd picked up on the possible diagnosis. The infections needed treating but I was not convinced that on their own they would have caused this cow to go down. That was possibly due to nerve damage, or potentially what's known to farmers as milk fever: a post-partum loss of calcium, which is vital for nerve and muscle function. Or they were now secondary issues having been down and not eating. Chicken or egg?

'I'd like to administer anti-inflammatories, and antibiotics, and some minerals,' I said, heading to the back of the Land Rover to draw them up. It took me longer than usual because my concentration was a bit off. I was distracted by Rob. As he patted the cow, I noticed his battered worker's hands, with their slim fingers and slightly thickened knuckles. How could such bashed and weathered hands be so pleasing, I puzzled to myself as I drew up the anti-inflammatory. Because, I answered myself, putting that syringe to one side and going onto the antibiotic, they were the mark of a grafter, an outdoors achiever, not someone who sat at a desk all day. My thoughts wandered to Sally's brother Max, of the dog's bollocks, and his soft, podgy, never-done-a-real-day's-work-in-his-life hands. (How much antibiotic did I need? I was going to have to calculate that again, I had forgotten.) I wondered whether my own unglamorous hands, covered in scratches and odd scars, and with thickened blobby knuckles scarred from bashing against crushes during TB testing, would ever be considered attractive by anyone. I picked up a third syringe, for the phosphorus.

And jabbed myself firmly in my left thumb with the needle. I swore softly – more at how unprofessional and clumsy it looked than from the sudden piercing pain. That was going to sting.

'Why does she need antibiotics?' asked Rob with a steady gaze when I got back to the cow with my syringes, trying not to stick myself again. His questions weren't in the least bit aggressive, but he was sure of his ground and not afraid to ask them. 'Phil will ask me and I will need to know. We're organic here so we have to prove to the Soil Association that we need any medicine we give.'

'To treat the infections of her uterus and udder. The names and batch numbers of the medicines will be on your monthly invoice.'

I administered calcium, a small amount of magnesium and phosphorus (just to cover all bases), antibiotics and anti-inflammatories. Rob expertly pulled the sick cow's head to expose the side of her neck for me with its big jugular groove. I pressed the base of her neck to raise the vein up and to my great joy the needle went in first time. Before I administered all her medicines I filled a glass test tube with some of the flowing blood from the inserted needle, capped it and put it in my boiler suit pocket.

In mild cases of milk fever, the calcium could have a magical effect: the cow could be up within ten minutes. We stood in the crisp, silent spring sun and chatted about nothing in particular while we waited to see whether the magic would work. I thought it unlikely but, hey.

'I've not seen you here before,' I said.

'I've been working off-site all winter – hedge-laying and coppicing mostly.' He had a slight West Country burr.

'You're from around here originally?'

'I'm from North Dorset. My family have a farm up there. How about you? You're not from round here?'

'I'm not really from anywhere.' I explained my itinerant childhood.

'Well, how are you settling into West Dorset?'

'We love it here,' I said, as Rocky bounded up to me, tongue lolling, for a quick pat. I bent to give his tummy a scratch. 'The landscapes are just fabulous. We go on lovely long walks all over the place.'

Rob nodded and went silent briefly. Rocky bounded off again.

'Well, I don't think she's getting up and it's been 15 minutes,' he finally said, glumly.

I talked Rob through the possible complications if we couldn't get this cow up: the muscles on which she was resting her half-tonne weight could become bruised and damaged; the blood supply to them would be compromised. Then it became impossible for the cow to stand. That usually meant the end of the line. The short line to a bullet and the incinerator for fallen stock.

None of this was news to Rob. He knew that no cow should be down for too long.

'She needs turning every few hours, I'm afraid. And please keep offering her as much food and water as she will take.'

'Okay. I'll do that.'

'Let me know if there's any change. In the meantime I'll run the blood sample to see if there are any deficiencies and come back in a few hours with the fluid pump to administer some intravenous fluids.'

'Okay. Will do. Thanks.'

It was time to go and I looked down the meadow for Rocky. In the distance I spotted him, cavorting dementedly with another dog. As soon as Rob noticed, he called out 'Soots' once and the little black Labrador started trotting over obligingly. I realised this was going to be a humiliating moment. I called Rocky, in as deep and commanding a voice as I could muster. Come on, boy, I thought. Just once, for me. Come on, Rocky. Gambolling up the field came Rocky. He was probably chasing his new friend, but I didn't mind. 'Oh what a good boy, good boy Rocky,' I told him as I led him back to the Landy.

I returned later that day as promised. Why was my stomach feeling flighty? Nerves at rechecking the cow, I told myself. Rob was talking to a couple of his colleagues as I arrived, but they seemed very busy and even more monosyllabic than usual, and it seemed they couldn't stay around to help. So it was just the two of us who walked down the field to check on my patient.

The cow had improved, Rob explained as we went. She had eaten a small amount of hay he had brought to her and seemed a little brighter. But, as I could see as we approached, she was still down.

'That's not good,' I said, pointlessly. Rob already knew that. I ran over what the tests had told me that afternoon. It might, I explained to him, be due to her low magnesium level: a case of hypomagnesaemia or 'grass staggers', so-called because of the staggering gait that is one of the possible nervous signs. Cattle do not have large reserves of magnesium and when they are heavily in calf they need more of it than normal so it doesn't take all that much for them to become low. Possibly, she had had a chronic shortfall over the winter, exacerbated by eating the spring grass which can be low in magnesium. Or possibly the double infection had put her off eating. Whatever the reason, we had to restore her levels and get her up in the next 24 hours or so.

We turned her together, pushing as one to shift her heavy weight, and then with Rob's help I administered more magnesium and fluids. To this end I used one of those plant killer sprays with a hose that you can direct and a pump on the side to build up pressure. I filled it with hypertonic saline (salty water which should then make her drink more) and a quarter of a bottle of magnesium, the remainder of the bottle going under the skin for a slow release. I then attached the hose to a large bore needle in 157's jugular vein and pumped in the fluid. It always seemed crude and somehow wrong to me but it did work well to rehydrate cattle.

'You need to keep on turning her I'm afraid,' I said to Rob as I packed away my gear. He nodded calmly, seemingly with no qualms about the long night ahead. 'We also need to speak to Phil about testing some of the other cows for magnesium levels to make sure you don't have an outbreak of grass staggers. You may need to supplement the rest. There isn't much else we can do for this one at the moment.'

And, with a final worried look at her, off I went again. Cow 157, though, was on my mind all evening. Looking up at the star-filled sky before bed, my first thought was not my usual one ('where's the plough?'). It was that without any cloud cover it would be bitterly cold for poor 157 overnight, and bitterly cold for anyone who happened to be out there with her, striding across the reserve in their chainsaw wellies.

The following morning, Judith was on the phone when I walked into the surgery.

'Oh, hang on,' she said, 'She's just walked in. I'll hand you over, Rob.'

I felt myself blush, and awkwardly rubbed my hand where I'd stuck it with the needle yesterday in front of him. Judith noticed my crimson cheeks, of course, but pretended not to. I took the phone from her and turned away, feeling like a teenager on the phone in her mum's kitchen.

Rob sounded exhausted and on the verge of tears. He

related how he had gone to turn this cow in the early hours of the morning and found her asphyxiated, dead. He thought she had bent her head underneath her on a hazel stump trying to finally get herself up, tipped herself forwards, and then been too weak to right herself.

What a compassionate man, I thought. And wasn't it sweet of him to bother to ring me when there was really nothing more I could do.

CHAPTER TWELVE

Tea and sympathy

Over the next few days I paid meticulous attention to the A4 paper diaries kept on Judith's desk, but there were no more calls out to the wildlife reserve.

This close attention did make me realise though just how comfortable I now felt working in Ebbourne. When I had first arrived, the diary – full of unfamiliar names and mysterious three-letter acronyms – had been a meaningless mystery to me. It had been the same with the working routine, the names of the medicines, the locations of the farms on the ordnance survey maps, how to drive my Land Rover. Everything had been new and I had gone through most days with that wide-eyed, rabbit-caught-in-the-headlights kind of look, desperately trying to take it in and retain it all.

Now, I had absorbed all of this new information. The three in one rota – one evening on, two off; one weekend on, one weekend 'second on call', one off – was second nature to me now. I reckoned I could pass the West Dorset equivalent of The Knowledge, such was my encyclopaedic understanding of every lump and bump of every road around Ebbourne. And the names of owners and patients and the scrawled explanations beside them now spoke to me loud and clear; in fact, they had the capacity to invoke feelings in me – sometimes of pleasant anticipation, sometimes of concern, often of amusement, and occasionally, when I saw the name of what was called a 'heart-sink' client written down there, of utter dread.

On one morning of consults, I looked down my list and read that I would be seeing Charlie and Lucy Cockburn (concern); Sophie and Tamara for a claw clip, ear clean and EAGs, or empty anal glands (amusement); Muffin and Mr Michaels for 'lump measure' (curiosity); and Esmeralda with Mrs Bromsgrove, the vicar's wife, who begged me not to call out 'Esmeralda' in reception – 'It's so embarrassing. Thomas named her you know,' – for a CBA or cat-bite abscess (pleasurable anticipation). I knew the vicar and his wife fairly well and could quite believe the reverend would have chosen that name.

Of course I saw lots of people on the list whom I'd never met before too, with unrevealing explanations for their visit such as 'off-colour cat' or 'check-up'. Penny had also cornered me on arrival when she had asked me to check her sweet-natured young collie, Jasmine, 'just when you have time as Jazz has slowed up a bit and developed a wet cough.' I pretended not to notice Penny's worried, watery eyes.

Charlie and Jazz were the only patients that morning who caused me real concern, coincidentally suffering from a similar problem. Charlie's chest was wet and noisy. When

I put my stethoscope on it there was a crackling noise on both sides; it should have been fairly quiet in there. And rather than a nice 'lub dub' for a heartbeat I heard 'lub shhh dub' with a longer, louder 'shhh' than previously. 'Lucy,' I began. (Mrs Cockburn insisted I call her by her first name which I found quite hard having had a rather formal upbringing on this matter: my mother still called the parents of her school friends by their surnames, that was just the way it was for that German generation.) 'Charlie's heart murmur is a little worse: his heart valve is more leaky so each contraction is not quite as effective as it was, and consequently fluid is damming back into his lungs – I can hear it.' I increased his diuretics to draw the fluid off and checked his dose of heart medication. 'He will drink and wee a bit more now,' I said. He lay quietly and stoically on the consulting table and I wondered with a heavy heart how long it would be before PTS (Put To Sleep) appeared beside his name in the consult list.

Jazz too had noisy lung sounds and a pretty impressive murmur. She was only two years old. 'Pen, it would be good to know if she has leaky valves or an enlarged heart, or possibly something else, although the treatment may well be the same. We should do X-rays and an ultrasound of her heart. I don't have that imaging ability yet but I'll read up and get the partners in on the case, okay?' Penny nodded bravely, hugging Jazz tightly to her.

Mr Michaels didn't turn up for Muffin's lump check. I felt a little uneasy about a lump in an older dog, so I asked Judith to give him a ring to re-book. Then I did the best thing I could think of to make us all feel a bit better: I popped to the patisserie and bought extra special strawberry tarts and, even though I knew I shouldn't really, I let Jazz have some of the pastry.

Glancing through the diary for the fifth time one day (I had started to try to time it for when Judith was on the phone, hoping that she wouldn't notice) and discovering that there were, as yesterday and the day before, still no calls out to Kingcombe, the idea came to me that Rob and his cute little black Lab, Soots, were probably personal clients of the practice. That meant that their details would be on our rudimentary database.

Once I had had the thought, it was hard to un-have it. My mind kept wandering there at inconvenient moments.

I had been shown how to use the database as part of my initial induction but that was definitely one of those things that had not become clearer to me over time because I'd had almost no occasion to use it. This was 1997. Appointments were still all run via the two A4 diaries in reception, and client records were still kept in paper files in the filing cabinets that lined the walls. We had two very old computers with huge box-like monitors and dark green screens – one on Judith's desk and one in Lois's office. The only thing we really used the database for was billing clients. Because it had every client's contact details on it, I had also used it once or twice, in a tight spot, for looking up a phone number for a client who had rung in for an out-of-hours appointment and then not turned up.

One quiet afternoon, Judith asked me to cover reception for twenty minutes while she nipped out to a dentist's appointment. I sat down and twirled on her chair a few times. I checked the diaries for the third time that day. I had a quick check that the coast was clear. Then, in full knowledge of how unprofessional I was being, heart beating slightly faster than usual, I found myself firing up the computer and searching on 'Soots'. (I didn't even know Rob's last name.) There she was. And there he was. And there was his home phone number. I scribbled it down and shut down the computer. The piece of paper sat burning a hole in my primrose wallet all week.

That weekend I was on call. I willed that phone to ring and I willed it to be Kingcombe with something easy but impressive for me to fix. But I couldn't just sit at home willing: I needed to be doing something. I decided I could build up a useful sweat in the garden and set to digging over the large vegetable patch bequeathed to me by the previous elderly residents of my cottage. That vegetable patch had obviously once been a thing of wonder, but it had been left unattended altogether for six months, and I speculated that before that it must have become too much for my predecessors to manage. It was overgrown with buttercups and bindweed, both of which I discovered had enormously advanced root systems.

I had got myself into a lovely steady sweaty rhythm by the time the phone finally rang, at three o'clock on the Sunday afternoon. As always, my heart raced a bit just at the sound of the phone: it was that slight stress of being pulled out of whatever I was doing, and not knowing what was about to be asked of me. I ran into the cottage and picked up.

It was not Kingcombe. It was instead the very last person I wanted to hear from.

I hadn't been out to Lizzie's farm since I'd accidentally voided her cow the previous December. Judith always assured me that she was a gentle soul who would have forgiven me easily, but I hadn't forgiven myself. In fact, when I had seen in the diary a few weeks ago that she was bringing in her little terrier dog for a booster shot, I had switched consults and made Stanley see her instead of me. I just couldn't face her.

When Judith had got to hear about this, she had issued an invitation I couldn't refuse to a cup of tea in the accounts room. 'Anna, you're taking this all too hard. There will be plenty more knocks like this. If Stanley and Mike stopped seeing clients they'd made a mistake with, the practice would soon grind to a halt. What's done is done. There's no use crying over spilt milk. You have to get back on the horse that threw you.'

I loved the old country sayings, but somehow I hadn't quite been able to act on them.

This time, though, I was on call and I had no choice.

'Anna, you've got the chance to redeem yourself,' Lizzie opened. Just the sound of her voice sent adrenalin coursing through me. My stomach squeezed itself into a tiny tense knot of horror. I was immediately the new girl again

– scared and incompetent. 'One of my old girls is in labour and struggling. Come and calve her.'

'Okay Lizzie, I'll be right there.' I was going to have to get back on that horse.

I abandoned my spade, donned a clean pair of wellies and a boiler suit and switched my home phone through to my pager. This involved tapping my phone number, then a hash, then another extremely long number, into the phone. Whenever I had to perform this task I was in a rush to be somewhere else and as usual it took me two or three clumsy and increasingly frustrated attempts. Once or twice I had forgotten to do it at all and ended up driving home after a call praying nobody had rung. As I finally succeeded in switching my phone through, I thought wistfully of Stanley and Mike having their wives to answer the phones when they were off on call.

I called Rocky in from whatever adventure he was on and, ignoring his excited 'where are we going' face, locked him into the cottage. Rocky's little surprised and uncomprehending face was heartrending. 'Surely,' he said to me with his big black eyes, 'we play together on the weekends.'

'Sorry Rocks,' I said, looking into those hurt eyes, 'I can't take you with me, boy. You're too naughty and this needs to go right.' I silently apologised to the neighbours for the howling I knew would ensue.

Driving over to Lizzie's in my Land Rover I realised that in my discombobulation at hearing Lizzie's voice, I hadn't taken any details from her. I knew she had a cow in difficulty but not much more than that. This left me free to imagine all manner of horrific and terrifying calving scenarios as I pelted down the familiar roads.

I had plenty of real-life experience to draw on now. Calving went on all year round, but there was also a calving season. Cows come into their peak milk about 100 days after calving and most farmers still tended to want their cows to calve in spring, to take advantage of all the sweet summer grass. Over the last couple of weeks we had entered the calving season, which meant you could guarantee a call out to a calving or the ensuing milk fever most nights and weekends.

And so I spooled out for myself a blood-curdling calving horror film.

Calves are supposed to come out in the 'Superman' position. Forelegs forwards and first, head forwards and next, hind legs behind them and last. Even when the calf is positioned beautifully and successfully delivered, a prolapsed uterus or a tear in the vaginal wall from a little hoof is always a possibility. Or a milk fever and a completely collapsed cow.

More likely, I thought, moving to scene two, the calf isn't presenting well. If one foreleg is twisted back, or if the head is twisted to the side, a calf can get stuck in the pelvic canal. Twins can get tangled up together so that neither can make their way out. Big beefy calves from big beefy bulls can be too big for a small cow to push out easily. All of these were bad scenarios.

Sometimes, especially with backwards presenting calves

coming out hind legs first, we could get them halfway out and then they got stuck. This was a real 'get a move on' situation because in this position the calf was putting so much pressure on the umbilical cord that it wasn't receiving oxygen and nutrients. Calves in this position seemed to have an instinct to try to take a breath inside the uterus, which is full of fluid: then they drowned.

And sometimes a calf that seemed to be a stuck calf was in fact a dead calf that still had to be delivered somehow. Sometimes in pieces, sawn up by cheese wire.

The worst of all scenarios was a dead mother. I'd never yet had to shoot a cow but I knew it happened. Perhaps I would put a finger through her uterus and give her peritonitis – an infection of the whole abdominal cavity. Perhaps I would manage to rip an ovarian blood vessel and she would bleed to death internally. I would deliver the calf, head home happily, and then Lizzie would get up in the morning and find her dead cow lying on its back, hooves in the air.

The credits of my horror film were running as I arrived at the top of the steep path that led up to Lizzie's farm. *Starring Anna Barrington as The Calf-killing Vet.* Lizzie was there at her gate to greet me, just as she had been that first time. My heart was in my mouth as I jumped out and offered a handshake. Lizzie nodded back, blue eyes level and unblinking, and shook my hand: no hostility but no reassurance either. 'Hello, Anna, thank you for coming.' I pulled on my plastic overalls, hauled out my calving box and followed her.

Lizzie led me through her large barn, past two happily delivered new calves quietly sucking with their mothers, to the very back, where a handsome Friesian cow with big anxious eyes was patiently and quietly straining.

'Daffodil's one of my favourites, Anna. I don't like to see her like this.'

I went around to the back end, where two buckets of warm water were already waiting for me. I could see she was an experienced cow, not a young heifer, from the size of her udder. That was a good sign: it was the first-time mums that were the most difficult to calve. Lizzie went to the front end and gave Daffodil's head a gentle scratch.

'Okay, Daffodil,' she muttered into her neck. 'You'll be alright now.' Daffodil gave a gentle grunt in reply.

I put on my long gloves and lubed them up. 'Is she an old cow? Has she had many calves before?'

'Old Daff's a third-timer. She's done her calves well. She had Aberdeen Angus semen this time too.'

Aberdeen Angus were meant to be easy-calving, not like these great big Belgian Blues or Limousins. Lizzie probably meant to be reassuring. What I heard, though, was 'This should be easy so only a fool could mess it up. The kind of fool who voids a cow.'

I could feel Lizzie watching me closely from her position at the front end as I gently introduced my arm into the other end. I tried to put Lizzie out of my mind and just focus on the job. I was able to get my hand straight through the cervix into the uterus. That was good – she was nice and open and dilated. Now I needed to orientate myself. What was where?

What was presenting? Was it dead or alive? My first finds were the tip of a hoof and a warm little nose. I felt around and put a finger in its mouth. It gave me a little suck.

'Well, the calf's alive, Lizzie.'

'That's good,' she nodded, unsmiling. It was good, of course, but it also put more pressure on me not to mess it up.

The next job was to distinguish the hocks (or ankles) from the carpi (or wrists). The evolution of the cow means that their joints are not quite in the same place as ours and it was easy to be confused. The technical term for this is 'doing the bendy thing'. To find out whether the limb you can feel is a hind leg (with ankles or 'hocks' as we call them) or a foreleg (with wrists or 'carpi' as we call these), you bend it at hock/wrist and fetlock (lower joint to both these joints). If the two joints bend in the same direction, it's a foreleg; if they bend in opposite directions, it's a hind leg. This is easier said than done when you are operating in a narrow pelvic canal that is contracting every couple of minutes. I had to push the nearly delivered head and leg against the tide, back into the uterus, to give me space to feel back to both shoulders. But much to my relief I quickly established that this situation, on the scale of terrible calving situations, was actually not too bad. The calf was coming out forwards but one of its front legs was positioned backwards. A complicating factor was that the calf did seem quite big for this cow's pelvis: not because it was a big calf but because kind-hearted Lizzie had overfed her cows and this mum-to-be had laid down too much fat in her pelvic canal, narrowing the gap through which her calf had to squeeze. But if I could pull the twisted-back leg forwards, there was every chance of delivering the calf alive.

I put a rope over the back of the ears and through the mouth to guide the head, slippery with membranes and fluid, and then around each slippery foot. The presenting foot was easy but to reach the foot that was twisted back I had to go in right up to my armpit, using my fingers as eyes to make sense of it all and be sure I didn't rope up a hind leg by mistake. I gently pulled, in time with Daffodil's contractions, while Lizzie scratched and stroked and encouraged Daffodil.

'Go on girl, you can have a good push now.'

Twenty sweaty, heaving minutes later, out popped the feet, then the pretty little head, in perfect Superman pose. One more pull in time with a contraction and the rest of it almost flew out and tumbled in a black leggy heap onto the straw. Waves of excitement and relief gushed through me, but before I got too carried away I needed to make sure mum and baby were both okay.

I could see the little thing was twitching. I got a piece of straw and stuck it up its nostrils to stimulate it to breathe. It shook its head. 'Oh, you little beauty,' I murmured.

'There's definitely good strong life there,' said Lizzie, wiping the calf down with more straw as mum came around to give him a nice big stimulating lick. What valiant, stoical beasts cows are.

Then Lizzie stood and watched in silence while I gathered my things together with shaky hands: I was starving, and relieved, and done in. When Daffodil delivered the huge salmon-pink placenta, Lizzie forked it up in one strong deft movement and put it on the dung heap before the cow or Lizzie's young terrier, Corky, could start eating it. (Cows are vegetarians so they can't really digest their placentas, but they eat them to get rid of the evidence, as an anti-predator mechanism.)

Finally, Lizzie's weather-beaten face broke into a broad smile. 'Mum and baby are doing just fine,' she said then. 'Come in and have a cup of tea?'

For once I said yes.

As I sat by Lizzie's Aga, cup of sugary tea in one hand, and doorstep of homemade farm fruitcake in the other, and Corky on my lap licking my wrist and asking to have his tummy tickled, I felt the stress of that phone call and the exertion of the calving fade into a warm glow of contentment. Lizzie and I didn't chat much: we just sat in a companionable silence, smiling. I drove home happy, apologised profusely to a whimpering, shaking Rocky – 'I'm so sorry Rocky, I'm so sorry I left you. What am I going to do with you, eh?' and slept a deep and uninterrupted sleep.

Reporting my triumph to Mike the next day, he was bemused.

'But why did Lizzie call you out?' he wondered out loud. 'An experienced farmer like Lizzie would surely have been able to pull a calf with a leg back herself no problem.'

CHAPTER THIRTEEN

Goodnight
sweethearts

It was a windy, rainy Tuesday morning in early April. Yet another windy, rainy morning. The lambs were paddling around in the pastures, the hedgerows were bursting into their spring tapestry, even Easter had come and gone in a flurry of unseasonal hail. But no farmers had yet been seen out in the fields fertilising or spraying the new spring crops: it was just too relentlessly wet. Those few beautiful days only a couple of weeks earlier, when I had felt the sun on my back and shed layer after layer of clothing, were now a distant, taunting memory. They hadn't, I now realised, augured the start of spring: they had been an all-too-fleeting interlude in the long slog through eternal winter. How could I have let my guard down so soon? How could I have laid up my winter coat, and all my thickest jumpers? They all came back out, along with my scarf, hat and gloves.

Even Mike's impeccable manners were being tested by this weather. He had a TB test today on a large dairy herd of around 200 cows – in fact, this was now our practice's third round of testing on the Porritt herd that I had first tested back in early December. When Stanley had re-tested in February he had got one or two borderline results, which meant the farm remained shut down, pending another time-consuming, stressful re-test of the entire herd 60 days later. We had an unspoken agreement to take it in turns to go – I suspect because we all hated to have to put old Mr Porritt and his decent, hard-working family through it, time after time.

Back in James Herriot's day, TB had been rife, causing terrible suffering in both cattle and humans. Later, bovine TB had been all but eradicated in this country. But by 1997, my first year of practice, disease control was starting to break down and the incidence was rising again at a worrying rate. So an increasing proportion of large animal vets' time – and farmers' time – was being spent on testing for bovine TB. 'Bloody thankless task,' muttered Mike, whom I had never heard swear before. We all feared the worst outcome: more borderline results, or reactors, meaning more cattle destroyed and the farm's continued closure. I didn't envy Mike his day. He would be on his feet for hours, handling nervous cows and an anxious farmer, in a biting wind. And my thoughts went out to Michael and the Porritt family: I so hoped it would be a clear round.

Stanley, on the other hand, was in fine form. I caught him whistling in the corridor. 'There's got to be some perks to this job,' he smiled (in a disconcerting way) as he put his coat on and headed out of the door. I looked across quizzically at Judith. 'Lunch with a drugs rep,' she smiled. 'What's not to like? Stanley's got a hard few hours of work ahead of him, being schmoozed by a pretty young girl trying to sell him something.'

As for me, I was worn out before the day had even begun. I'd been on call overnight and had been called out twice: once just as I had dropped off to sleep and then again at five o'clock in the morning. In calving season one could expect a call most nights, for a calving or a milk fever. But two calls, and at either end of the night, was particularly unlucky and particularly spirit-crushing. I was going to need a day of easy consults and a ready supply of croissants to get through today.

A morning of consults, though, was always something of an unknown quantity. Despite the scribbled notes in the diary, and my growing familiarity with the clientele, I never quite knew what might come through that consulting room door at me. On this particular miserable day, quite by chance, it was a relentless stream of very sick animals.

By eleven o'clock I had already put three animals to sleep, including a lovely chocolate Burmese with a huge abdominal mass who purred right up until the anaesthetic took effect, put her head in my hand, and gently slumped to the table. It was a peaceful end to all her vomiting and pain. But she was not an old cat, and she reminded me of my Kiska – who was fit and well and curled up somewhere warm no doubt. I felt a terrible wave of sadness wash through me as her owner, the woman who ran the local Chinese takeaway, said her goodbyes.

Next a mother and her eleven-year old son had brought in their gorgeous, playful, uninsured ten-week-old puppy for the start of its vaccination course, and on examination I'd detected a heart murmur. Often puppies and kittens have innocent murmurs that never cause any harm but this one did not sound very innocent, and she had been the runt of the litter which made me even more suspicious. The options were return to the breeder (but they had already fallen in love with her) or referral for expensive tests (but they couldn't afford that). Or, see what developed and possibly foot the bill for years of future treatment. Mother and son were both in tears as they left my room.

So I was hoping for some respite – something cheerful. Ideally, a healthy new kitten to vaccinate, with nice owners? A cuddle with a little kitten would go down really well at this point.

But next through the door came a sturdy, roughty-toughty chap in workman's trousers with pockets and tabs everywhere – an electrician, I thought, or a plumber maybe – with his elderly tom in his muscular arms. The cat looked painfully thin with a spiky ginger coat. 'Sammy's just drinking and drinking like a good 'un, but he won't touch his food, and he's being sick,' said roughty-toughty.

I did a full clinical examination. Poor Sammy did not seem to care what I did to him. He barely noticed me as I opened his mouth and saw the ulcers on his tongue; as I felt over the individually palpable ribs heaving a little with each shallow breath; and as I gently squeezed his abdomen and detected very empty intestines and small kidneys. I put my stethoscope to my ears to help me think. Diabetes? Kidneys? Heart failure? At least his heart sounded okay. I looked at the single index card that held his life's simple medical history.

I'd never met Mr Turner before, but I was going to need to build a relationship quickly, and have a difficult conversation.

'Mr Turner,' I began, quietly but firmly, wanting his full attention, and trying to convey that he needed to prepare himself for some serious news. 'Sammy is not well. Not well at all. To find out more, I would need to run some tests.'

The big man in front of me seemed to shrink as he bent his broad neck down over his cat, whispering to him. He nodded his assent to the tests. Sammy was a much-loved cat.

I took some blood for testing, sticking myself with the needle in my haste, then left Mr Turner cradling Sammy in the waiting room, and leapt up the stairs to the lab, two at a time. Spinning the sample seemed to take forever. Loading it and priming the machine took another era. But twenty minutes later the printer spat out a sheet: Sammy's urea and creatinine levels were sky high. My heart sank. That could only mean one thing.

'Well,' I said softly, back in the consulting room, 'it is not great news I am afraid.' I studied his face for a reaction. He refused to meet my eyes. I forced myself to swallow, forced myself to continue. 'Sammy has severe kidney failure. There is no chance he could have drunk some anti-freeze, is there? You haven't drained your car recently maybe?' If he had, that would certainly have explained Sammy's woeful condition, as anti-freeze is so toxic to the kidneys.

Mr Turner was struggling to hold it together. 'No, he hasn't left the house for days now. Can we do anything?'

This was slightly easier: I could at least set out some options, take refuge in the technical. 'We have some options. I could inject some fluids under Sammy's skin to try to perk him up, and then send him home with you. But if I do that you will almost certainly be back here again with him in the same state in 24 hours. His kidneys are just too far gone.'

Mr Turner nodded, his serious eyes focusing hard on the scuffed tip of one of his working boots.

'Or,' I went on, 'I could admit Sammy and put him on a drip so that we can get some fluids into him intravenously. That would be a more costly option.'

Mr Turner nodded again, eyes still on his toes.

'But Sammy's 15 years old, Mr Turner. That's better than average for a cat. He's very sick, his enzymes are very high, and he's suffering. I think that even with fluids, we are not going to get much further. Anything we do now is probably just going to be prolonging the inevitable, and prolonging Sammy's suffering.'

'Sammy's in a lot of pain, you think?' asked Mr Turner, looking me in the eye now, for the first time since I had told him Sammy was unwell.

'He is in discomfort and feeling sick.' I wanted to be as objective as possible with the information I was giving him.

Mr Turner looked urgently around the room, as if there might be something on one of the walls that could help Sammy. 'And there's nothing you can do to make him better?'

'There are things we can try – the IV fluids and some injections. But with renal parameters this high, they're unlikely to work.' Oh Anna, stop hiding behind the vet talk.

'So you're saying I should let him go?' There was a slight quiver in his voice.

'I'm saying that's an option.' I knew what I thought best, but I couldn't insist.

There was a pause as Mr Turner tickled Sammy's ear. 'An option you would recommend?'

'An option I would strongly support. In the end, it has to be your decision.'

With a heavy exhalation, Mr Turner asked, 'Can I have a minute to think?'

'Of course.'

We stood in silence while I pretended to hunt for something in a drawer and Mr Turner stroked Sammy gently with his strong working man's hand. Then he looked up at me and said, 'Yes, okay.'

For the fourth time that day, I explained the procedure and we completed the paperwork. Penny brought in that day's fourth fleecy vet bed. Then, for the fourth time that day, I drew the barbiturate up into the syringe.

As I was gently euthanising the tom, I felt a weight on my shoulder. 'I'm so sorry,' blurted out this big roughty-toughty man between sobs. 'I'm so sorry. I just wish they could have done this for my mother.'

It was not the first time I'd heard this in my consulting room, and it was a sentiment I sympathised with. It seemed inhumane to leave a loved one lingering and lingering and lingering, being tube-fed for months or having their teeth removed so they couldn't do damage to themselves champing, and being pumped full of a cocktail of drugs, each one countering the side effects of another. Wasn't this just prolonging their suffering? When I saw suffering, I wanted to take it away. Why should I – when that awful time came – not be able to grant to my own mother what I would grant to a suffering animal? I knew that was what she would want, she'd told me often enough. 'When I'm on my way out, just give me some blue juice, Anna. Please.'

I'd never before had a client literally crying on my shoulder though. Oh, I felt so awful for Mr Turner. But I wasn't sure what the policy was – was it 'no touch'? I gave him a slightly awkward hug. He composed himself, and backed out of the room.

By lunchtime, I felt like Dr Death and I desperately needed some food and a moment to myself. I strongly believed I was doing the right thing by taking away these creatures' suffering; and I did my best to do it at the right time and in the right manner. But I felt overwhelmed by the responsibility of guiding these poor pet owners through these decisions, and drained by the effort of managing their emotions as well as my own. Vets don't cry, I told myself, vets don't cry. In which case, I wasn't sure I really was a vet. I needed to become hardened to this. But how could I become blasé about the end of an animal's life? And, if I did, would I like what I had become?

I caught sight of my latest needle stick injury. The previous one – nearly healed now – I hadn't minded so much. Each time it hurt, I had thought about Rob's hands and smiled to myself. This new one had no redeeming features.

One bite into my sandwich, an apologetic Judith put her head around my door. 'Anna, it's Charlie. I think you're going to want to see him.'

I jumped to my feet and ran downstairs to the reception area. There was Lucy, half-staggering under the weight of her splendid spaniel, Charlie.

Judith and I took Charlie from Lucy and carried him awkwardly up the narrow corridor to the consulting room, where we put him down gently on the consulting table. Penny had already read the situation, and had laid out the biggest, fleeciest, vet bed she could find. No expense spared for Charlie. We all loved him.

Charlie didn't resist. He was coughing and struggling to breathe, and he was going blue.

'Alright Charlie, it's going to be okay,' I said, as I lifted his lip, looked at his eyes, and put my stethoscope to his chest. His chest was so wet and noisy it sounded like the wind blowing through the trees as he wheezed in and out: his lungs must have been full of fluid. There was a galloping chaotic rhythm to his heartbeat too, which meant that the murmur I'd heard the last time – the regular heart sound, like a washing machine – had now been joined by an arrhythmia like a mixed up fast and slow spin cycle. Looking at Charlie's chest I could even see the heartbeat.

This was beyond tinkering with the medication. This old chap had no quality of life left. Fondling Charlie's ears, I started to talk quietly to Lucy.

'Okay. We can admit Charlie for some intensive therapy. I could give him some more diuretics right into his vein and try to get some of that fluid off his chest. And we would need to start some anti-arrhythmic therapy because he is going to go into total heart failure if we don't get this beat under control. But he's already on a high dose of diuretics and I don't hold out too much hope for that helping that much. And he's got such a significant heart murmur here, and I'm just not sure ... '

I didn't need to go on. Lucy looked at me with pooling tears in her eyes and said, 'It's not fair to continue. This is Charlie's last day.'

I called Penny back in and we exchanged a look. She started prepping everything we needed.

'Okay,' I said to Lucy. 'What I'm going to do is put this catheter in. I'm sure he will be fine with it. It's just like a needle prick that he has had before for a blood test and he is always so brave about that.'

I could have administered the anaesthetic the usual way, straight into the vein, with Penny applying pressure to raise the vein up. But Charlie's poor circulation meant his veins might not have stood up very well. I couldn't bear the thought that any anaesthetic might go out of the side of his vein and sting him and make him howl, or hurt him in any way. Using the catheter was a way of making sure I was definitely in the vein.

The catheter went in fine.

'Okay,' I said. 'I'm going to use the anaesthetic now. I will just give him too much, so that he goes into a very deep sleep and doesn't wake up from it. It will start to slow the beat of the heart down until it fades away to nothing.'

Lucy nodded, and a tear escaped down her cheek. I felt a bitter pricking in my throat.

'What we might find,' I went on, 'is that he takes a few big breaths as he is going. And then he will slip into sleep. He may take a while, because his heart isn't working particularly well. You are very welcome to stay if you want to, but you don't have to at all. I can do this with Penny.'

'I'll stay please,' said Lucy.

'Okay. So, you stroke him, you let him know that you're here.' Lucy slowly moved round to the head of the table so she could look into Charlie's eyes while she stroked the top of his head. 'Now, I know this is a difficult question,' I had to continue, 'but what would you like to do with Charlie when we've put him to sleep? Would you like to take him home and bury him? Or would you like to have him cremated? And if you would like him cremated, would you like to have his ashes back?'

'I'd like him cremated, and his ashes back please. He can go with my husband, John.'

'One last thing Lucy. I'm sorry to have to do this but can you just sign this piece of paper for me, giving me permission to put Charlie to sleep today? It is a legal thing, we have to do it.'

Lucy couldn't really see through the tears and she signed her name with tears splashing on the paper. How many pieces of brine-stained paper had I seen that day? My own eyes filled up but I was no use to Lucy in that state. I pulled myself together and drew up a good dose of the blue barbiturate into a syringe.

'Here we are, Charlie. You can go back to chasing the bunnies again.' And I just very gently injected the barbiturate into his vein and he slowly, slowly, peacefully, sank down. Then he took a few breaths. And that was the end. I listened to his chest; took his pulse. There was nothing.

'He's gone. We might still have another breath or two. That would be reflex, that is normal. He might even twitch a paw, that is normal too. But he's gone.'

Lucy and I both stayed there for a few minutes, gently stroking Charlie, while Penny quietly pottered around preparing for the next stage.

'We'll just give you two minutes on your own with him,' I said, and Penny and I left the room. Then I went and locked myself in the toilet and had a good cry.

I stumbled through the rest of my day.

I wondered whether I ought to call Lucy and check she was alright. Watching her walk away from the surgery, alone, had been heartbreaking. I knew she would have gone home to an empty house and I wanted her to know my thoughts were with her. But perhaps it was none of my business. I found an appropriate card from Judith's card collection: water and ducks flowing under a bridge, because I remembered Lucy telling me how much Charlie had loved it down by the river. I wrote a note to express our sympathy for her, and to say what a lovely patient Charlie had been, and that we would miss him loads too. Oh crumbs, was that too much? Would it make her cry all over again? Seeing me upset and dithering, Judith rescued me. 'Why don't you put it in the post-tray with a note saying "Do not post until Thursday",' she suggested.

I drove back home through the rain.

Back at my silent cottage, my lovely Rocky picked up that all was not well. He did his best to comfort me, coming to sit beside me and putting his great big head on my knee. It did make me feel a bit better, looking into those big sympathetic eyes, and rhythmically stroking his soft head, but I needed to talk to a human being.

Sitting there scratching at Rocky's back, I ran through the options. My parents were in Germany for my mother's birthday; Angus, my brother, wouldn't be sympathetic, and would just turn the conversation around to ask me something about his dog; and my sister Henry had surprised us all and gone off travelling for six months with her accountant boyfriend, now fiancé. A vet friend, then. But I knew Lena was still in Ethiopia and Sally and Athena, when I tried them, both went through to their pagers. They must be on calls.

Rocky licked my hands with his soft tongue, making my newest needle stick injury sting.

Hmm. There's a thought.

I took out my wallet and found the little scrap of paper that had been lying there for a week and played back to myself a phone conversation I had had with my friend Lexi two nights ago. During our student days I had grown to love Lexi's refreshing take on the world, she loved life, loved people and had been urging me to make the call: 'for the company; it's not brazen'. I hadn't been convinced, and I still wasn't. But … oh, what the hell. My day couldn't get any worse.

My nerves at what I was about to do at least broke through my melancholy. I'd never been this bold in my life. I picked up the phone and dialled the number. 'Oh hello, Rob? It's Anna Barrington, the vet. From Dryden and Dalrymple. I hope you don't mind me ringing. It's just, I'm really interested in hedge-laying. I was wondering if you could tell me about the courses you run?'

There was a pause. I wondered what he was thinking. I cringed. *I'm really interested in hedge-laying.* Ugh. Actually, I was. But it had to be the worst chat-up line in history.

Then that lovely, deep, friendly voice replied. 'Hello Anna. Um, hedge-laying, yes we do that on the reserve. The centre runs courses. Generally in the autumn and winter because the bird-nesting season stops us from touching the hedgerows right now.'

We chatted comfortably for a while, just about this and that. We compared notes on how our lambing and calving seasons were going; complained animatedly about the vagaries of the rules of the league at the squash club and plasters floating in the swimming pool; and swapped tips on the best locally-sourced meat and cheese and breads and cakes. I advocated strongly for the Chelsea bun with cherries from Peighton Lubbock. Rob couldn't believe I'd never tried the apple pie from the Ebbourne patisserie.

'What did you do at the weekend?' Rob asked after about twenty minutes of easy chat.

CALL THE VET

'I drove back to see my parents. They live in Leicestershire.'

'Just you?'

'Yes. Who else?'

'Your partner. Is he a vet too?'

I was puzzled.

'I haven't got a partner. Unless you count the cat that sleeps on my bed, or the dog, Rocky, and you've met him. He's an excellent travelling companion so yes, he came with me.'

'Oh. Oh, I see.' Rob chuckled softly. 'I thought you did, because down at Kingcombe I asked you how you were settling in, and you said "we love it here".'

Now it was my turn to give a nervous little laugh. Yes, I suppose I might have said that.

'Oh. I don't remember. Well. I will have just meant me and Rocky. It's just me, Rocky and Kiska, the cat.'

'Oh. So ... ' said Rob. 'What are you doing this weekend?'

I couldn't help the smile that spread across my face, but I kept it together.

'I'm on a one in three so I'm on call all weekend,' I said, with more than a hint of disappointment.

'Oh.'

'But I'm only second call the following weekend. That's just Friday evening and Saturday morning. Then I'm off for the rest of the weekend.'

'Would you like to go out for a drink then?'

Yes, yes, *yes*.

'I'd love to.'

242

CHAPTER FOURTEEN

Best intentions

Thanks to the tedious on-call system, it was nearly two weeks until my date with Rob and the time would have dragged if I hadn't been so busy. As it was, it went by in a blur of consults and call outs, with any spare moments devoted to elaborate daydreams. Rob was on my mind a good deal. Things that happened in the surgery reminded me of him, and I had to restrain myself from dropping references to him into conversation. Eventually, with only two days to go, Penny pulled me aside, eyebrows lowered in reprimand. 'You're not being fair. I tell you all about me and Den. What's going on with you and this Rob?'

It was true, Penny was always open about her feelings for Den, and her frustrations with his approach to the relationship. She was clearly devoted to this strong, gentle, silent man, and I was convinced, from all I had seen and heard, that he was to her. But Penny was an open and effusive young woman who would speak a thought as soon as she had it. And Den was quite the opposite, happy to let

Penny do all the talking in the relationship, and sharing his thoughts like they were precious jewels, to be shown off only on rare special occasions. My guess was that Penny was under the misapprehension that if Den wasn't declaring his love – in general terms, and preferably with a proposal of marriage – then he couldn't be feeling it, and I was pretty sure that Den was under the misapprehension that Penny knew exactly how he felt about her.

'It's just a date,' I said, with a poor pretence at nonchalance. 'On Saturday. With one of the naturalists from Kingcombe. Nothing might come of it.'

'Okay, but I'm going to need details on Monday.'

I knew she meant it: she had her 'gentle but firm' face on. Come Monday, I would get away with nothing less than a blow-by-blow account.

The drive over to the branch surgery in Peighton Lubbock the following day was more breathtaking than ever. As I passed the turning down to Kingcombe Meadows I thought of Rob and felt a lovely little twang of the heartstrings. A moment later, as I drove alongside a small brook, a kingfisher shot up in a thrilling flash of metallic blue. I'd never seen a kingfisher before: surely, it was a good omen.

But the afternoon was a trying one. The surgery was a Portakabin in a car park, and afternoon surgery coincided with school pick-up time. It wasn't difficult to make it feel crowded. It must have been particularly testing for Deloris in the reception/waiting room trying to keep all the clients happy, answer the telephone, take payments and hand out medicines to local farmers. I was not as fast as the other vets so numbers could build up and there were times when it sounded like she was doing the can-can to keep everyone amused.

First Molly Smethwick had come to afternoon surgery with her cat, and her four young children. Six people and a cat in my tiny consulting room would have been a squash in the best of circumstances. But three of the children seemed completely out of control. They buzzed manically around the tiny space, opening and closing drawers, rifling through cupboards, pulling themselves up on the consulting table. The eldest – who couldn't have been more than eight years old – and Molly herself, on the other hand, seemed almost catatonic they were so laid-back. I was at a loss: I didn't know how firm I could be with someone else's children, even when they were swinging my stethoscope round their heads and helping themselves to syringes and latex gloves.

But I felt for Molly Smethwick. It must have been difficult for her, trying to give me a history, hold her animal on the table, and manage four young children.

'Careful there,' I said, ineffectually, to the youngest, who had caught the second-youngest across the cheek with the stethoscope. I felt uncomfortable and self-conscious, aware of the silly 'talking to children' voice I had adopted. 'We don't want any injuries, do we?' He looked up at me for a moment and then carried on swinging at his brother, who was now crying. 'Best not open the needle packets,' – this was directed at the second-oldest – 'I'm not very good at the sight of human blood.'

'Why? What will you do?' asked the freckle-faced goofy-looking little chap. He was about six, I guessed.

'I'll faint,' I said, attempting to be amusingly dramatic now.

Wrong answer. He seemed to think that was some kind of a dare and continued trying to tear open the packet, keeping half an eye hopefully on me. I looked at the mother for help – usually I preferred to let the parents take the lead – but something about her demeanour made me think I needed to take control of the situation.

'I'd better take those, I think,' I said to freckle-face, holding out my hand and switching from chirpy children's entertainer mode to strict teacher. It seemed to do the trick. He handed over the needles and went and stood dejectedly next to his mother, shooting me occasional hurt glances. His younger brothers carried on swinging the stethoscope and crying, respectively.

Molly Smethwick had brought in her five-month-old kitten, ostensibly to check that he was no longer limping since I had treated an injury to his left leg the previous month. In fact, he seemed to have accrued a further injury. The last one inch of his tail was at a 45 degree angle, and the skin was missing down to the bone.

'How did this happen?' I murmured as I carefully examined the poor kitten. The injuries were consistent with several traumatic scenarios.

'We don't know,' said Molly, rather too quickly, I thought. My hunch was confirmed by the oldest of the boys, who spoke now for the first time.

'It got slammed in the door.'

I looked through the kitten's notes. February: squashed foot. March: fall from window. March, again: fall downstairs. This was in fact the fourth injury he had suffered in the three months he had been owned by the Smethwicks. Either he was a very accident-prone little kitten, or something else was going on. But how was I going to broach it with all the children around? I was very conscious too of how thin the door was in the Portakabin consulting room, and of how many people were waiting in silence just on the other side of the door. I said, as assertively as I could, that Jasper the kitten really needed the end of his tail amputating. 'No, my husband would never agree to that,' murmured Mrs Smethwick with a quiet finality. I should have been more persistent but something held me back. I offered that we could try peace and quiet, preferably keeping Jasper in his own crate, plus daily antibiotics and a painkiller that I would administer now. 'And bring him back please in a week's time, or sooner if the tail looks worse or he seems off-colour.' It was a perfectly reasonable treatment plan but somehow I didn't feel happy: I would raise this with Judith – she would know what to do – or perhaps the partners, as soon as I got the chance.

My final patient of the afternoon was Trevor. Trevor was an enormous fawn-coated mastiff-cross who belonged to Sheila Warren, the Peighton Lubbock pub landlady, and always smelt of cigarettes and salt and vinegar crisps. He looked worried as he came in, but then mastiffs often bore a permanently furrowed brow on their huge faces, and in fact he wagged his tail when he saw me.

'Silly bugger went racing after a deer and caught himself

on a barbed wire fence,' opened Mrs Warren. He had a nasty four-inch tear on his flank. The edges of the skin around the tear, about an inch and a half apart, were ragged and flapping, with the glistening muscle clearly visible underneath.

'Mrs Warren, if we don't surgically close this tear, the wound will have to granulate and heal by secondary intention.' There was a pause. 'That is to say, it will have to close by filling with granulation tissue and contraction.' Mrs Warren folded her arms across her chest and cocked her eyebrow at me. 'If we leave it,' I tried again, 'it will take some time to heal. It will be more open to infection while it's healing, and Trevor will probably try to lick it all the time.' I chastised myself inwardly for the elaborate vet-speak. When making a diagnosis, I had discovered, it was all too easy to fall back on the technical stuff we learnt at college and spout it at my clients. Learning to translate the medical jargon into a human message that made sense was part of my job as a vet, but it was sometimes just as hard to get this right as it was to complete a difficult procedure or diagnose a mysterious illness.

'He'll need stitching then,' summed up Mrs Warren for me.

I smiled gratefully at her. 'I think that's the best option. And the sooner the better, to keep the risk of infection to a minimum. But we don't have the facilities to do a stitch-up here. Could you bring him over to Ebbourne and I will do it there?'

'It's difficult. I've got to get the pub ready for this evening. I'm already running late and even if I call someone now they won't get here for an hour. It's a Friday night, I can't not open.'

'Trevor really needs this doing as soon as possible and I just can't do it here. I wonder though – how about if I drove him over to Ebbourne myself, and you could come and collect him when I'm finished?' (Thank goodness I had left Rocky at home after a good lunchtime run.)

It seemed to both of us to be a sensible solution, but we didn't have such a thing as an animal ambulance – or even a dog harness – so I rang through to check the protocol. Judith put me onto Mike, who said airily, once I'd explained the situation, 'You'll be fine. Just bring him back in your Land Rover.'

Mrs Warren thought that sounded okay. 'He's my guard dog, but he's really friendly,' she reassured me. 'Never bitten anybody.' I hadn't treated Trevor before but he did seem to be a gentle fellow. He had submitted to my examination very calmly.

So I took Trevor by the lead and put him in the passenger seat. Trevor wagged his tail as Mrs Warren said goodbye. 'He looks happy, doesn't he?' she said as she hurried back to the Duck and Drake.

As soon as I pulled out of the car park, with Trevor sitting beside me, bolt upright like a statue at the gates of a grand country house, my travelling companion changed his demeanour. As I put the car into second gear, Trevor raised his lip and started growling. It was such a deep, guttural noise that I didn't just hear it, I felt it.

My hair stood on end and some tiny part of my brain thought 'Oh, my piloerector muscles are contracting.'

I glanced sideways at Trevor. He was a solid mass of muscle and he must have weighed 65 kilos or more: easily as much as me. With his fawn coat and rippling, rumbling chest, he was doing a decent impression of a lion. Oh, how attractive healing by secondary intention suddenly seemed. Why had I not had faith in the power of the doggy body to heal itself? I could have left Trevor's wound to the beautiful physiological process of healing, and put a bucket over his head to stop him licking. Instead of which, I was putting myself through this.

I went to change up a gear. The growl got louder and angrier. I put my hand back on the wheel, gear unchanged, as sweat beaded on my brow. The growl reverted to its previous, still blood-chilling, level.

I was on the top road now, and I wanted to put my foot down – not least to get this journey over as soon as possible. I reached for the gear stick again. Trevor opened his massive jaws, showed me his huge teeth – which he had not long ago happily let me look at as I had given him the once over to check he was fit for an anaesthetic – and turned the volume on his growl up to eleven.

After a couple more attempts at changing up out of a now whining second gear, with the sweat trickling down through the erect hairs on my neck, I got the message. Trevor was adamant: if my hand so much as touched that gear stick, he was going to bite me.

So I drove the eight miles from Peighton Lubbock to Ebbourne in second gear, crossing my fingers at every T-junction that it would be clear and I could chug straight on. Behind me, I acquired a small tail of irritated and incredulous drivers.

Above the complaining of my engine and the growling of my passenger, I kept up a steady gentle murmur of my own, in an attempt to calm my frayed nerves and perhaps soothe Trevor.

'Hey, Trevor, you great lollop. Why did I agree to take you in my Land Rover? Without your mum? Do I have some kind of death wish? Why couldn't I have left you to heal? Mmmmm? Trevor? What's that you say? You say *grrrrrrr, I want to bite you*? Oh. Fascinating. *What's healing by secondary intention,* you say? Funny you should ask that. Well, it's a most beautiful physiological process that has started already, and that does not require your vet to drive you across the countryside in second gear. First a clot forms at the injury site. That's happened already, hasn't it Trevor? We saw that when you pretended to be a nice dog back at the branch. Then you get the inflammatory phase. Oh Trevor, couldn't we try third gear – no? Okay. Anyway, the white blood cells move in like little pac men – you know Trevor, from the 1980s computer game – and they eat up the bacteria and the dead cells and the dirt that has got into the wound. Next, collagen-exuding cells are recruited to come and help to bring the wound together. Still with me, Trevor? Keep up because this next bit is a good bit. The collagen and new blood vessels form the granulation tissue, which is that lovely shiny pink tissue you see over wounds, and the bit that you would have wanted to lick constantly. And then, as the collagen contracts – oh, wait, let me just concentrate on this T-junction – as the collagen contracts, the wound heals. It's an amazing process. But yes Trevor, you're right, even if we'd given you one of those collars, you would have managed to rub it against a wall and re-traumatise it and we would have just ended up with a bigger problem. What's that you say? I've done the right thing not the easy thing? Yes, thank you Trevor, I suppose you're right.'

I came to a halt outside the surgery and switched off the engine. Trevor wagged his tail happily and transformed himself magically back into a good boy.

There was an atmosphere of strained hysteria in the surgery when I got back. Once I'd settled a now placid, pre-medicated Trevor in the kennels, I demanded to know what was going on.

Strange looks shot all over the place – between Stanley and Judith, Judith and Penny, Lois and Mike. Finally, Judith spoke up.

'Stanley's been telling us that funny story – haven't you, Stanley?' Rabbit-in-the-headlights look from Stanley. 'You know? The one about the dog?' Still nothing from Stanley.

'The dog in glasses,' prompted Lois.

'Yes,' agreed Stanley, nodding vigorously. 'You must have heard it Anna?'

I hadn't.

'Well, this was a few years ago now,' he began. 'I had to put to sleep a huge Great Dane who had simply reached the end of the road. The owner was a big hairy biker, quite a mean-looking bloke in leathers, and he was distraught. When it came to the moment, the biker broke down completely. He took off his glasses to wipe his eyes and looked me right in the eyes and said, "I'm going to leave the room now. You're going to put him to sleep. When I get back I want his eyes to be closed. I don't want him staring at me with those dead eyes. Understand?" So I nodded and scary hairy biker left the room and I put the Great Dane to sleep. But you know, when you put to sleep with barbiturate, the eyes almost always stay open, and I just couldn't get them to close. I was getting in a bit of a panic. There was no way I could let the owner back in the room with those eyes still open. So in a moment of madness I resorted to the surgical glue. I glued his eyes shut. Back came biker. Loads of tears, bent down, hugged his dog, stood up. And his glasses were stuck to this Great Dane, who was now wearing back-to-front glasses, with the arms sticking out into the air.'

It was amusing, but I wasn't fooled. 'Okay, so what were you really laughing about?' I demanded. Another set of looks was exchanged. Finally Stanley blurted it out.

'Penny seems to think … we … are you going on a date with a naturist? Have you decided what to wear?'

Then they all giggled like schoolchildren. There was no point trying earnestly to explain the difference between a naturist and a naturalist. They had their story, it amused them greatly, and they were sticking to it.

*

I anaesthetised Trevor and stitched him up without a hitch. By the time Mrs Warren arrived, Trevor looked like butter wouldn't melt in his mouth, and I had recovered sufficiently to be able to lie as convincingly as a childminder with a naughty child. 'Oh, he's been no trouble at all. Absolutely fantastic, no problem. What a lovely boy.'

I immediately set about buying myself a dog harness.

Rob had arranged to pick me up from my cottage at eight o'clock that Friday evening.

At 7.30 the telephone rang. It was Rob.

'I'm really sorry but I'm running late. There's been a surge in lambings and because it's so cold we have to build pens for them all. I've just finished the last lambing pen. I should be there by 8.30.'

At least, I thought, he'd had the decency to ring, and to be honest about it. And I could see that this needed to be done – the lambs needed sorting out. But the delay gave me an extra thirty minutes to worry about my outfit. I'd decided on my usual comfortable jeans; my low, practical, battered leather boots (I couldn't walk in anything with a heel higher than an inch); and a cerise, low-ish cut, long-sleeved T-shirt. I wasn't sure about the T-shirt though – was it, first, too bright, and, second, too low-cut, for a date in rural West Dorset with a conservation worker? It wasn't that low-cut – it didn't show any cleavage or anything. But the neckline did dip down. I pulled an over-the-head fleece on as a top layer, and felt better. Now I was in my usual casual look. If I decided my top was going to be a little bit too flash, I could just keep the fleece on.

At 8.30 Rob drove up the steep path to my cottage in his metallic blue pick-up truck, decorated with mud slashes along the front doors and traces of hay on the seats. To my relief, Rocky was asleep in his basket and I crept out of the cottage, closing the door softly behind me. I heard Rocky stir and give a small howl, then settle back to sleep. Rob came round to open the passenger door for me to get in. I found the old-fashioned courtesy – and his pride in this bashed-up but practical vehicle – rather sweet. And I was relieved to see that he was as relaxed in his dress code as I was: he was wearing a pair of clean jeans, well-worn hiking boots, a faded check flannel shirt and a fairly awful navy blue chunky-knit woollen jumper with a hole near one cuff. But if anyone could make a holey blue jumper work, he could. I thought he looked lovely.

Rob was a good driver and the conversation flowed easily. Before I knew it Rob was parking in Bridport, the handsome local seaside metropolis, and filling me in on its history as a flax-making, rope-making town. He led me to one end of the wide high street (built so wide so that the rope could be stretched out across it and down the narrow alleys leading off it, and spun into great lengths of twine), then down some stone steps to the basement of a Georgian-looking building.

'The Cavity Club,' he grinned, pointing at the first floor brass plaque and the dental practice overhead that had inspired its name. We walked into a loud, low-ceilinged, under-lit room with a bar along the back right wall and a juke box on the left. It was cocktails or South American beers at the bar, and we both chose a Sol, which came – excitingly – with a lime slice jammed in the bottle neck. It was nice to have to stand pretty close to Rob and half-shout into his ear, his thick wavy hair sometimes tickling my nose or lips. It was equally nice to feel his warm breath on my ear. But I was quite pleased when he suggested we move off after just one beer. From trendy young Bohemian Bridport bar we strolled just across the T-junction to the old-fashioned George Hotel. Here we found ourselves amongst older, more staid, but still merry Bridport folk. Now we could hear each other properly we talked and talked, on and on, about everything and nothing. There was no posturing, no nerves. He was easy to talk to, easy to listen to, and easy to make smile, with a slightly lopsided grin that involved his green eyes too. We ordered a bit of food, I suppose, but for once in my life I wasn't really hungry. By the end of the evening, I was smitten.

As he drove me home, I did a quick mental inventory of my front room. Had I washed up my breakfast things? Did I have underwear drying on the storage heater? Were my wildlife books prominently on display? Yes, No and No. Two out of three wasn't bad.

But when Rob dropped me back home it was all rather formal. He opened the car door for me, and let me walk back into my cottage on my own, without so much as a peck on the cheek.

CHAPTER FIFTEEN

When the gorse
is in flower

For two days my phone did not ring.

On Sunday morning I decided that a watched pot
never boils, and went to church. As I headed off down the
lane, alone, the sound of Rocky's protests howled down
to me on the wind. On my return to the cottage though,
all was quiet. My initial buoyancy at this development
was quickly deflated. A thorough search of the cottage
revealed that my cat-flap had been gouged into a dog flap
– a 35-kilo dog-sized dog flap – and that Rocky himself
was missing, presumed in action. I was even less inclined
than usual to tramp around calling after him: I had a
hole in my cottage that needed fixing, and a phone that
might ring.

But it didn't ring. In fact, my only human contact in
the rest of my day was a second unpleasant interaction
with the gamekeeper. This was more or less a re-run of
our first encounter, complete with another poor dead
pheasant, except with a ramping up of the gamekeeper's

obscenity levels – which I met with a humble increase in the abjectness of my apology.

I knew I would have to face Penny with an account of my date on Monday morning. In fact, I realised I was quite looking forward to sharing my excitement with her. But in the event, Penny came in that day with such pink cheeks and such a spring in her step that I knew that whatever was going on with her had to take priority.

'How was your weekend?' was all I had to ask and the floodgates opened.

'Anna, it was great. I could not be happier. I'd got it all wrong with Den – you were right. Have you got time for a cup of tea?'

Penny brought the tea through to my consulting room and propped herself against a white cabinet. Out it all tumbled. 'On Saturday night I finally got up the courage to have *that* conversation with Den. You know: where are we going with the relationship, what are we doing here? I'd had a couple of drinks, to get up the nerve, and then I just went for it. Well, he hated it of course. Just sat there gazing into his pint glass for such a long time. Then he looked up at me and just said, "Penny. I love you." Imagine. Just like that. Well, I told him I loved him too, of course.'

'Penny, that's wonderful,' I managed to interject into this stream of happiness.

'And then it got better. He said, "I want to be with you

forever, Pen. But we have to have somewhere to live first. We can't have nowhere to live."'

Penny paused here to make sure I'd got the point. She looked at me meaningfully.

I smiled so broadly that my cheeks hurt, and nodded. 'I know,' nodded Penny. 'I know. Amazing. It's not the most romantic proposal. But this is Den we're talking about here. For him that was the equivalent of a ring in a cake at a fancy restaurant, and flowers, and violins. Now all we need is to find a house we can afford. Anna, I feel like I could burst.'

I was absolutely delighted for Penny. She deserved this. And – I admitted to myself – I was a bit envious.

On Monday evening, just as I was wrestling with Rocky in a futile attempt to cut his nails, a sudden *brrrrring brrrrrring* made me jump. Rocky seized the moment and shot off under the table. I picked up the phone, heart beating a little faster.

'Oh, hi Athena,' I said, trying not to sound disappointed. I wasn't really in the mood to talk vetting.

I soon warmed up though, and after an hour of swapping animal stories we moved on to romance and I told Athena about Rob. 'I thought you might be him, actually,' I confessed.

'Better put the phone down then, he's probably trying to ring you.'

Five minutes later, Athena's pager went off and she had to go. Almost as soon as I put the phone down, it rang again. I knew it would be Athena again, pulling my leg, so I picked it up with a terse, 'Yes?'

A deep West Country voice said, 'Oh, hi Anna. It's Rob.'

My stomach turned a somersault.

'Oh, Rob, sorry, hi, hi, I thought it was someone else,' I kind of blurted out.

'Oh. Well, it's not,' said Rob, deadpan.

There was a short pause while I gathered myself and tried to think of something sensible to say, then realised that that was his job: he had rung me.

'I'm sorry I disappeared so quickly the other evening,' said Rob now.

'Oh – no – that was fine,' I said, slightly holding my breath at what was going to come next. Please not some complex former relationship. Or, worse, some current relationship.

'I was shattered,' Rob went on, 'and I knew I'd be up early, checking the ewes and the lambs.'

Phew. I took a deep, happy breath.

'We've had another fifteen lambs born, including five sets of twins and one set of triplets. That's a complete pain, as ewes only have two teats. It takes a bit of managing.'

'It is a bit of a design fault, isn't it?' I said, delighted at the way this conversation was going. He had a genuine reason for skipping off early, plus this was familiar ground for me. 'And isn't it odd that cows have four teats but usually only have a single calf?'

We chatted on about lambing and calving – and teats – for a bit until I began to wonder whether his apology had been the sole reason for his call. Finally, he said, 'Anyway, it was a good evening, and I wondered if we could do it again. Maybe not the Cavity Club this time – I was thinking more of a curry? Are you free next Saturday?'

'Yes – great – me too. I'm off all weekend next weekend. That would be great.'

A curry might not have been my first choice for a date, but it was a date. I replaced the handset with a grin I simply couldn't wipe from my face.

That Saturday, Rob turned up on time, in the same blue holey jumper, and back we drove to Bridport. We parked up and headed down the broad main street to the town's square, where an impressive-looking cream-coloured marquee had been erected. This wasn't quite the dark, red-flock wallpaper-ed restaurant I had been expecting. We ducked inside, the brief accidental touch of our heads making my scalp prickle. Beyond the curtain was another world. There were no tables or chairs – just bejewelled and colourful cushions on rugs, placed around a solitary sitar player whose beautiful stringed instrument seemed to have a body made from a highly-polished gourd. The mouthwatering smell of Indian spices filled the air. 'It's a new environmentally friendly catering company called Henry's Beard,' explained Rob as we found a secluded spot on the floor. 'They're based in Dorset and use local, organic ingredients.'

It could have been Ravi Shankar himself playing, but

I would not have noticed. I was much more aware of Rob's laugh – frequent, and slightly high-pitched for a man with such a deep voice – and of the pressure of his shoulder leaning into me as we half-sat, half-lay relaxing on the cushions, surrounded by others in similar poses. I was concentrating too on eating the delicious vegetarian curry being served up from this laid-back position without spilling it down me.

Around ten o'clock the sitar-player was replaced with recorded music. The marquee started emptying out, while a few of those remaining started gently dancing in the middle of the space. It was one of those times to either leave, or stay for another two hours. Since I didn't much rate my chances of impressing Rob with my Indian dancing, I suggested we head back to my cottage for a herbal tea. To my delight, Rob agreed.

We talked and talked and talked. At one point I showed Rob my photos from my post-A-level trip to the United States, when I had built a walking trail with the American Hiking Society in Arkansas – mostly retirees, the odd hippy, and a fireman from Dallas Fort Worth Airport. We had camped in the Buffalo River National Park and canoed down the canyon. 'The fireman called my sections the Rolls Royce trail,' I boasted. I guess I wanted to show I was an outdoors type and a hard worker.

I even made Rob leaf through my prized possession, my natural history book from the area. 'It's signed by the ranger who wrote it – look. He was one of the first men to be documented with Lyme disease, that he got from tick bites out there.' I suppose I wanted to show I knew a little bit about nature, the countryside. Rob did a good job of looking interested.

By two o'clock in the morning we were both yawning uncontrollably.

'I think I'm going to have to get some sleep,' I said. To my disappointment, Rob readily agreed to being kicked out. I walked him out to his car, wrapping my arms around me in the cold night air.

'Good night, Anna,' he said, and drove off.

Nothing, still nothing. I liked a gentleman, I thought, as I fell into bed, but this was taking it a bit too far.

At eight o'clock the next morning, I was enjoying a lie-in when the phone rang. Who would ring me this early in the morning on my day off? A family emergency? A vetting emergency?

'It's Rob. I've got to work today, on the reserve, but do you fancy coming along? You could walk Rocky around the wildlife reserve.'

'I'd love to.' I put the phone down and did a little dance. 'Come on Rocky, we've got a date.' I took the back roads from Redcombe across to Kingcombe. The eight-mile journey took me half an hour, and incorporated a couple of tricky five-point turns, when I took a wrong turn on one of the narrow green lanes that barely held back the forest around them. I was, of course, hot and sweaty by the time I arrived.

'I've asked someone else to take my amateur botanist group on their walk today,' said Rob. 'I'm doing an inspection of the state of the hedgerows instead.' And off we went, for a hard day's work.

The hedgerows and the meadows on this brilliant spring morning had never looked more beautiful or more alive. I let Rocky off the lead and he and Soots immediately ran off and got lost with each other in the long grass while Rob and I wandered slowly around the reserve.

I became an educated rambler as Rob named the riot of pinks and whites and yellows for me. In the hedgerows, he pointed out the pale yellow wild primroses and brighter yellow cowslips; the green leaves and white flowers of the gelder rose and wayfaring tree; the deep purple of the early bluebells. The flowers were in such prolific bloom that they competed with the fresh green leaves of the hedge itself – the dogwood, the blackthorn, the hawthorn – all themselves also in glorious pink and white flower. He found wild garlic flowers – 'an ancient woodland plant' – and crushed them under my nose, releasing that pungent heady scent. He encouraged me look for moschatel, or clock tower flowers, very pale yellowy green. These tiny plants were almost impossible to spot at first but then once I'd found them and got my eye in I saw them everywhere.

On the meadows, it was the shocking pink campion – 'the same colour as your top' – the delicate pinky-white cuckoo-flower or lady's smock, and of course the deep orangey-yellow of the gorse that grew everywhere. And I hadn't appreciated how many different varieties of grass there were that had yet to flower: fox meadow, foxtail, quaking grass – that beautiful grass you see sometimes in flower arrangements with little seed heads that literally quivered in the wind – all ancient varieties being nurtured and protected on the reserve.

The sun shone and a warm breeze delivered the coconut-scent of the gorse flower and the calls of the song birds. 'Do you hear that?' Rob would ask. 'That repetitive, beautiful song; that bird that is singing everything twice? That's a song thrush. And overhead – look – a hobby.'

We must have walked across the entire reserve, across meadows, through coppices, past streams and ponds and gnarled old tree trunks, along the river. We walked slightly too close to each other, knocking into each other every so often. Rocky and Soots checked in with us from time to time, tails wagging madly, before becoming distracted again by something only they could hear or smell and running off. Just as on our two dates, the talk flowed easily and naturally. Even after two evenings of fairly solid chatting, punctuated only by the sitar player, there seemed to be so much to talk about.

Rob told me about his plans. He didn't want to work on the reserve forever. He had all kinds of ambitious ideas about organic farming that he wanted to try. He came from a farming family, knew the local farmers, appreciated how their businesses worked, had clear views on exactly what was wrong with the countryside and how to put it right. 'I'm not going to be a warden all my life, Anna. Definitely not.'

In turn I harangued him with my favourite theories and worries. What was the best way to talk to a grossly overweight pet owner about their obese pet and all the risks it was facing if it didn't lose weight? When was it okay to perform a Caesarean on a pedigree dog? Why do we keep breeding bitches with small narrow pelvises that then had to try to give birth, often unsuccessfully, to pups with large heads – the chihuahua, and the Westie, to name just two. Why did we go through all the pain of battling to save a farm animal that was going to slaughter the next month?

Rob was thoughtful, practical and straightforward to the point of bluntness in his responses. Obesity was bad for animals and humans, and it was our duty to tackle it, whatever the cost in embarrassment. Extreme pedigree dog breeding was immoral. And on farm animals: 'It's economics. It's how people make their living. It's just life. If a lamb dies too soon, the farmer gets nothing for it.'

We chatted about the rural issues we both kept coming up against, day in day out: farmers eking out a living on the edge of bankruptcy; our lovely nurse Penny and her boyfriend Den, who wanted to move in together but couldn't afford it while my closest neighbours were wealthy Londoners who visited every third weekend. It turned out Rob had first-hand experience of this: for his first few months at the Wildlife Trust, he'd lived in a mobile home with no heating. 'I had to be local so I could check on the animals all through the night and this was all I could afford locally. The owner was very sweet and used to bring Sunday lunches over. It was freezing cold though so they said I couldn't stay there through the winter. Then I moved to a converted stables but they kept putting the rent up. I live in a house now: I managed to persuade the Trust to buy it for the Deputy Warden to live in.'

There was so much I found admirable in this: his ability to suffer through a cold autumn in a mobile home; and even more so the confidence and nous it must have taken to put a business plan together to persuade the Trust to buy a house for him to live in.

I confided in Rob a dream I had never shared with anyone – a long-held hankering to one day become self-sufficient. It felt silly because I really had grown up with little connection to the land. My parents were town people really, my brother was in the Royal Marines, my sister lived in London: none of them seemed to want to live in the country. But, I confessed, I already felt part of the community here in Ebbourne after just a few months, already felt an affinity for the country lifestyle and a yearning to live it more fully. Rob, who had lived in Dorset all his life, didn't think it was silly at all. He found it difficult to understand why anyone would ever want to live any other way.

After a couple of hours of meandering and chatting, it occurred to me why this all felt so effortless: I wasn't trying to be impressive at all. I was just being me, completely. And Rob, it seemed to me, wasn't the kind of person who ever went out of his way to impress anyone. I meant that in a good way. He was simply at ease with himself and it wouldn't have occurred to him to try to be anything other than completely honest and completely himself.

I hadn't been in particularly complicated relationships in the past, but I'd been with people where it was clear I was going to need to put in a lot of effort to really get to know them, or to be the person they wanted me to be. I couldn't be doing with any of that any more. I wanted someone like Rob whose signals were clear: 'This is me, this is my life.'

Finally, having climbed gently up to a high point on the reserve, we sat down side by side to look at the view. It was spectacular. In front of us a huge meadow peppered with cuckoo-flower sloped gently down to a hedge line punctuated by tall mature oaks. From there, the land angled itself gently up again through a diamond-shaped pattern of fields towards the scruffy cotton wool clouds, barely moving now the wind had dropped. Towards the steeper side of the brow, over to our right, a small wooded area with scrubby edges nibbled into the field.

'That's ancient woodland hedge,' explained Rob, pointing to the hedge line. 'It would have been left as a hedgerow when the ancient woodland was cleared for agriculture. The big oaks are remnants of ancient woodland as well. They would have been boundary markers – property boundaries, or parish boundaries. And you see how the hedge follows a windy route, it's not laid out geometrically? That means it probably dates from medieval times or earlier. Enclosure Act hedges tend to be straight lines. We know the hamlet of Kingcombe dates from medieval times.'

'Mmmm,' I said. It was interesting, and I loved listening to his voice, but I was enjoying feeling a bit dopey and sleepy from the walk in the warm sun. And to be honest, I had got a little bit lost just watching the movements of his eyes and lips as he talked.

There was a long silence. Then Rob turned towards me. 'Do you know the country saying,' he asked, 'about the gorse?'

I didn't.

'Well,' he went on. 'They do say that when the gorse is in flower it's kissing season.'

I was suddenly wide awake. I turned towards Rob, looked into his brilliant green eyes, paused to take a deep breath of the coconut, and surrendered to my new favourite country saying.

After that day, we spent almost all our free time with each other. If I wasn't vetting, I wanted to be with Rob. One day I glanced at my hall table and saw a small pile of *Veterinary Records* still in their plastic wrappers. Before Rob, I had read these weekly missives from cover to cover, eager to be fully informed, keen to stay up-to-date. Now, they had lost their appeal, and I silenced the guilt pangs by convincing myself that surely most vets didn't have time for such things. Did it feel like a whirlwind? Perhaps. No, not quite. It felt more like a bubble.

If we were both off work, we would go out to Bridport or one of the more local pubs. If Rob was working and I wasn't, I'd go out to the reserve. Sometimes I'd help him, especially when he was very busy lambing and calving, but other times, I just joined in with whatever he was doing.

And if I was working and he wasn't, he'd come and be my nurse.

Rob led fabulous nature walks. I tagged along on one walk for a rambling club interested in orchids and other hay meadow flowers. I knew Rob was focused on casting around for signs of the early purple orchids, but every now and again he turned to look at me, with a grin that made me melt. The Reverend Bromsgrove and his wife were among the jolly ramblers and I felt slightly shy airing my relationship with Rob amongst people I knew, but as the group straggled up an uneven field, Rob took my hand. When Rob eventually spotted the glossy dark green leaves with dark spots on, he beckoned me over and made sure that I was the first one to see the cluster of purple flowers just emerging.

The following week Rob led a walk for blind naturalists to hear the dawn chorus. The dawn chorus is always an amazing experience but this was something really special. The blind folk couldn't see the stunning sunrise over the meadow but, whereas I still couldn't tell a black bird from a black cap, they could identify all the different bird calls individually.

I loved the walks and I relished the strong tea and home-made cakes that were always served up afterwards at the Education Centre.

I loved, too, watching how Rob handled the stock. He could turn a sheep over quite easily, which was something I often struggled with. He knew how to approach cows so as not to startle them – gently, and talking softly, and from the side rather than head on because their eyes are on the sides of their heads – and how to move them by standing at a certain point that made them move away from him. It sounds easy, but it's a real skill. One time, he had so many wild Soay ewes lambing that he ran out of pens again – just like on the night of our first date (the ewe and the lamb need to be penned together to bond for their first 24 to 48 hours). So he just constructed a load from straw bales and hazel twigs, which I thought was pretty clever. He picked up these heavy bales so easily, and he knew exactly how to arrange them, and exactly how to wheedle the hazel twigs in to pinion them together. There was no huffing and puffing, he just quickly and deftly got on with it.

Rob even seemed able to handle Rocky. On one of our walks together in those early weeks, we passed through a field of peacefully grazing sheep. There must have been thirty or forty of them, quietly keeping the gorse levels down, minding their own business. 'Is Rocky okay with sheep?' Rob asked. Instead of telling the truth and saying 'no' I crossed my fingers and hoped for the best. 'Mostly,' I lied. These were Soay sheep, which are quite skittish. It might just have been okay if they hadn't scattered, but once they started running around in every direction Rocky couldn't control himself. His bloodlust was up and he went bounding after them, barking at the top of his voice. (Soots, in the meantime, was being absolutely gorgeously good, bumbling along obediently at Rob's heels.) As quick as a flash, Rob was after Rocky, yelling at him loudly from right down the bottom of his register. He rugby tackled him at speed and stopped him in his tracks. Rob proceeded to give Rocky a jolly good telling off, and Rocky came back to me with his tail between his legs. I was pretty embarrassed by Rocky, and pretty impressed by Rob.

On one of my half days, a couple of weeks after that kiss in Kingcombe Meadows, Rob mysteriously asked me to leave Rocky at his house to keep Soots company. 'We've got a dog-free mission ahead of us.' I was nervous about how Rocky would behave on his playdate but Rob assured me it would be alright. 'Soots will keep him in his place.' I knew that was true. Soots was a little sweetheart and considerably smaller than Rocky – he was at least 35 kilos and she couldn't have been more than 25 – but she was clearly the top dog and had no difficulty putting Rocky in his place if he ever tried to get too boisterous with her. Like a good teacher who never has to raise her voice to her pupils, Soots had only to lift her lip to Rocky to make him toe the line. (I wondered whether I should learn to lift my own lip: certainly it couldn't be any less effective than my current methods.) Rob had a quiet, firm, deep-voiced conversation with Rocky as well before we left.

From the reserve car park we walked at pace for about twenty minutes. There was no point asking Rob what we were doing – he wanted this to be a surprise, so it was going to be a surprise. Rob led me up a slope between two hedge banks and along the shallow bed of the stream that bubbled through Kingcombe. After another ten minutes we emerged onto a meadow with a large eastern-facing bank bathed by late afternoon sun. We silently navigated the edge of the field, staying near the hedgerows, towards the bank. Then we sat down. Rob gestured to me to stay quiet and look at the bank, which had a darker patch in the middle. After about half an hour, a little nose on a chestnut face and floppy body emerged from the dark patch, to be quickly joined by four yellow fox cubs. I had to force myself not to 'oooh' and 'aaah' as they tripped and tumbled together, hunting down long grass stalks and each other's tails. I had never seen fox cubs so close and they were so very very cute. We just sat there until it got dark.

In fact, as time went on, much of Rob's courtship involved some wildlife theme or other. I suppose he was so at ease with it, and keen to share the countryside that was his life. We ate salads laced with citrus-tasting sorrel leaves and long wild garlic leaves from the woods. His floral offerings were handpicked posies or blossom, delivered with a shy grin. A wildlife warden's position is pretty poorly paid so there was no question of extravagance but that suited me just fine. I was paying off seven years of student loans so I didn't have much money either. In truth, there had been times at Oxford when boyfriends had lavishly wined and dined me, but somehow, driving to a secret location with Rob to hear nightingales sing for the first time, and then sharing a flask of tea and some locally made biscuits, was even better.

In return for these experiences I offered a tour of my beloved 13th-century church, with its graveyard overrun with what I learned from Rob was comfrey and wild garlic and bright yellow celandine; plus a diagnosis of Soots' PMT. I noticed one day that Soots wasn't herself.

Instead of tootling around the place after Rob, with her little beaver tail wagging away in a full circle, she had retired to his pick-up truck and curled up, snarling at anyone who came near. I recognised all the signs: Soots was feeling hormonal. On questioning, Rob volunteered that his usually obedient and affectionate dog got like this every six months just as she was coming into season. I spayed her three months later, as nervous as I had been since my very first ops, with Rob sent on a distraction-mission – there was no way I wanted him there clucking around like a mother hen and asking anxious questions – to buy a new dog bed.

I also cooked up good, wholesome meals for the two of us, incredulous at how much Rob ate. My food bill more than doubled as the rest of the poacher's pie or Bolognese that would normally have gone in the freezer (for those nights when on call) were merrily tucked away. Plus puddings were considered de rigueur. But Rob usually bought the wine, chosen with help from Jonathan, a friend who ran a local bakery and general store. On one occasion Rob left the brown paper bag containing a particularly dark bottle of merlot on the side in the kitchen. I could not help but read the scrawled writing on the bag: 'For Hedge, So you did get the vet!' I raised an eyebrow and quizzed Rob. 'Hedge? Get the vet?'

He grinned his lovely grin. 'Ah yes; that's my nickname – big hair, so "Hedge" … and I confessed my interest in you to Jonathan, just after we met, but I didn't think a vet would want to date a conservation worker. In fact, to be honest,

I didn't think a lowly wildlife worker like me could even approach the vet, so if you hadn't phoned me that time to ask me about courses on the reserve, I don't think anything would have ever happened.' How ridiculous, I thought. Why on earth not? I knew Rob read a lot of Hardy but I had thought it was for the local landscapes, not the misery-inducing social conventions.

'And while we're on confessions,' Rob went on, putting his arms around my waist and smiling down at me, 'The gorse. I don't know when you would have finally noticed this, but I might as well tell you now. It's in flower somewhere all year round. Every day of the year. That's the whole point.'

I remembered our first kiss up on the reserve and smiled. Now I loved that country saying more than ever.

And then I remembered something else, and I started giggling. I thought back to our first phone conversation when I had asked him about hedge-laying. And I remembered the pause that had followed, which at the time I had attributed to his shock at my terrible chat-up line.

'So, you're Hedge? And when I phoned you I asked about ... '

'Yep,' laughed Rob. 'You asked me about hedge-laying, and all I could think was "Yes, please".'

Then we both stopped laughing. Rob gently tucked a particularly wild piece of my hair behind my ear. 'I'm glad you phoned,' he said.

I took his hand and subjected one gnarled knuckle to a detailed examination.

'Blimey, Hedge,' I said, 'so am I.'

PART FOUR

Summer

CHAPTER SIXTEEN

A proposition

'Leave,' shouted the owner of the standard poodle. 'Off. Now.' His tone was increasingly threatening.

'Rocky, come,' I called rather feebly. 'Here, boy.' I started marching towards a perfectly-clipped apricot-coloured standard poodle, her rear end being sniffed by a very excited and frisky Rocky. He should not be doing this, I thought to myself. He's castrated. (Two testicles floating in formalin flashed in my mind's eye.) My neutered four-legged friend was at this point on two legs, attempting to mount Pandora, the poodle.

We could now do 'sit' and 'stay' when there were no distractions, even from ten metres. But there was so much going on here: the smells of other canine companions; the sardine cake for training; and now this lovely lady who was presumably in heat. She was rather beautiful with her long eyelashes and curly fringe tied up in a pale blue bow but it wasn't the front end that was of most interest to Rocky. I put him on his lead and we slunk to the back of the hall.

The dog trainer joined me soon after, bag of baked liver and sardine treats hanging from a pouch around her waist and dog slobber wiped across the thigh of her black jeans. The rest of the class had been given a break so that she could deliver some intense one-on-one training to me and Rocky. She was very patient with us both, but when, after ten minutes, she sent us to rejoin the rest of the group, her final piece of advice made my heart sink to the floor. 'Perhaps,' she said brightly, 'you should go and see your vet.'

The following evening I was sitting outside enjoying the early June sunset when a familiar trio – dog (dirty), pheasant (dead), gamekeeper (livid) loomed up over the horizon. Rocky had killed several pheasants over the last few months, and the local gamekeeper was becoming wildly angry about it. Now, returning Rocky to me for what had to be the third time, eyes bulging and veins popping, he announced, 'I'll shoot the bugger next time I find him in my pheasant pen' and stomped off before I had time to protest. I believed him.

'What am I going to do with you?' I asked an unrepentant Rocky. He gave me an inscrutable look back. Dogs were happy when they knew their owners were the alpha dog, the head of the household. Was Rocky happy with me, I wondered? Were we right together?

The phone interrupted my thoughts and Lena came through on a crackly international line.

'Is everything okay, Lena?' Earlier in the year Lena and I had talked quite regularly. Over the last few weeks we hadn't talked at all. I felt a brief pang of guilt – with Rob around I had been much less attentive to my friends – then remembered that the main reason we hadn't spoken was that she was, I was pretty sure, still in rural Ethiopia, assisting with a programme to protect the endangered Ethiopian wolf population.

'Everything's fine. It's amazing out here. But I'm under-experienced and overwhelmed. I was wondering whether you might like a break from cats and hamsters. Just for a few weeks.'

'Lena, it's so lovely to hear from you, but I can't just drop everything here.'

'I know, I know. But don't say no straightaway. At least let me try to convince you.'

Lena described what she was doing. She told me about the programme of visits to outlying villages up in the mountains where as a research assistant she was charged with capturing, vaccinating and neutering the semi-domesticated (which meant semi-feral) village dogs. This in turn prevented these dogs from passing on disease to the Ethiopian wolf, the rarest canid in the world, and stopped inter-breeding which was watering down their gene pool.

'But I really need an extra head and an extra pair of hands. Especially as we're working at altitude with no anaesthetic gases.'

Lena said that last bit very quickly and quietly.

'No gaseous anaesthesia?' I checked.

'No. We're using triple combination anaesthetic, topped up.'

'Well, I've never done that. I'm in a first world country here, we do neutering with gaseous anaesthesia.' I was intrigued by the idea of working in those conditions, though, and Lena knew it. She pressed home her advantage.

'I've thought about how it would work. I just need someone who knows the castrating procedure well and who doesn't mind the dog fleas: someone like you. Plus, it will be fun,' she pleaded. 'Exciting. Operating 4,000 metres above sea level; living in the mountains; seeing Ethiopian wolves. This is once-in-a-lifetime stuff, Anna.'

'But I can't get away from here just like that. I've got a job, and a cat and a dog. And a boyfriend.'

'Woah – a boyfriend? Okay, I need to hear all about this. But Anna, of course you can get away from all of that. Your job comes with holiday. Your boyfriend can manage without you. Maybe he can even look after Kiska and Rocky. Picture it. Promise me you'll at least think about it?'

'Okay, I'll think about it.'

'Only I need to know quickly so we can get your jabs and visas sorted. Can you let me know tomorrow?'

I promised Lena I'd sleep on it. Mike was on duty so there were no calls to keep me up but I didn't sleep much that night as I turned the African adventure over and over in my mind. I kept going round in circles, repeating the same series of thoughts.

I didn't want to let down Mike and Stanley. But was I really so crucial to their enterprise? I was still learning and certainly not pulling my full weight yet – sometimes I felt I was more of a hindrance than a help. I knew Mike and Stanley still ran an informal second call system for me anyway. I shouldn't kid myself that I had become indispensable to them. I was sure they would be able to manage just fine without me for a few weeks. But I was not sure I could ask for more than two weeks off and if I was going I absolutely had to see the sights; just a busman's holiday was not so appealing.

I had fallen in love with Ebbourne, it was true. And I was enjoying my quiet, settled life here. But there was a bit of me that still wanted adventure too. And why shouldn't I? After all, wanting to live somewhere forever didn't mean never leaving at all. Then again, why did I think I needed to leave to taste adventure? Wasn't my life here full enough of adventure? Here I was, being paid to be outdoors in a beautiful place doing something I loved. Why did I need anything else?

And what would I do about Kiska, and Rocky? I was their family, I had responsibilities to them, I couldn't just take off on a whim. Kiska would be an easy sell and there were several people I could ask to come in and feed her, but there was no one I really felt I could ask to take on Rocky. Except perhaps ...

And that brought me to Rob. We might have only been together for a couple of months, but we were clearly already serious about each other. I'd miss him terribly. Then again, I wasn't emigrating: he'd still be here when I got back.

As these thoughts were circling around and around I also realised that I knew almost nothing about Ethiopia. From some sketchy school geography I knew it was a large country in North East Africa, land-locked but fairly close to The Red Sea. I had strong memories, from an impressionable age when I'd been at school in the mid-1980s, of the drought and famine that had killed so many, prompting the enormous money-raising by Band Aid and Live Aid. More recently the news had covered a small-scale war with one of its neighbours. That was the extent of my insight.

Towards early morning I decided it all came down to Mike and Stanley really: if they said it was okay, I should go. If they really couldn't spare me, well, then, I would just have to accept that.

All day I was distracted, rehearsing in my mind what I was going to say and trying to find the right moment to speak to Mike.

I knew it wasn't going to be easy because things were even more hectic than usual. Stanley was away on holiday (just for the one week), which meant Mike and I were holding things down between us. The usual one-in-three rota had become a one-in-two – and of course every night had seen either a late call or an early call or both. During the days we were sharing three vets' worth of work between the two of us, including re-testing of a number of farms for TB. The previous day I had been back to the Porritt farm. Thankfully, I'd been able to give them the happy news that they were finally free of TB. I'd had to turn away and fiddle with my paperwork to be sure not to witness the reactions of this stooped old farmer and his hulk of a son. It had been a worrying, expensive, time-consuming few months for them, and of course even now they knew that at any time they might have to go through it all again.

In short, I had done two thirteen-hour days in a row already this week with no lunch break to speak of and not enough sleep – and I was sure Mike had done the same, probably more because he had all the practice management to take care of on top of the vetting. The backs of my legs ached with all the standing, from behind my knees down to the Achilles tendons, and my throat was dry from talking to clients so much. Both of us were exhausted, and rushed off our feet.

The day started early with a 6.30 a.m. dash to a down cow with milk fever over in the Marshwood Vale. My favourite veterinarian magic trick worked, happily, and she was up within ten minutes of the calcium injection. (I would tell Mike I wanted to use my skills to help those most in need of them, I thought. No – that sounded really crass, and he would say he needed my skills here.)

From there I raced through the crisp clear morning, barely taking time to enjoy the stunning views, to Rankin village, north of the practice, for a calving. It was to the Jasons of Manor Farm, a very pleasant, hard-working, younger farming family who were tenants on a larger estate that was split into three separate dairy herds. The couple must have been in their late 30s, which was unusually young to be running your own farming set-up. Most of the younger farmers I met were the sons or daughters of a still-working farmer who remained in charge. As I walked up to greet the anxious-looking young couple, I wondered whether I could have worked on a day-to-day basis with my father. Colonel Barrington's Law Of Time (Always early) and Law Of Place (Everything has a place to which it must be returned) would probably drive me potty, much as I loved him.

I snapped my attention – already shared between the Jasons and the Ethiopian wolf, and now wandering off on flights of fancy about working with my father – back to the task in hand: delivering a large calf backwards. I donned the calving gown and slid a well-lubricated hand into the cow. The cervix was fully dilated, I noted, so she was ready to push; and I could feel the calf's large rump. I could feel, too, that the fur on this big, backwards-facing calf was dry, which was not such a good discovery: it meant that the waters had broken some time ago and already run out. I explained what this meant to the Jasons, wanting to be up front about the situation: 'Usually the waters lubricate things and make it easier to slide the calf out, but we aren't going to be getting that help today. And because the calf is coming out backwards, the fur is piled the wrong way too, creating even more friction. And, as you already know, we've got a big calf here.'

They nodded in unison and exchanged an anxious look.

I started to sweat: even at eight o'clock in the morning, the warmth of the coming day, combined with the adrenalin now surging through me, was enough to challenge my never-reliable personal thermostat under my plastic calving gown and wellies. I found the tail and pushed the rear end of the calf forwards so that I could pull the hind legs up to the birth channel. It sounds so easy in the textbooks, I thought to myself, as my cheek brushed the cow's damp rump, but there really wasn't much room to manoeuvre and I had to protect the cow's uterus from the dangerous little hooves. Cupping the hooves, with the sweat now dripping down my back, I pushed up, flexing all the calf's back leg joints to get the left hind foot high enough to pull it up and out. I did the same again with the right hind, except this was even harder, because the left foot was in the way now, and there was consequently less room for my squeezed and bruised arm to operate. Sweat stung my eyes. I attached ropes to the calf's feet. Crumbs, those were big hooves. I squeezed more lubricating gel into the palm of one hand.

I started pulling, with Mr and Mrs Jason each providing stronger and stronger traction, exchanging worried glances all the while. (I would tell Mike that I had learnt so much from him and become so good at neutering that my colleague needed me. No, that's ridiculous. Anyone with any experience of neutering would be just as good as me out there and we both knew it.) Meanwhile, back at the cow, nothing was happening. I remembered a trick that Mike had mentioned once.

'Mrs Jason, could you find me a clean plastic food sack?'

'Annette, please, and this is Tony,' she said, leaving her post at the rear end. Annette Jason quickly found a sack, rinsed it thoroughly under the outdoor tap, and opened it up. I slid the bag between the calf's back and the cow's upper vaginal wall, hoping this slippy food sack would reduce the friction enough to allow me to pull the calf out. By this point, drops of sweat were dripping off my chin and down my calving gown.

I pulled again, with the Jasons again providing traction. Still nothing, and this had been going on too long for my liking. I headed back to the Land Rover to collect the calving jack: a long pole with a ratchet mechanism that could be winched or made to slide up and down, with a saddle on the end forming a T-shape. I breathed deeply as I tried to steady my hands, then placed the saddle under the cow, attached the dangling ends of the calving ropes – which were looped around the calf's feet – to the hooks on the ratchet, and slowly started to winch the calf out, using the ratchet only with the cow's contractions at first. The damn thing kept slipping. I swore quietly. Gradually, gradually though, the huge calf started to emerge.

And then, halfway out, it seemed it would move no further, no matter how hard the three of us tried: Tony on the ratchet, Annette keeping the saddle in place and me with my hands in the cow trying to lubricate and guide things, and pull as much as possible.

I felt a prepuce. It was a bull calf. 'And again, another notch,' I demanded, feeling a tension in my throat.

'Won't go,' hissed Tony. He had no breath for anything more.

'Try,' cried Annette, almost hysterical.

But the shoulders were locked, and so broad that there seemed no way this calf could make it out of this cow. I'd gone too far now for a Caesarean to be a possibility.

Perhaps I should have made that call 40 minutes ago. Easy to say in retrospect. Shit. We were going to lose this calf. We were going to have to stand here while he died from lack of oxygen, with his umbilical cord squashed against his mother's pelvis, his head and shoulders still inside her. And I was facing down a possible embryotomy to get this huge calf out: a horrid procedure in which a dead calf is cut in half with cheese wire, in order to remove it from a still-live cow. I could taste bile in my mouth. I had actually never carried out an embryotomy before, but I had heard about it in grim detail from one of my vetting friends.

'Mrs Jason, Annette, I'm so sorry but I think we've lost the calf.'

She nodded. I was confirming something she already knew. 'We shouldn't have put her to such a big bull. Tony said no, don't be greedy, but it was me, I thought it would be alright. Tony said no.'

She looked at her husband. He put his arm around his wife.

Then the cow went down, rolling onto her side, possibly the effect of the pressure on her nerves and blood vessels. The Jasons exchanged more anxious looks. I knew what they were thinking. Were they going to lose the cow as well?

I, though, saw a silver lining in this development. With the cow on her side the anatomy changed somewhat. With the three of us working together over another twenty minutes, we managed to twist and finally pull out the calf – a fine-looking animal, and still-warm but motionless. I listened with my stethoscope. Mrs Jason pushed a piece of straw up his nostrils. I heard nothing, but moved round to take a pulse to be sure. Annette knelt beside the calf where I had been listening and started pumping on his rib cage, trying to resuscitate the lifeless figure. With her elbows locked she pushed firmly on his chest, counting. 'One, two, three, four ... ' After twenty pumps, she moved to the calf's head, cupped her hands around his nose, and blew desperately so that his chest rose. Pumping and breathing, pumping and breathing, Annette kept going.

I felt inside the cow again just to make absolutely sure there was no twin, or a tear. Annette's farmyard CPR became more urgent and her cheeks flushed with the effort. Tony and I exchanged looks and I shook my head.

'Stop, Annette, please,' pleaded Tony. 'He's dead.'

Annette stifled a sob. Her actions were becoming more laboured but she would not stop. I glanced at Tony, now cradling his chin in one hand, eyes closed. I checked the calf's eyes.

'Annette,' I said, trying to sound sympathetic but firm. 'There is nothing there. I'm sorry, but he's gone.'

The words had the opposite of the effect I'd intended. Annette pumped on the ribcage with more vigour. Then, suddenly, she collapsed forward onto the calf. Tony lifted her up and she put her face in his chest and sobbed.

'I am so sorry,' I said rather hoarsely. And then, trying to salvage something, 'But let's treat this cow now. Give her anti-inflammatories to get any swelling and bruising down, make her more comfortable, and if you turn her regularly, even lift her – you may be able to borrow a lifting cradle from John Jones – then she should be back up soon and at least you will have the milk, and you can try again.' I was gabbling now, I realised, but I needed to get away. Away to reflect, to change my soggy clothes, and to let these good people move on. As I pulled out of the farmyard I glanced in my mirrors and saw Tony dragging the calf away while his wife stared, wiping her eyes and nose with the back of her hand.

It's a fine line between life and death, joy and sorrow. Could I, should I have done something different? I really didn't know.

It would be a tough time around their kitchen table for a while.

A few weeks in Ethiopia with no calvings to perform seemed extremely enticing as I left the farm, wet and slimy both inside and outside my calving gear, and with my sugar levels and spirits low. (Perhaps I should tell Mike I needed a break. God, no, I could see how that would go down with someone who had been working one-in-three for twenty years.)

I arrived back at the surgery in this state at eleven o'clock. Usually I would have sat down, had a cup of tea and a reviving snack, and gone through all the gory details. But the atmosphere was slightly tense, I thought. There was no Stanley to lighten the mood, and Mike was running consults on his own – as he had been doing all morning while I was out on the farm. Judith and Penny were rushing around trying to hold everything together, exuding a kind of 'where have you been?' resentment. I changed my top and headed downstairs to pick up some consults. Perhaps I'd talk to Mike about Ethiopia at lunchtime.

'Anna, there's a routine lumpectomy in,' said Judith as I came down the stairs. 'Mike's behind with his consults. Can you do it?'

A large and very friendly yellow Labrador dog had been booked in for a mass removal. I looked over his notes, written in Stanley's unmistakable and almost unreadable scrawl. With Judith's help I deciphered them: a firm mass had been slowly growing on Paddy's left flank over about 18 months. It had been sampled and identified as a benign lipoma – a non-spreading fatty lump – and the owners had opted to monitor it. But it had continued to grow and although still benign was preventing Paddy from moving his left elbow freely. So the owners now wanted to have it removed. It all looked pretty straightforward.

Penny brought Paddy through to the operating theatre to be anaesthetised and clipped and cleaned. Or rather, Paddy and his amazing rotor blade of a tail brought Penny in. As always, the soft furry body seemed incongruous against the bright hard surfaces of the theatre: all stainless steel and white tile glinting under the harsh theatre lights. But Paddy had a huge grin on his wide face and was happy to see everybody – he had no idea of course what was about to happen to him. He lifted my mood immediately. Here I was with a lovely happy Labrador, about to use my hard-earned skills to make him better. Why would I even think of leaving Paddy and the surgery and Rob and Rocky and Kiska for some unknown adventure? I had everything

I needed right here. (I wouldn't talk to Mike at all. I'd just have to tell Lena.)

'Hey Paddy,' said Penny, struggling to lift his back end onto the operating table. 'Let's get you asleep and remove that lump, shall we?' I took the front end of this 48-kilo canine, heaved him up, and got my first good look at the lump. It was huge, the size of a gala melon.

'Mmmm, Penny, this is going to be more like a Paddy-ectomy than a lumpectomy. I think we'll be removing Paddy from the lump rather than the lump from Paddy.'

I clipped a vein over the top of a foreleg, Penny used her thumb as a tourniquet and the vein stood up like a hosepipe. Beautiful, just beautiful, I thought. Strange what one could find aesthetically pleasing. I slowly injected the anaesthetic and within a few moments, Paddy's lolling tongue hung even further out of his mouth as he rested his huge head against Penny. We lay him on his side and while Penny opened his mouth even wider I secured a rubber tube down his windpipe and turned on the anaesthetic gas. (Lena won't be working with anaesthetic gas, I thought. What fun, what an adventure, to be working in those kinds of conditions. I would only be away for three weeks, maybe four. I would be honing my skills. Maybe I should talk to Mike. Arrrrgggggg. Anna. Make up your mind.)

The vastness of this lump made the surgery less straightforward than I had anticipated. With the surgical lights blazing down on my be-hatted head, I could feel the sweat beading out on my forehead between my damp curls.

'It's shelling out okay, Penny, but it's leaving a lot of dead

293

space. It will need a drain.'

'I've never heard of dead space,' said Penny. 'Is that like a house where no one lives except every other weekend so local people can't get on with their lives?'

I smiled and raised a sweaty eyebrow. Since Penny had finally confronted Den about his intentions towards her, she had been getting more and more agitated about her housing situation. 'You know I'm going to end up an old maid because of bleeding dead space?' exclaimed Penny. 'You and Rob will be grandparents before Den will ever marry me.' Den was still insisting that they needed somewhere to live if they were going to get married. They were both putting aside whatever they could, from their wages as a veterinary nurse and a countryside contractor, and their evenings out with the Young Farmers or just down the pub had dried up as they tried to save all their pennies. But getting together a deposit was going to take them years, and in the meantime renting was just money down the drain. So they were both living with their parents.

I felt for them. They were cheerful, hard-working people who were being ground down. They deserved better.

'It's an empty space in the body where there was once tissue. The body reacts to the space by filling it with serum or blood, which creates a fantastic place for bacteria to breed. I'll stitch as much as I can, but I want to leave as little suture material in there as possible, because that could be a focus for infection and reaction too.'

'Okay,' said Penny, dropping the subject at least for now. I guessed that this was distracting her at least as much as

Africa was me. 'We've got 6mm, 13mm and 19mm flat soft latex drains. Which do you want?'

I took a length of 13mm. I placed the end of one flat tube in the gaping hole I had left, then created another hole through the skin near the top of Paddy's shoulder, and stitched the drain in place. I was feeling much happier with my stitching and knots now, and I felt myself working quickly and confidently.

'Anna – do you think it's going to drip out from there?' asked Penny.

Bugger. Stupid girl, Anna. No, of course it wouldn't. Gravity dictates that the open end of the tube should be lower than the end inside the dog. I sighed, cut my lovely neat sutures, and restitched lower down near the elbow. I glanced at the clock on the wall. We were now into the 63rd minute of the procedure and the sweat was running freely down my head and into my eyes. I wished rather forlornly that I had removed my shirt from under my operating gown. (Good practice though, all this sweating, for Ethiopia.)

At 90 minutes I placed the final stitch, a nice secure mattress suture to try to relieve some of the tension from the edge of the wound. Penny and I heaved Paddy's sagging 48 kilos into the kennel, arranged him comfortably with his neck straight, and covered him with a blanket. How did little vets manage, I wondered, not for the first time? I was nearly six foot tall and fairly fit and strong, and I found all this hefting and heaving quite physically challenging.

I slumped down in a glowing heap next to Paddy to monitor his coming round. I was completely knackered.

The afternoon went by in the usual flurry of consults. I tried my hardest to focus but a combination of sleep deprivation and Ethiopian thoughts meant half my mind was somewhere else much of the time.

So I didn't pay enough attention when Molly Smethwick and her children turned up with their sorry-looking kitten again. The three younger boys chased each other around the reception area and ran in and out of the consulting room banging the door. The oldest boy wouldn't catch my eye and seemed to want to disappear through the floor. I examined the kitten, and admitted it for treatment of its broken tail. As they were leaving, Molly turned and seemed about to tell me something, then two of the children started fighting. She put her face in her hands and hustled them all out. I had a nagging feeling that, despite having taken good care of her kitten, I had failed her somehow.

Eventually at around six in the evening I approached Mike in the operating theatre, where he was working on a fat brown rabbit. I'd decided to take the most direct approach I could. This wasn't an altruistic mission and it wasn't about honing my skills – it was simply something I really wanted to do, and would probably never get the opportunity to do again.

Mike exploded.

'I've done this for over twenty years. One weekend in three, one night in three, for twenty years. I have never – never – had more than two weeks off. Ethiopian wolves? This is not how it works. No.' He stripped off his gloves, marched out of theatre and banged the door shut. 'Rabbit's dead.'

I went and sat at my desk in the vets' room upstairs. Of course I shouldn't go.

There was a knock on the door, and there was Judith with a cup of tea and a custard cream. 'Anna, you do know you're a good vet and we need you? That's what Mike was trying to say. Don't worry. Stanley will talk him round, I'll make sure of it. Just don't come back with rabies.'

That evening the phone rang. I picked it up, expecting Lena to be on the other end. Instead it was Sally. Her voice was choked.

'What's up, Sal?' I asked, concern rising.

'Have you heard? Heard about Mary?'

'Heard what?'

There was a pause, then Sally sniffed and replied, 'She's dead. Committed suicide. Oh God, Anna, poor, poor Mary.'

I felt the blood drain from my face. 'What? ... How ... it wasn't that long ago I saw her ... '

'She hooked herself up to a drip and ran in a bag of barbiturate. I can't believe things were that bad. Can you?'

My thoughts were racing, my stomach churning, my heart thumping almost audibly. I thought of Mary sitting on her deck chair looking forlorn. Why? Why? Why had I not rung her again and gone to see her? Would it have helped? Her poor family. What a waste. Why, Mary, why? My thoughts circled round and round this track, but I kept returning to Mary's family.

'God, Sally, why?'

'I think it was the pressure,' said Sally. 'I feel it too. We all do, don't we? Long hours, no sleep. Then another day with

Mrs Bloggs weeping on your shoulder, begging you to save her much-loved Tibbs. It's a lot of responsibility.'

She was right, there was a lot of pressure on us. Exacerbated by our inexperience, and our own personal struggles and flaws. I wasn't a perfectionist, but so many vets were. And all of that was topped off with our access to an 'easy' way to end it all. We knew, because we had been told at veterinary college, that vets had a terribly high rate of suicide, but it is easy to know something in one's head without really, truly knowing it.

I couldn't think of anything meaningful to say to Sally, but it didn't matter. We stayed on the phone in quiet companionship, pledging always to try to support each other through difficult times.

Finally I put the phone down and breathed deeply. I didn't know what I was feeling. Was it guilt? Or was it 'there but for the grace of God'? Whatever it was, it made me feel sick to my stomach. I washed my face and said a prayer (to whatever force was out there) for Mary and her family. Suddenly going to Africa really did not seem so very important.

CHAPTER SEVENTEEN

In a stew

'Of course you should go to Ethiopia. Of course you must. It will be fantastic experience for you,' declared Stanley. 'I'll work it out with Mike, don't you worry about that. We'll expect you to do a one-in-two rota when we go off on lengthy sabbaticals, mind, but we're not going to stand in the way of something like that. And you do realise that when you get back you will be expected to treat any and all Ethiopian wolves that come through the door?'

I hadn't even had a chance to ask him how his holiday had gone.

Now I just had Rob to deal with. He seemed to take it quite well. 'I can see why you would want to do it,' he said, and then immediately changed the subject. Great. That was all okay then.

Work continued to be relentless. Almost as soon as Stanley had come back from his holiday, Mike had gone off on his, so that I ended up doing a one-in-two rota for a fortnight. Finally, Mike and Stanley were both back and I had a whole weekend off duty. Amazingly, Rob was off duty too, and to celebrate our rare weekend of leisure, I'd invited Rob to supper at my cottage. He said he had a particularly fine bottle of Bordeaux. In between consults and call-outs I had put a lot of thought into the menu planning and how the evening would go.

On the Friday morning, a glorious crisp clear early summer morning, I headed to work with a spring in my step, and plans to use my lunch hour to run around the Ebbourne shops picking up a shoulder of lamb, some juicy tomatoes and aubergines, and a couple of delicious hunks of local cheese. With Mike and Stanley around, finding half an hour at lunchtime to do some shopping shouldn't be a problem. I saw the weekend stretching luxuriously in front of me. I could almost touch it.

At eleven o'clock, Stanley burst into my consulting room. 'I'm so sorry Anna, I'm going to need to lean on you a bit today. I've just taken a call from my aunt and she's had a bit of a fall. Probably on the gin again! Nothing serious I think, but I need to go and see her. Could you manage the rest of my appointments this morning do you think? Mike is picking up all the farm calls. The book isn't too full. I should be back to be second-on-call this evening.'

'Yes of course, Stanley, you go.'

The book wasn't too full, and if I worked into my lunch break I should be able to get through all the consults and ops. Perhaps I could find a moment to make it to the shops in the afternoon, if things weren't too busy here.

Of course, things were busy though. All afternoon I kept looking for a shopping slot but none appeared. Penny and Judith, who would happily have zoomed round to the butcher's for me (if I could bear the ribbing) were rushed off their feet too so I couldn't ask them. Lois didn't seem over-stretched but we didn't have that kind of relationship. As the afternoon wore on, I came to terms with the fact that Rob was going to have to eat some store-cupboard staple tonight. I had lentils, beans, onions and a few old tomatoes. I was sure he would understand: he was actually pretty easy to cater for just as long as there was plenty of it.

Just as I was leaving work, too late for the shops, Stanley rang through. 'Anna, I'm so sorry, I wouldn't ask if I could help it, but could you cover my second-on-call for me tonight? I'll be back in the morning but my aunt's actually in a pretty terrible state and I think she needs me to stay with her overnight.'

'Of course I will,' I said.

'I am sorry Anna. I hope you didn't have plans.'

I put the phone down. All was not lost. Most evenings the first-on-call vet managed to cope with all the work and didn't need to call on the second-on-call. But it meant I couldn't drink, in case I had to drive. And I couldn't completely relax. There's something seriously relaxing about knowing that there's no chance that the phone is going to ring and you're going to be asked to jump into action.

When I got home, I was greeted by a sight that at

other times would have made me laugh. There was Kiska, my avid little hunter, trying with all her might to drag a dead pheasant over the fence into my garden, like a miniature cheetah hauling its antelope up a tree. But, exhausted from the long week of work, and disappointed about the way my longed-for evening was turning out, I could have cried.

My biggest worry was that Rocky would get the blame for this. Remembering the gamekeeper's threat the previous week, my blood ran cold.

And yet … and yet. The phrase 'killing two birds with one stone' seemed both inappropriate and strangely apt. I had no supper for Rob, and a dead pheasant to dispose of. It would be a bit fresh for some palates, might be a little chewy but …

When it came to it, though, Rob refused to eat the pheasant: he didn't think it would be legal. So lentil and bean stew it was. As Rob chopped onions and I opened tins, I confided to him my worries about Rocky. Somehow the incident with Kiska had brought them to a head.

'I feel terrible,' I said. 'I love the handsome little bugger, I really do. But I just can't control him.'

Rocky must have sensed I was talking about him because he chose this moment to put on a demonstration of all of his most charming features. He came and nuzzled his big head against my legs, wagging his tail and looking up at me with his irresistible big brown eyes. I bent down and gave him a little kiss.

'You're so naughty Rocky, you're such a bad boy,' I told him.

And then, to Rob, 'I feel like a complete failure admitting it, but I'm just not sure I can look after this dog anymore.'

Rob had already seen how Rocky behaved around sheep. Now I filled Rob in more honestly than I had previously on Rocky's other crimes and misdemeanours: the teeth-baring, the howling, the door-chewing. The difficulty of either taking him on farm visits or leaving him at home while I went to work. 'He just isn't cut out to be a vet's dog. And the worst thing is, he runs off all the time. All the time. And kills things. I've tried really hard and I don't know what else to do, and I'm really worried that he's going to be shot if he stays here. Aren't I, Rocky? You're going to get yourself killed.'

As I had known he would – it was part of what I loved about him – Rob gave the problem serious thought. 'You don't have to give up on him yet. There are other things we can try. Have you done any training with him?'

'Yes. Loads of training,' I wailed. I explained how Rocky and I had attempted dog training, with me going under a false name out of embarrassment at being a vet who couldn't manage her own dog, and how Rocky had been by far the worst-behaved dog in the class, and how we had finally been more or less kicked out for being a disruptive influence.

I'd even gone on a dog behaviour course one weekend, as part of my Continuing Professional Development, where I had learnt that more dogs are put to sleep because of behavioural issues than die of parvo virus. That was a sobering revelation.

'Actually,' I said now to Rob, taking the deep breath of one making a shameful confession, 'I'm so desperate

I've even been thinking about getting him one of those electronic collars.' These were devices you could buy that enabled the owner to issue an electric shock to their dog. I knew most behaviourists were against them because if you pressed it accidentally when a dog was coming back to you and being good, they would get terribly confused. I hated the thought of shocking my dog at all, but Rocky had me at my wits' end. I had to control him somehow or the gamekeeper was going to take matters into his own hands.

Rob was outraged. 'No, you can't do that. Don't even think about it. I won't let you. I'll have Rocky if you're going to do that to him. Okay. You need to manage the situation. Let me think. What about Miriam Williams? She's the best dog trainer in Dorset according to my dad. We could see if she's got any suggestions. If you can just get him better on the recall, that's going to make life so much easier. Let's go for a really concerted effort with him over the next few weeks and see how that goes.'

I agreed to try Miriam Williams but I didn't hold out much hope.

Just as we were about to eat, the phone rang.

I prayed that it was a friend I could fob off, or failing that a vetting call that could wait until the next morning. A lot of times people rang in with things that could wait: a mild bout of vomiting, a cat scared of the dark (!) or even just a request to order medication. Sometimes, if I had nothing better to do, I would go out anyway, but tonight I would definitely be providing reassurance and advising the owner to 'try to get some sleep and come and see us in the morning'.

But of course it wasn't a friend, and it wasn't something that could wait. Natasha's voice informed me that Mike was doing a caesarean on a cow some distance away and this was a tom cat having difficulty peeing, with a possibly blocked bladder – a genuine emergency. Natasha was an experienced vet's wife, she could probably diagnose half the problems down the phone herself.

I took a deep breath. Okay, I thought, the stew can just simmer in the oven for a couple of hours. I can see this cat and still be back in time to rescue the evening. I rang the owner and arranged to meet him at the surgery in fifteen minutes.

I put the phone down and immediately dialled Penny. I was possibly going to need to flush the bladder, and the anaesthetic can be tricky to get right with this particular condition, so I'd be needing a nurse. Penny wasn't at home and her mobile phone went straight through to answer phone. I remembered that she and Den were going on a rare night out at a pub at the bottom of the Marshwood Vale. How sensible, I thought, to have a date somewhere with no phone signal. I wish I'd thought of that.

'Sorry Rob, grab some bread and butter to keep you going. It's nursing time.'

I filled Rob in as we drove. 'Cats – especially male neutered cats on dry diets – can get a condition called urolithiasis, where they get a sludgy kind of crystal, like sand, in their bladders. It's because they can't manage the amount of magnesium, ammonium and phosphate in their diet. Mostly it just causes inflammation and irritation to the bladder lining. They might pee blood and struggle a bit to pee, but they'll still be passing small amounts of urine. Sometimes though they get great big crystals, whole stones, or a load of sludge and inflammation that block the urethra – that's the tube that goes from the bladder and out through the penis.'

I sensed Rob tensing just a little.

'If the urethra blocks,' I hurried on, 'the cat can get kidney damage as the urine dams back up to the kidneys – and possibly a ruptured bladder. If this poor chap is blocked, and I can't manually express it, by squeezing the bladder and making him pee through the blockage, then I'm possibly going to have to sedate him, pass a catheter up the penis, drain the bladder, and flush it out.'

'Okay.' Rob had gone a little white but he was a farming lad, he was holding up.

'It's a fairly simple procedure.' I didn't have much truck with squeamishness about these things. What had to be done, had to be done.

Unfortunately when we got the tom on the table, he was completely blocked. Completely and utterly. There was no way I could pass a catheter at all. The bladder urgently needed decompressing somehow, or it could burst. I could have stuck a needle in and sucked out the 100 mls or so that was in there, just to give relief for that night. That would have been a relatively quick procedure and Rob and I could have been back in my cottage within 30 minutes. It was definitely tempting. But this cat had a long history of urethral blockage – I'd seen the poor thing several times with the same problem, though it had never been this bad before – and it needed dealing with properly. Sticking a needle in tonight could make the bladder even more fragile, and would only leave us with the same problem to deal with in the morning.

'Right, Rob.' I paused, then decided the only way was simply to say it. 'The salvage procedure in this case is to cut off the penis. We create a false stoma – a hole – at the back of the tom, so it can pee that way. Like a female.'

'Okay.' Rob shifted his weight uneasily.

'Usually I'd book the cat in for Mike to do tomorrow but I know the consults list is chocka already, and there may be some farm calls to pick up, and for all I know Stanley won't be back. I think I'm going to have to operate tonight.'

'Okay.'

'I've never done it before.'

'Okay.' Rob's face was the colour of the shiny white tiles in the operating theatre.

'You're not going to hit the decks on me, are you?' I remembered the owner of the German shepherd who had done just that the other day when I'd inserted a catheter into his dog's penis. It was a large catheter, granted, but then, we were talking about a German shepherd.

Rob swallowed hard and managed a weak smile. 'No.'

So with Rob holding the book open at the right page, and helping with the anaesthetic, and breathing hard, I removed the poor tom's penis. The operation – which

I performed that night for the first and only time in my career – seemed to be a success.

It took a good hour, and then another hour to clean up and wait for the poor little soul to come around fully. We tucked him up with a hot water bottle, litter tray and some food and water and left him for the night.

On the drive on the way back I attempted some humour. 'We should be having coq au vin, not lentil stew!' And then, 'I've got a bottle of wine that says it smells of cat's pee on a gooseberry bush. Just the thing!' I thought the supper just needed some rice and our evening could be resumed, but as we drew up to the cottage Rob claimed he wasn't hungry any more. He said a hasty goodbye and hurried home. It was unlike him but, I reflected, it had been quite an unlikely date night all round. I ate lentil and bean stew on my own, and went to bed.

CHAPTER EIGHTEEN

Cut and blow-dry

I wasn't, perhaps, ever going to be the most academically-minded vet. I might not be destined to be the most brilliant surgeon, or the most ambitious. But as I settled into working life, with my trip to Ethiopia now gleaming on the horizon like a distant exotic palace, I began to think I was developing one useful strength: I knew how to talk to people, how to read them. (Perhaps that psychology degree hadn't been a waste of time after all.) Sometimes though – like with Mr Michaels – even that went wrong.

This particular Thursday, Mr Michaels was finally coming in with his golden retriever, Muffin, for a re-check on the lump I had examined several months ago. I had first seen Muffin in February, when I'd asked Mr Michaels to come back in two weeks so I could monitor the lump, as he hadn't seemed keen on anything more invasive. It was now late June and despite several reminder phone calls from Judith, this was going to be my first re-check. In all likelihood, Mr Michaels had missed his appointments because he was a busy farmer and the lump hadn't been growing and he had better things to do, but nevertheless I was anxious to set eyes on Muffin so I could judge for myself.

Mr Michaels looked defiant as he walked in, mud clinging to his wellies. I crouched down to Muffin and felt for the lump. Even without measuring it, I could tell that it had grown to twice the size it had been in February – it had gone from walnut to large apricot. And, oh no, *all* the lymph nodes were up: it felt like ping pong balls in front of the shoulders, and there were swellings under her arms and at the backs of her knees. A feeling of dread crept in. I performed my standard work-up on Muffin, not least to give me two minutes to think. What was going on in Mr Michaels' head? He obviously doted on this dog and yet by not bringing her in he had put her life in danger. Had he not felt all these other lumps: after all, he had picked up that first one?

Work-up completed, I turned to Mr Michaels and gave him a look that I hoped would help to prepare him for the bad news that was about to come.

'Mr Michaels, I wish I had seen Muffin earlier. I am afraid the lump has grown a lot since I last saw it. And there are several more, all over her body.'

Mr Michaels looked down at his boots. 'She seemed fine,' he mumbled. 'I thought since she didn't seem ill I didn't need to come back. And anyway, like I said, I don't like operations and that.'

There was a long pause while we both took in the situation.

I had completely misread Mr Michaels back in February,

I now realised. While Muffin had been deteriorating, I had, in blissful ignorance, been assuming that all was well. I didn't know why he had kept Muffin from us – some people just had a natural, visceral fear of medical procedures – nor did I know exactly what was going through Mr Michaels' head as these thoughts went through mine. All I knew was that, whatever the reason for Mr Michaels' aversion to medical interventions, my job was to convince him that Muffin needed some diagnostics today.

'Mr Michaels,' I said gently, keeping eye contact. 'I need to sample this lump today and it would be good to take a blood sample too. I am worried it is not good news.'

Mr Michaels slumped, as though defeated. 'Okay then. You doctors always do what you want in the end.'

I had two clients waiting so I handed Muffin over to Stanley for him to take some blood and a needle aspirate from the mass, berating myself for all my failings in this case. It was possible that, because of me, poor old Muffin had been fighting cancer with no help for months. If I had seen her after two weeks, I would have spotted the increase in growth, and the additional growths, and we could have acted immediately. I suspected lymphoma, a cancer involving solid organs like the lymph nodes. 'I handled it all wrong, Stanley. I had bad instincts on this one. I think all the medical talk at that first consult scared him into not wanting to come back.'

'Anna, you didn't do anything wrong. Everyone did their best. You asked him to come back, you explained why it was important, and Judith rang him to remind him. Ultimately, we can't force people to bring their sick animals to us. You know most cases of untreated lymphoma proceed more rapidly than this – dead in two months without chemo – so maybe it was something completely unrelated on first presentation.'

Now an awful thought occurred to me.

'I'm sure I would have told him to come back, but honestly, Stanley, I can't remember doing it. What if I didn't? What if, just that time, I forgot?'

'Well, what does it say in your notes? You are generally very thorough on those notes.'

'It says "check in two weeks". But just because I wrote that down, it doesn't prove I told him that.'

Stanley screwed up his mouth and looked up at the ceiling as though thinking something through. 'Anna,' he said, 'I actually know you told him he needed to come back. And what's more I know you explained very clearly why it was important he kept the appointment. And the reason I know is that I just happened to be in the next-door consulting room during that consult, and the slats on the windows at the top of the wall there just happened to be open. And when I just happen to be in the room and the slats just happen to be open, I just happen to be able to hear everything a newly qualified vet is saying to our clients. You can be pretty entertaining at times but what was said to Mr Michaels was fine, Anna. Those notes though,' he continued, 'you're right, they are a little sketchy. You could afford to work on that.'

Stanley had written some of the sketchiest, untidiest

case notes I'd ever seen and there had been times I'd had to skirt around the issue with a returning client, asking 'how is Fifi?' in the hope of somehow winkling out the information I needed without admitting I knew nothing about the case. He gave me a wink and a hearty pat on the back, scooped up Muffin and strode off. I shook my head at him and went to call in my next patient.

Just then, I heard a plummy woman's voice rising angrily from reception. 'May I help you,' said Judith sweetly, in an attempt to defuse whatever this new situation was.

'I want to see Miss Barrington,' said the woman. 'It's about this bill.'

Dismayed, I stayed where I was, in the corridor, hidden from view to anyone in the reception area. I remembered this lady now. Her name was Marion Baxter and she had brought her cat in three weeks ago, in tears, saying that he was her only link with her dead husband, and I must do everything I could to save it. The cat had advanced kidney disease but I had treated him as aggressively as I could, as she had asked me to, and had managed to send him home with her. I had blood-tested him, put him on fluids to rehydrate him, and given several injections, and Penny had hand-fed him for two days to get him eating.

I'd had a premonition on this one, at least, and had written my case notes up especially carefully. I knew too that Judith would deal with the situation – sadly, this memory lapse about what treatments a client had insisted on in the emotional heat of the moment was something veterinary reception had to deal with too often. Still, I was surprised to hear Marion Baxter's parting shot about the 'last link' with her dearly departed husband as she stalked out. 'If I'd known it was going to cost that much,' she spat, 'I would have had it put to sleep.'

I poked my head out into reception. Judith looked at me, raised an eyebrow, and shook a despairing head. I did know how to talk to clients, but occasionally it was impossible to do the right thing.

'What's up?' asked Penny when I slumped into a chair with a piece of paper from the fax machine in my hand. It was a week later. I handed her Muffin Michaels' faxed report from the cytology lab. Penny screwed up her face. It was lymphoma. 'You could offer chemotherapy,' she tried.

'I'm not sure Mr Michaels will go for that. He wasn't too keen on biopsies or surgery before,' I replied dismally.

'Did you know his wife was the sister of my dad's sister's best friend?' asked Penny. Was Penny's family history relevant right now, I wondered. 'She died of cancer. She had ops and chemo but it was pretty quick.' Well, that explained quite a lot, I realised.

I dialled Mr Michaels' number, almost hoping he wouldn't answer.

'Anley 472.'

'Hello, Mr Michaels? It's Anna Barrington, from the vets. I am ringing with Muffin's results. You might like to sit down.' Couldn't I do better than that?

'Yes ... ' he said, giving nothing away.

314

I explained that Muffin had a cancer, one that would spread, affecting all her glands and maybe even her liver, spleen or intestines. There was an option to try to halt it with medicines but they were not guaranteed and not without side effects.

'So how long has she left if we don't use these drugs?' asked Mr Michaels, his voice still expressionless.

How I wished I could not say what had to be said. 'Well, each dog is different.' I waited. Mr Michaels was silent so I plunged on. 'On average about one to two months. But Muffin might not be average.'

We agreed to try some prednisolone to slow things down a bit and at least make her feel better. And to re-check Muffin in two weeks. I thought I heard a cough, or a sigh.

'Are you still there, Mr Michaels? Are you okay?'

'Yes. But she's not, is she?'

That afternoon, Stanley and Mike had given me a half-day to sort all the admin for my trip to Ethiopia, and I tried to put my clients and my patients out of my mind. I sorted out my visa application, then called in at the doctor's, to collect my anti-malarial medication and get my jabs. I had administered vaccinations to dogs, cats and rabbits most days for the past ten months, but I still found it best not to look at the needle going into my own arm.

Next, the painful bit over, I headed into Bridport and spent a happy afternoon locating the bits and pieces of kit that I needed, and exploring touristy gift shops, hippy alternative shops, and an array of wonderful independent book stores. Although I already had a dust-stained guidebook I had borrowed from my sister Henry, I was also beguiled by a new one, full of glossy photographs of rock-hewn churches and colourfully clad Ethiopians.

Browsing in a gift shop, I couldn't resist buying an oversized handmade mug with a heart on it for Rob, and filling it with his favourite dark truffles. In the queue, waiting to pay, I turned it around and saw that it said, 'I love you' on the back. Should I put it back? No, it was true. Crumbs, had I just had that thought? I tried saying it to myself. 'I love Rob.' Yes, that felt comfortable. It felt real. It made me smile. And giving him the mug would certainly be easier than saying it.

Next, I'd been tasked by Lena with buying half a dozen rubber sealing rings for the lids of pressure cookers. My first happy thought when I had received this request was that catering was obviously a top priority. Alas, though, the pressure cooker was the veterinary autoclave – the device we would be using to sterilise our equipment.

My final purchase had nothing to do with Ethiopia. Cauli, my ever-reliable odd-job man, had been painting the bathroom in my cottage and needed two more pots of a particularly vibrant primrose yellow mix I had chosen to finish the job.

All tasks executed, I bought a locally made ice cream and found a sunny spot on a wooden bench on the main street. Feeling like a proper tourist, I drank in the views of the rolling hills and marvelled at the width of this magnificent high street. I sighed contentedly. I could have sat on that sunny bench all day but instead I hauled myself up, knowing I would thank myself later. I still had a spare couple of hours before I was due at Rob's (he was going to cook me dinner for a change), so I took myself off to Bridport's lovely light swimming pool. Large animal work kept me fairly fit but I still felt the need for regular aerobic exercise to really blow the cobwebs away. When confined to small animal duties for too long, as I had been for the last week or two, I started to feel almost itchy in my own skin. I dashed off 50 lengths then headed off to deliver the tins of paint to Cauli, feeling like I had earned supper and a rest.

Arriving back at my cottage, though, I caught sight of the back of the Land Rover and immediately saw that both supper and a rest would have to be postponed. The lid on one of the paint pots must have not been quite on properly after mixing, and I had possibly taken the roundabout coming out of Bridport a little fast. Now that I thought about it I recalled a muffled clanking sound as I had taken a bit of a racing line around its empty lanes. My beautiful yellow paint had slopped everywhere and was brightening up my boot well, my foot box and my calving gown, and forming an inch-thick primrose carpet on the floor of the boot. After pointing out what an idiot I was, Cauli fetched a hose and I spent an hour returning everything to its former, paint-free, glory.

Finally I was done with all my chores. I drove over to Rob's little house, collapsed back onto his battered sofa and put my feet up while Rob opened a bottle of wine and pottered about making supper.

'I've had such a lovely afternoon getting ready for my trip,' I announced, taking a glass of wine.

'Oh, good,' said Rob. 'I've been on the reserve, same as always.'

Was that a cutting remark, or just a remark, I thought to myself. But Rob didn't go in for cutting remarks so I decided it was simply a statement of fact and asked him what had been going on at the reserve that week.

'Nothing out of the ordinary,' said Rob, and he talked me through the events of his week: moving the cattle from one part of the reserve to another; rounding up the sheep for shearing; preparing barns and machinery for the future grass-cutting and baling; repairing a fence; and leading an orchid walk for the education centre.

He seemed a little low so rather than depress him further with the too-large lumps that had actually made up my day, I decided to regale him with our latest crop of funny stories.

'It's been crazy at the surgery,' I offered. 'I can't remember a week quite like it.'

It was true.

The main event of the week had been the poor old husky, Tess, whom I had had to put to sleep after her long fight with a suspected gastro-intestinal cancer. (I admit this doesn't sound like a promising opening to a 'funny story'. Bear with me.) She had had amazingly piercing blue eyes and a gorgeous thick white coat flecked with pale grey. The owners were a lovely couple – he a GP, she a solicitor – who had taken early retirement from their London careers to come to Dorset. According to Judith, the fount of all local knowledge, they had holidayed on the Dorset coast with their young family in the 1970s and had harboured ambitions to retire there ever since.

The owners, Dr and Mrs Dorrington, were beside themselves at the death of their faithful family pet, and hadn't been able to decide what they wanted to do with her body. There were phone calls being made to their grown-up children about funeral arrangements, and evidently each child had a different opinion about what should be done. Finally the husband suggested that she could donate her body to science: I could post-mortem her. I suppose he was a doctor himself and recognised how helpful that could be to a new vet.

So that afternoon I slit this beautiful dog from just under her chin right down to her pelvic brim and had a really good look. It couldn't hurt her now, and it would help the dogs who came after her. Just as I was having a good rummage around, Penny put her head round the door, took one look at the table and whispered, 'Ohhhhh … crap … ' Apparently, Mrs Dorrington had just rung. She had changed her mind, and wanted Tess back to bury in the garden with full funeral rites. Tess was not looking her best at this point. Her guts were out and her white fur was comprehensively covered in blood and other internal gunk. Penny and I spent the afternoon putting Tess back together, stitching her up, then shampooing and lovingly taking the hairdryer to her. Ten minutes after we'd finished,

Lois came in looking very sheepish. She thought maybe she'd got her wires crossed with Penny earlier, sorry. The owners definitely didn't want Tess back.

Normally Rob's sense of humour was as dark as mine. He should have loved this story. But not tonight, although I thought I was being very entertaining.

I tried again.

'Something else really funny happened on Monday.'

Two huge chaps from the local council estate, father and son, had walked in with their German shepherd and looked at me shiftily. After a pause, while I smiled encouragingly, the son said, 'he's got a lump on his tail.' So I set about examining the dog's tail really closely, but I couldn't find anything. Up and down and up and down I went, quite a few times. Eventually I said, 'sorry, I can't find anything on his tail at all.'

The son coughed, blushed bright red, and said, 'his other tail.'

I thought for a moment. Dogs do only have one tail each. Then the penny dropped. They meant his penis – more specifically, an organ called the bulbus glandis, which is a circular bobble at the body end of the penis that expands during erection, but can be quite large even when quiescent. I explained that its presence was normal and nothing to worry about, though since they were here I would check it out to make absolutely sure. 'Bet you didn't want to see the lady vet today!' I had remarked good-naturedly as they made a swift and sheepish exit.

Rob just smiled weakly. Perhaps he wasn't in a chatty

mood. I picked my guidebooks up again, thinking I would sit and read quietly and leave him to whatever thoughts were on his mind. Soon though I forgot my vow of silence and was enthusiastically reading whole chunks out loud to Rob.

'Listen to this: "Ethiopia has a culture dating back over 3000 years, what we know as Abyssinia."

'Wow. You know "Lucy" – the oldest hominid bones ever discovered – well – they were found in Ethiopia.

'"There is a varied landscape from mountains to desert, savannah to lakes." How am I going to fit in "the burning furnace of the Danakil Depression, the mountain monastery of the Tigray region and the awesome splendour of the Blue Nile Falls" *and* a spot of vaccination and neutering all in three weeks?

'Rob – have you heard of Lalibela?'

'No – what is it? Some kind of funny dog disease that you vets like to laugh about?'

'No. It's amazing, I hadn't heard of it either. Look, here in the guidebook, look at these photos. These churches are literally carved out of the rock, some several stories high, either hidden below ground level or in opened quarried caves. Isn't it incredible? It's the eighth wonder of the world, apparently.'

Rob stopped washing the salad leaves, dried his hands on his trousers, and came over to where I was sitting. He looked over my shoulder at the photos in my book.

'Yup,' he said, walking away. 'It's pretty incredible.'

He went back to washing his salad leaves and, with his back to me, continued, 'Have you taken a look at what's around you, Anna? That's pretty amazing too.'

'I know,' I said. 'I love it too. I really do. But it's exciting to be going exploring.' Rob turned to face me now.

'It's great that you want to go exploring, I get that. But isn't there enough to explore here? I've lived here most of my life and I'm still finding new things.'

'It's just something different and exotic and something I'll probably never get the opportunity to do again.'

'Mmmm.' He shrugged. 'I suppose I just don't really get it. I'm happy here.'

'I'm happy here too. That's not the point. I can be happy here and still want to see other places.'

'Good. That's great then. I'll just stay here on my reserve in Dorset, and you go off to Africa and explore.' He picked up the salad bowl. 'Supper's ready.'

Over supper, the conversation didn't flow as easily as usual. Trying to keep off Ethiopia and the black humour of the surgery, I tried his territory, boasting to Rob about how much better I was becoming at recognising the local flora and fauna. He seemed distracted and unimpressed. In fact, he seemed more interested in feeding a delighted Soots titbits from his dinner, and petting her, and telling her what a good girl she was, than in anything I had to say.

As Rob finished his meal, he pushed his chair back from the table and ran his hand through his thick hair. 'I've got a long day on the reserve tomorrow,' he said. 'Maybe you should head off. And you know, that poor dog, Tess. Maybe you need to pay a bit more attention to people's feelings sometimes.'

I was speechless. We both always had long days, but that had never before interfered with our long evenings. Rob knew, too, that I cared deeply about my patients – surely he knew that? I'd obviously post-mortemed Tess with the best of intentions. And how could he not see the funny side of me spending an afternoon blow-drying a completely dead dog?

I picked up my things. I was heading out in two weeks: maybe a break would do us good.

When I got back to the cottage I unpacked all my bags. Right at the bottom I found the mug and truffles. I'd completely forgotten to give them to Rob, and now I wasn't sure he deserved them. I made myself a big cup of hot chocolate and scoffed all the truffles myself.

CHAPTER NINETEEN

Somewhere over the rainbow

'Mmmm, this smells familiar.'

Lena and I were sitting, exhausted and exhilarated, in front of a camp fire on an Ethiopian mountain plateau. We had spent the day climbing in our pick-up truck to 4,000 metres above sea level and then neutering several of the potentially vicious semi-feral homestead dogs of the local settlement, using the fold-down part of the truck as an operating table. Now the local project workers and guides had roasted a goat by torchlight, and as the honoured 'doctors' we had been offered the most highly-prized parts of the meat, which was a half-cooked testicle each.

It was one week into my Ethiopian adventure, but so much had happened it felt like one month. And to think that it had crossed my mind not to come. The small-scale conflict on Ethiopia's north-eastern border had nearly been the final 'anti' as I continued to weigh up the pros and cons right up until the last moment. As a responsible tourist I had consulted the Foreign and Commonwealth London

Office for travel advice and had received a worrying fax:

'The Ethiopia/Eritrea land border is closed due to military action. Do not travel near or attempt to cross the border.' There had then been a description of a recent aircraft attack in this area and *'Fuel supplies are erratic throughout the country. Ensure you have enough fuel to return to your point of origin before setting out. Travelling with another vehicle is recommended. All Ethiopian Airlines flights from Addis Ababa to Asmara have been suspended. Heavy rains have started and will continue until September. Travel to Lalibela and other outlying areas by road will be impracticable during this season. Do not travel after dark in rural areas.'* It went on.

I knew we would be travelling widely and in rural areas. Long distances, too, and possibly alone. And Lalibela was on the itinerary. But Lena had been there some time now and had local help and insight. Should I err on the side of caution or curiosity?

With gung-ho bravado and some butterflies in my stomach, I had failed to consult my parents, or Rob, or Mike and Stanley on the matter. Instead I crossed my fingers and packed the usual travel clothes plus the pressure cooker rubber rings, a pair of walking boots, several cereal bars, a strip of water chlorinating tablets (just in case), multiple pairs of knickers (just in case) and a copy of *Fugitive Pieces* (had been meaning to read that for ages).

The journey was complicated. On the last leg, the plane emptied and we proceeded to Addis Ababa with only a quarter of the seats full. A little ominous, I thought but at last I had some leg room.

We touched down in Addis Ababa, Ethiopia, Horn of Africa and taxied to a small-scale airport building. On disembarking I grinned inwardly at the signs directing our exit: 'Ethiopians; Aliens; Diplomats' and went to stand with a handful of other extraterrestrials. The wait was not too onerous, and customs largely disinterested, so soon I was striding out into a surprisingly fresh climate to meet a man called Solomon.

Lena had helpfully arranged for this friend of hers to meet me. He lived on the outskirts of the capital city with his wife. A short, slight, closely-cropped, very smiley black man who looked to be in his late twenties was calling my name. We got into a dusty maroon hatchback and drove to his home, weaving through pedestrians, as he cheerfully explained that he was actually Eritrean, and it was becoming quite difficult for him.

'I am one of the few remaining Eritreans in the city, the rest having been taken away or fled. My aunt left last week. Luckily I have some helpful political connections looking out for me at the moment.' Perhaps I should have been less relaxed in the knowledge that I was to be staying under his roof, but he was so disarming and charming I was not concerned. We arrived at his home, a brick-built three-bedroomed house complete with a wet room which seemed rather a luxury to me, even by European standards. (I soon discovered though that running water was sporadic and definitely a luxury.) Like most middle- to high-income city dwellings the house was surrounded by a high wall and guarded by a man who stayed in the compound all night.

I had the following day to acclimatise and sort out travel arrangements to Bale, the mountainous region to the south of the capital where I was to join Lena. In fact the weather was not so different from back home: my summer wardrobe would do fine. I thought of what Rob would be wearing right now: his green combat trousers and a faded flannel check shirt, no doubt. The thought of him made me smile as I picked out my own outfit for the day ahead.

Clad in some simple khaki trousers and a white cotton shirt, I set off for the airport with Solomon to book my tickets for my local flight. The plan had been to fly to the region using Ethiopian Airlines, but as it turned out, I was not to experience their service just yet as fuel was in short supply having been stockpiled for the dispute with Eritrea.

Instead, we looked into booking a bus trip to Dinsho, the small town where Lena was based. On the way to the bus station, we drove through the mercato, a huge market. It was almost a town in its own right with blocks of stalls or undercover shops mostly sheltered by corrugated tin roofs. It was enormously dusty and alive with people everywhere: milling around the stalls, on the road, even sleeping on the central reservation. This included young children and beggars and a disturbing number of amputees. And donkeys. I caught sight of earthenware pots, colourful umbrellas and fabrics, tin lamps, wooden furniture, baskets and shields and then enjoyed the visual and olfactory bombardment from the fabulous fruit, veg and spices on display. I promised myself this would be revisited on my return to the capital. I wanted to buy Rob a souvenir.

Buying the ticket for my journey was an interesting process: the trip was discussed, at length. Solomon was my interpreter, speaking in Amharic, Ethiopia's language of administration. After much debate my ticket was ordered and after more gazing at this foreigner, or 'fereng', I was sent to a different office to pay.

Lunch was an introduction to 'injera' and 'wat'. The former was a shared dish that looked like a pile of thin chapattis, and was made from a fermented grain called teff that my guidebook disparagingly told me was fed by most other nations to their animals. This staple, which on investigation tasted both sharp and sour, was then decorated with servings of wat, a stew-like and very spicy dish. When I exclaimed at its intense heat, Solomon told me that wat was in fact flavoured with nutmeg, cardamom, ginger, coriander and fennel as well as chilli peppers, garlic and onion. Although at some later meals I managed to make out the more delicate flavourings, on this occasion I had to take his word for it, as they were overwhelmed by fire.

The next morning I set off on a stifling ten and a half hour journey, on an old bus with firm, upright seats of worn and faded red striped fabric. After two hours the firmness was just hardness. I was not allowed to open any windows as my fellow passengers did not like the draught or the dust. Fortunately we had several stops where one could purchase coffee and food (injera and wat) from local stalls. On one such stop there was much wailing and angst in the marketplace where a large set of scales had been set up and was being supervised by several men with guns slung around their shoulders. I had noticed that there were more and more weapons on display the further from Addis we travelled. Young boys stepped up onto one end of the scales and if over a certain weight were then apparently recruited for the army and the current border conflict. The shrieks from the womenfolk when the scale ends containing their sons tipped downwards were utterly heart-wrenching. I was glad to get back on that airless bus.

The road became a dirt track as we headed into foothills. The valleys and hillsides were mostly farmed and there were oxen in the fields pulling ploughs of single ploughshares with men following dressed in white. Rather biblical, I thought. And how did they keep their clothes so white? I found farm work messy enough in a full set of overalls.

The track was badly potholed and we were so shaken in our seats that we hardly touched down on the striped red fabric. My teeth chattered with the bumping; reading was not possible. After six hours we were climbing higher and navigating barrier-free hairpin bends. Outside, people walked under black umbrellas sheltering them from the sun. The settlements were more of the mud hut variety now. As the hills became steeper the villages spread out and flowers were evident – it was the rainy season and there were red hot pokers radiating their colour everywhere. There was a wild sort of lobelia and sagebrush and juniper trees lining the road. Rob would have loved these plants: he would have brought a botanical library with him to help identify them all. I hugged myself tightly as I thought of him – partly with pleasure, and partly to stop my innards from bouncing any more.

Finally, with dusk falling, we arrived in Dinsho. The whole village seemed to be there to greet the bus. Being the only white traveller I was obviously of interest, particularly to the children. So many smiling, welcoming faces. It was great to see Lena, if not a little strange, as the last time we had been together was at our graduation, in a marquee in a manicured English garden. Now the smell of thyme was overwhelming as Lena led me to the lodge, her current base, where we were to spend the night. There was no running water but plenty of coffee I noted. (Coffee originates from Ethiopia so that was hardly surprising.)

The lodge was a one-room log cabin currently inhabited by Lena and her boss, Susan (at that time vaccinating dogs in the field further north) who had funding from the Wellcome Trust to help with the University of Oxford's Ethiopian Wolf Conservation Programme. They were vaccinating the local semi-domesticated farmstead dogs to prevent them spreading rabies and distemper to the native wolf population, and neutering them to prevent over-population and cross-breeding with the wolves. Sounds straightforward, but the logistics of this in Africa, at altitude, often with no drivable tracks and in the rainy season, was not so easy. Fortunately the lovely Lena had a Zen-like aura, a quiet determination, and a love for the African people and wildlife. She had been meticulously planning our trip into the higher mountains and we spent the evening sitting on the veranda discussing working protocols, exchanging news in the ring of light thrown by our gas lamps, and watching a comical family of visiting warthogs and the endemic nyala antelopes with their beautiful big eyes and long twisting horns.

Inevitably, Lena wanted to quiz me closely about Rob, and in that relaxed, exotic, peaceful atmosphere I found the words came easily.

'Okay, so tell me about this Rob?' demanded Lena as one particularly graceful nyala came a little closer.

'He's the Deputy Warden on a local wildlife reserve where they use cattle and sheep to graze the pastures. We met over a sick cow.' The nyala ventured a little closer.

Lena smiled and raised her eyebrows at me. She wanted to know more than that.

'He's a farmer's son, he has a degree in geography, he's passionate about ecology. He has a very cute dog. He loves Dorset.'

Lena nodded approvingly.

'You'd like him.'

'I probably would. We could certainly do with some passion about ecology out here. Tall?'

'Yes. And very handsome.' I laughed at myself.

'Well,' said Lena, 'I've never heard you so positive about a boyfriend before.'

I grinned. We went back to watching the local wildlife. No, I thought, I've never felt so positive about a boyfriend before either.

*

The following day was spent meeting the group of local project assistants, including a delightful and ever-helpful young man called Abiott, who was to gather and pack our provisions before accompanying us into the mountains. These included a coffin-sized tin trunk absolutely full of food – rice, dried beans, chickpeas, oats and milk powder.

We set off early the next morning, a cool, misty affair with the mountains shrouded until late morning and everything touched with a light but constant drizzle. My hair hung in damp ringlets, more curly even than usual, and my clothes stuck to my skin impeding every movement. As we climbed we drove through barren moonscapes, escarpments peppered with scrub and red hot poker plants. The dusty tracks had become slippery with the drizzle and we bounced and slid our way to the Northern plateau of the Bale Mountains National Park, 4,000 metres above sea level. The mist lifted, or maybe the clouds had just passed over, I could not tell, and the trees and scrub of the lowland had been replaced by heather moorland. Lena calmly slowed the pick-up to point out a very smart-looking and very leggy chestnut-red creature with a white bib and legs and a long nose, standing motionless and concentrating on the ground some fifty feet away.

'Your first Ethiopian wolf. It's probably hunting; waiting at a burrow for a tasty rodent. If it gets a giant molerat it can take the rest of the day off – they weigh up to a kilo!'

That was the weight of the average guinea pig. Unless it was Amelia's guinea pig. Bubbles had recently tipped the scales at 1.6kg and been put on a strict diet and no more

Jaffa cakes. Having a yummy orange-flavoured topping had not been a good reason to continue feeding them to him, I had remonstrated just last week with Tamara.

After two more exciting sightings of the fantastically leggy wolf, we arrived at our camp. Set on a large, flat grassy area, reminiscent of an alpine meadow, on the edge of an escarpment, it had an immense view. There in the middle of the closely cropped grass was a tukul, a mud hut, with one of the best vistas ever. I gazed across a high-altitude plateau carved up by a gorge, jutting volcanic peaks at odd angles, lakes sparkling in the distance and uneven rugged ridges further still. Wow, what a temporary home this would be. I couldn't wait to tell Rob about it.

After ten months of honing my new veterinary skills in a reasonably well-equipped, slightly sleepy rural western practice, I was now going to spend ten days doing similar procedures but with very different pets, owners and supplies.

That first day we set up shop in a small mountain village made up of mud huts. The semi-domesticated dogs that were each associated with a farmstead were not pets as we know them. They were loosely owned by a villager or herdsman and his family and would often be fed scraps and attention but would largely fend for themselves. We still needed permission to catch and vaccinate or neuter these dogs so interpreters had spent weeks talking to and educating their owners before we had arrived. Permission granted, there was no chance for a full pre-injection check-up.

Idris, one of the more expert local project workers, was to snare my first patient for me, using the standard equipment: a long metal pole with a steel band at one end that could be drawn tight from the other end. Idris enticed the wiry-coated black dog, somewhat larger than a spaniel, with a lump of goat's meat. As soon as he came within range of the end of his pole, Idris snared his neck in the steel band, lightning fast, and pulled the band tight. Next he held the dog's head down while the semi-feral beast, crazed with anger and fear, did back flips and tried to bite Idris, me, anyone who came near. Rabies is an issue in Africa so we did not want to get bitten. I jabbed the largest bit of moving muscle I could see, on the back leg nearest to me, and jumped away, my heart racing. Idris loosened the collar and the dog raced round in angry circles before disappearing up the mountain path.

My second reluctant patient – and all my patients that morning and every morning – reacted in the same way. Anger, fear, backflips, biting. Every time my heart raced, every time I felt that surge of adrenalin. Often something about a dog – its breed, its colour, or just the look in its eye – would remind me of Rocky. I would try to calculate what time it was in England and what he might be doing. Mostly I imagined him curled up in Rob's living room with Soots, the lucky boy.

There was always a sense of relief after the dog was safely released, and the owners clearly felt it too. So the sociable aspect came after. It was like James Herriot in Africa, as we were asked into house after house to share food and hospitality. Only the houses were sparse mud huts and the sustenance often soured smoked milk mixed with ghee and passed around a circle to share from one cow horn.

After a few days we had vaccinated as many dogs as we could catch in two small mountain villages and were feeling confident enough to try some surgery. There was however no sanitised steel table, no operating light and no quietly calming Penny at the end of an anaesthetic tube. The pull-down back flap of the pick-up truck's rear carrier was the operating table and Kassim, an elder from the village, was our nurse (promoted from dog-catching) whom I was to train whilst Lena got her hands on, and in, the bitch to spay her. I was painfully aware that the local people were trusting us with this new project and losing a dog under anaesthetic would not build their confidence. I was not used to administering a general anaesthetic purely with injectable top-ups to keep the animal asleep. Back in Dorset if I needed to extend anaesthesia beyond the initial few minutes that the first injection gave, the animal would be intubated. I did not top the first spay candidate up quite quickly enough and the poor thing became very light, giving an unhappy Lena a moving target. It was not just the midday Ethiopian sun at altitude that made me sweat!

And so it was that one week into my trip we had returned to our camp high in the Bale Mountains, exhausted but exhilarated, filthy and flea-bitten. And always hungry. It was not so easy to snack in Ethiopia – there were no quick fortifying cereal bars and bananas were apparently difficult to get. Whilst up in the mountains we had a camp cook, which was good. However after only four days we had run out of food, which was bad. The end result was that with several days' work remaining we had only some rice and dried beans left. So Lena had sent Abiott and his cousin to a local village to purchase a goat. This was duly slaughtered, the goat receiving a halal death as there were several Muslims in our party. There was much chanting and ritual. It gets dark quite early and suddenly – always between 6 and 7 in the evening, and always almost instantaneous – so our supper was finally butchered in the twilight. I felt like some treacherous accomplice as my head-torch was borrowed to help finish the process, but less so once the mouth-watering smells of roasting goat wafted our way.

That night, we huddled around the campfire (it got very cold at night high in the mountains) and as the honoured 'doctors' we were offered those highly-prized, half-cooked spheres of loveliness: the goat's testicles. After a little more cooking they were actually welcome sweetmeats. There was much merriment and enchanting African singing that night before I happily but wearily made my way to my freezing cold tent. My head-torch had, it seemed, been loaned for the entire night, so as I gazed again at the amazing stars I slipped on the dead goat's intestines.

As I climbed into my sleeping bag, with a sharp pang, I suddenly missed my two boys. My last thought as I fell asleep was that I had forgotten to tell Rob that Rocky always had a Bonio dog biscuit at bedtime.

*

I awoke at 5 a.m. to more Muslim prayers and a slightly dodgy tummy. I snuck out of the tent into the undergrowth and discovered en route that what I had slipped on the night before was in fact multiple coils of tapeworm – from inside the goat's intestines. My slightly dodgy tummy became a decidedly dodgy one.

Our final castration was carried out one morning ten days later, in a clearing in a village of mud huts, in the relentless drizzle. The dog's owner was an elderly lady with a wide, toothless smile that disappeared after we injected her dog with the anaesthetic mix and within minutes it fell motionless to the ground. She was obviously petrified that we had killed her dog and sat wringing her hands and using her ear picker distractedly. These are ornamental implements worn around the neck by many Ethiopians, usually in silver with one decorated end and one small spoon-like end for gouging out earwax. I tried not to be distracted by the old lady's ablutions and tried not to panic when the dog's pulse dropped to a rather low rate. Modern anaesthesia is pretty safe but no anaesthetic is without its risks and this field setting rather ramped up the risk a bit.

Thankfully, the castration was completed quickly and efficiently. Compared to neutering a bitch it's relatively straightforward. I reversed the anaesthetic with another injection and the dog started to wake up. It was a rather rough recovery; I'm sure it was seeing psychedelic dogs, or pink trees. It was too wild to comfort and I worried for the ligatures and stitches as it threw itself about in its tripping state. The toothless old lady started laughing hysterically – probably with relief. I wanted to do the same.

Early the next morning we decamped and headed back to the lodge in Dinsho, through sticky mud and down steep slopes with minimal tread on the pick-up's tyres. People appeared from everywhere to help us unload, the cutest of children with bare feet and ringlets helping us carry our equipment into the building that was the clinic. Then we enjoyed a last night at the lodge where we entertained some of Lena's local friends, including a delightful statuesque woman for whom Lena had helped fund a trip to the dentist in Goba and a petite, quiet woman whose teenage daughter Lena had driven to the hospital after she had spent five excruciating days in labour. The baby had been dead long before they reached the hospital; the daughter had died a few hours later. Lena was starting to question whether she could ever return to veterinary practice in the west where people regularly spent more money on their pets' health than any of these people could dream of spending on themselves or their children.

The following morning we were overwhelmed with the generosity of people giving us leaving presents; people whom I had only known for one week. We received lumps of carefully wrapped frankincense, local dried thyme from Abiott and a handmade wooden cross on a piece of leather. Lena and I said fond farewells before climbing into the now-lighter pick-up and setting off towards Addis Ababa.

It was another long journey with our one and only tape playing over and over again on a loop: half westernised African songs, half familiar slushy lyrics that had me dreaming of Rob thousands of miles away, and thinking how much he would enjoy this leg of the trip, a tour for the naturalists that took in wildlife and geology in abundance. That night was spent in the luxury of a hotel with running water, beer and – best of all – pizza. I hadn't appreciated that there had been 40,000 occupying Italians in Ethiopia by 1940, with a plan to introduce a further two million, until the British helped the Ethiopians defeat them. I was glad Italian cuisine had become embedded before that moment!

Lena stayed in Addis Ababa to write up her project whilst I embarked on Ethiopia's northern tourist circuit. I flew to Lalibela, a UNESCO World Heritage Site where I marvelled at 'the eighth wonder of the world', eleven rock-hewn churches excavated from the very ground in the 12th and 13th centuries. It was even more incredible in the flesh than in the picture I'd shown to Rob. Later, I set off on a four-hour hike to a mountain monastery – again a church completely hewn out of the mountainside. It was amazing, but my residing memories are watching three tiny children playing very happily with a homemade doll of sticks and rags and having coffee with some local people – one of whom, a young man wearing a poorly fitting pair of 'Diesel' jeans, told me that the previous year his father and six other family members had died after a rabid dog bit them. If I needed it, this was a reminder that the disease control programmes really were necessary.

I flew onwards to Gondar, once the Ethiopian capital, home to emperors who entertained in their castles complete with banqueting halls and battlements, where Lena rejoined me, and then again to Bahar Dar for a hippo-spotting trip on the vast and glittering Lake Tana. This was the very source of the Blue Nile and we planned to trek to it. We left early, with a guide, hiking through verdant landscapes, turning to lush rainforest the closer we came to the din and spray of the waterfall: the Blue Nile Falls. Here the lake pours out over the edge of an ancient lava flow, some 45m high and 400m wide. Being the rainy season the water was brown and we stood giggling like schoolgirls as we turned into chocolate figures bathed in the spray of the thundering waters. We quickly stopped laughing when we and our guide were marched away at gunpoint by a rather fierce and unhappy looking man in tattered camouflage gear. I remembered a dear fellow student who had been shot whilst travelling in China and tried to keep calm.

It turned out to be a dispute between rival tribes about who had the rights to guide tourists to the Falls. We were glad to be set free and released our tension over a boozy lunch. This was now a proper holiday as I spent an afternoon in the warm breeze in the gardens curled up with my book. My fellow travellers stayed up until 1 a.m. watching a nail-biting England vs Argentina football match in the bar, while I wrote another letter to Rob (who was probably watching the penalty shoot-out back home). I had rarely written letters home when travelling before this trip, but here I had found myself constantly describing the landscapes to Rob. I needed to tell him I loved him. While we'd patched up the coolness from that awkward evening before I'd left, and he had happily taken on Rocky for me, he had been a bit more taciturn than I was used to of late, and I wanted to be sure everything was okay. He was too special a man for me to lose.

Two days later, back in Addis, I said sad goodbyes to Lena as she headed back to Dinsho, then went shopping, spending my very last birr on presents and souvenirs. I bought Rob a fine pair of silver cufflinks with an embossed horned goat motif and a wonderfully soft cotton cloak with a Coptic cross embroidered on the back, which would make a great dressing gown. I bought myself an ornate silver ear picker. When in Rome ...

On my flight home I picked through my impressions and memories of a land full of contrast – such varied geography from high damp plateaus to low arid savannah; different religions, architecture and cultures. It was an astonishing country full of beautiful people. I had been rather dazzled by it all – the poverty, the generosity of spirit, the colours, smells, sounds and unforgettable tastes! But as I made my way back across the skies my thoughts wandered back to Rob, and Ebbourne – the place I was starting to think of as home.

Rob and Rocky came to meet me at the airport. Rob was standing amongst the crowd gathered at the arrivals gate. It was easy to spot his blond head, taller than most. He must have come straight from work: still in his army surplus green trousers and a faded checked shirt, just as

I had been imagining him, and with that wide, familiar, heart-stopping smile on his lightly tanned face. I could smell the deep earthiness of woodland as I buried my nose in his collar. Tears prickled my eyes.

In the car park, Rocky had never been so vocal to see me. 'I missed you too,' I crooned, as I hugged him close. We drove back to my cottage, chattering away. I opened the door, and smelt the sweet coconut-y smell of gorse in flower. Rob had hung gorse everywhere – from the lampshades, in the bathroom, the kitchen, the bedroom. The whole cottage was yellow. It was heavenly.

'I did a lot of thinking while you were away,' said Rob, as he put the kettle on.

I'd been doing a lot of thinking too. I'd thought about Rob the whole time I'd been away.

'Me too,' I said lightly.

I held my breath, crouched on the floor with Rocky. Had he been thinking what I'd been thinking?

'You know I think you're amazing, Anna. All that energy, adventure, get up and go.'

He turned to face me. I stood up, smiled. Then I stopped smiling. This pause was going on for far too long. I scanned Rob's face for clues. Rocky licked his bottom.

'Well, I've got get up and go, too. I'm not going to be a warden of a nature reserve forever, Anna. I've got a new job. I'm moving to Somerset.'

CHAPTER TWENTY

Moving on

It was difficult to see Rob in the couple of weeks we had between me coming back from Ethiopia and him leaving for Taunton: I was working non-stop, on call or second call three weekends in a row as penance for my Ethiopia jaunt, and he was busy finishing off on the reserve and finding a new place to live and packing up, and then moving and unpacking. We barely saw each other and had to manage on long nightly phone calls.

I felt bereft and empty. The vetting expanded again, to fill the void that Rob had left. I got through my backlog of *Veterinary Records*. I had to step out of my bubble and go back to spaying, castrating, and squeezing anal glands. (Oh yes, Mum, it's such a glamorous job.)

'Penny, come and look at these.' I was hunched over the microscope and the smell of X-ray developer and cat's pee was all-pervasive, like a bad sauvignon blanc. No wonder

I preferred red wine. 'They're almost beautiful. And there are lots of them.'

Penny squinted down the microscope. 'That would explain why poor Monty's having difficulty peeing,' she said. We were examining a urine sample from a young cat that had been struggling to wee, and it was full of coffin-shaped crystals. It was that all-too-common scenario in cats, unfortunately.

'We'll sedate, X-ray and flush the bladder to make sure there are no stones. Can you prep him for me, Penny?' As we headed downstairs, we passed Judith coming up.

'Girls, it's not great news about Muffin, I'm afraid. Mr Michaels has just rung to say she doesn't want to get out of bed today and hasn't eaten for two days. He thinks the time has come. He'd like a home visit.'

For a couple of seconds nobody said a word, nobody moved. I broke the silence. 'Could you ring him please, Judith, and say we are just operating but we'll be with him in about an hour.'

Penny and I left the practice just before midday, syringes prepared, emotions in check. There was no conversation on the way there. Mr Michaels opened his front door and gestured wordlessly for us to come in. In the warm kitchen with its flagstone floor, in front of the Aga on a thick tartan dog bed, lay Muffin. Mr Michaels lowered himself into a rocking chair in the corner of the room while I examined my patient. Muffin looked up but did not raise her head. I saw that her collar had been removed and it now looked like she had mumps, with egg-sized swellings below her jaw, in front of her shoulder, behind her knees, everywhere. I tried to read what she might be feeling but her dark brown eyes gave nothing away. With my stethoscope in my ears I could still hear the gentle rhythmical sound of wood on stone as Mr Michaels rocked himself. I went into autopilot and explained the procedure to Mr Michaels, got a signature and quietly asked what he wanted to do with Muffin's body. 'I've already dug the hole, my dear. Beside the cat she used to chase. Puss always outwitted her. Now Muff's finally going to catch her.' He continued to rock backwards and forwards.

There can't be many more peaceful ways to go, I reflected, as I withdrew the needle from Muffin's vein and she took one last big sigh. She had felt nothing, been aware of nothing. And now there was nothing but the sound of wood on stone. Penny packed the medical kit away. Mr Michaels did not want any more help. We crept out of the cosy kitchen leaving an old man rocking with his thoughts, and his dog seemingly fast asleep.

The very first Friday evening I wasn't on call, I drove the one and a half hours from West Dorset to Somerset as soon as I finished work.

Rocky came with me and was, as usual, a super driving companion, sitting up like a passenger beside me for most of the journey and then lying his big head on my lap when he got weary. It ought to have been a pleasant drive, with no major roads until Taunton – just lots of twisty, turny country roads with the views changing slowly from the rolling fields of West Dorset to the higher, more dramatic hills of the Quantocks, with those starkly vivid patches of rape interrupting the gentle native greens. But the incessant rain meant I had to concentrate more on my driving and less on the landscape.

The journey took longer than I'd expected – I took a couple of wrong turns (characteristically, Rob had found a tiny, remote hamlet to live in); I had to curb my speed a bit because of the water on the roads; and getting through Taunton, jam-packed full of grumpy people in cars, all wondering where the summer had gone, was a nightmare.

My thoughts wandered as I drove. It occurred to me that West Dorset really did feel like home to me now. It had been good to get away, good to have an adventure, but it was true that there was no place like home: and West Dorset was, now, most definitely my home. I had lived there almost a year – which was a long time for me, certainly long enough for me to put down roots. I had a wonderful, funny, supportive set of colleagues (plus Lois, whose negativity I had learnt to accept and ignore). And my Ethiopia trip had brought home to me too how much I really had learnt during my first year in practice. It was partly being with Lena and realising that I did have things I could impart to her. But even more striking was returning to the surgery and feeling how much more competent and confident I was, walking in now, than on that first day.

Finally, I pulled up at Rob's new address. Nice spot, I thought, as I drove into the gravelled courtyard and parked outside a country pile with a majestic but slightly ruined, 'once-was-great' air about it. It was built out of the local Quantock stone, a lightish sandstone, and set about with pillars and climbing flowers that were soaking up the still-lashing rain. Hovering at the foot of the Quantocks, it belonged to a local country set family, who had converted part of their family pile into apartments that they let out – I guessed to cover inheritance tax and upkeep on this fabulous and probably Grade 1 listed property.

It was easy to see why Rob had picked this place to live. The magnificence of the architecture would probably have featured low down in his calculations: it was the location. I could imagine him leaping out of bed and almost immediately taking his long-legged strides up the slopes with Soots at his heels. I couldn't wait to see them.

I found the buzzer for Rob's apartment and Rob buzzed me in and told me to come up to the third floor. Up we climbed. I had a big smile on my face, in anticipation of an open door and open arms. Instead, arriving at the third floor, I found all the front doors closed. I rapped on Rob's door but he didn't answer. I knew he was in there, I could hear him shuffling around. I was banging on the door, and he wasn't answering, and I had been driving in the rain for a long time at the end of a long week because Rob had moved to Somerset, and I needed a wee, and Rocky was scratching at the door, and I was getting really cross.

When Rob finally opened the door he wouldn't let me in further than the little bathroom in the hall, and only then because I insisted I wasn't going anywhere without having a wee. He stood shiftily outside the bathroom door and then hustled me out, insisting that we went straight out for a walk up to Wills Neck, the highest point on the Quantocks. I wasn't really up for walking in the filthy summer rain at this point. I wanted a cup of tea and a bun and a sit down. But I supposed Rocky probably needed a walk. Fine, I'd come.

We stormed up to the top, Soots trotting happily at our feet, and Rocky – who had resisted the ministrations of both dog-sitter Rob and dog-trainer extraordinaire Miriam Williams and was as poorly behaved as ever – barking loudly and chasing around after rabbits, his tail, the wind. After twenty minutes, the exertion and the silent scenery – heather-clad hills, decorated with clumps of trees that loomed out of the slanting rain – lulled away my irritation. Grey footpaths scarified the pink and furry face of the Quantocks. At one point we saw a pair of doe down in the valley, too far away for them to hear us or smell us.

I relaxed enough to try out a couple of the best stories from the last week on Rob.

Sophie the Labrador's latest trick had been to jump out in front of the post van. The careful driver hadn't had a chance of avoiding her and was of course utterly mortified. Sophie had survived, but had fractured her front leg quite badly, so we had sent her for advanced surgery from an orthopaedic specialist. Amelia had found it all terribly exciting and was now fired up to become an orthopaedic surgeon.

It was really bothering me that I had seen Mrs Smethwick and her kitten again with another injury. Mrs Smethwick had come on her own, during the school day, this time, and wearing sunglasses. It was a sunny day, but she hadn't taken them off, even in the consulting room. Again I had felt she was on the verge of telling me something. Again I had held back from asking. And again something had stopped her. Was I just being nosy and dramatic or was there something more going on here than an injured kitten? And if so, was it my place to do anything? In fact I felt so uncomfortable about this case that I didn't really feel I could share any of the details with Rob.

And – joy – I had finally treated a llama. Rocky had been finding their regular treks past our cottage very interesting, and I had too: they looked so great ambling along with those colourful South American rugs, and I had been dying to get my hands on a camelid or two. I had finally got my wish this week when a client had phoned through and asked to have her two new 'lawnmowers' checked over and wormed. Not glamorous work, but still, pretty exotic.

Rob ummed and ahhed obediently in most of the right places but his mind seemed to be elsewhere. I asked him how his new job was going but it was like asking a small child how their day at school had been. 'Fine,' he nodded, returning to distracted silence. The thought flitted across my mind that maybe it was going to be too hard to make this work long-distance. Or maybe it had just been a long week for both of us.

When we got to the top where a stone cairn stood, with its stony debris littered around it, Rob suddenly became animated. 'There's something in the heather over there,

Anna, go and have a look.' I didn't think I could face an animal in trouble at this point but off I tramped. 'No, three paces to your right, no, a bit further.'

As I searched through the heather, rain was streaming onto my face and down my neck. I bit back the urge to tell Rob to come and get whatever it was himself just before I found it. There in the heather was a bunch of flowers and the sweetest card, with a declaration of his love that I just about managed to read before the rain made it all smudge down the page. He must have climbed all the way up here earlier in the day to plant them there.

'Rob, that's … '

'Keep your back turned, don't look,' said Rob. 'Okay, you can turn around now.'

Spelt out from the stone debris I'd seen earlier, on the top of the highest point in the Quantocks, Rob had written, 'Marry Me.'

We'd been together four months: it had been four months since that first gorse-scented kiss on Kingcombe Meadows. There was no gorse in flower that I could see, but the heather, the stunted, wind-bowed Scots pines, and the driving rain, provided a perfect backdrop to answer the question with a long kiss. We both laughed nervously, almost hysterically. I felt so light and happy I wanted to launch myself into the air and fly with the rooks in the buffeting wind.

'Of course I bloody will,' I said. 'What took you so long?'

Acknowledgements

It is with heartfelt thanks that I would like to mention the following people:

My ever-loving parents who have been excited and encouraging about the whole adventure, from getting a place at vet school to getting a publishing deal. And my sister for giving me an insight into owner psychology and for her expert copyediting.

To my husband, my hero for his quiet encouragement and invaluable technical help with all things computing. And to my parents-in-law for their support and loving childcare. So, of course, also to my two gorgeous children for not minding being childminded when it was Mummy's turn.

Special thanks must go to Deborah Crewe who originally suggested that I put my story down on paper. She skilfully helped it happen, and happen on time, with professionalism, fun and cake on the way. I am also grateful to Andrew Lownie, my agent, for his faith from the beginning and Kate Moore and Elen Jones, my editors at

Ebury, who have been so enthusiastic and welcoming in the world of publishing. Dr Eve Pleydell also deserves a special mention for her invaluable comments on the Ethiopian episode, and similarly Ellen Berkeley who generously lent her journals and provided wonderful suppers.

Lastly, but most appreciatively, a very big thank you to my wonderful friends and colleagues who have been most game about the entire project, and of course to my clients and patients. It has been a privilege to know and work with you all.